Beginning Windows Mixed Reality Programming

For HoloLens and Mixed Reality Headsets

Second Edition

Sean Ong
Varun Kumar Siddaraju

Apress®

Beginning Windows Mixed Reality Programming: For HoloLens and Mixed Reality Headsets

Sean Ong
Tukwila, WA, USA

Varun Kumar Siddaraju
Covington, WA, USA

ISBN-13 (pbk): 978-1-4842-7103-2
https://doi.org/10.1007/978-1-4842-7104-9

ISBN-13 (electronic): 978-1-4842-7104-9

Managing Director, Apress Media LLC: Welmoed Spahr
Acquisitions Editor: Jonathan Gennick
Development Editor: Laura Berendson
Coordinating Editor: Jill Balzano

Cover image by Sean Ong

Distributed to the book trade worldwide by Springer Science+Business Media LLC, 1 New York Plaza, Suite 4600, New York, NY 10004. Phone 1-800-SPRINGER, fax (201) 348-4505, e-mail orders-ny@springer-sbm.com, or visit www.springeronline.com. Apress Media, LLC is a California LLC and the sole member (owner) is Springer Science + Business Media Finance Inc (SSBM Finance Inc). SSBM Finance Inc is a **Delaware** corporation.

For information on translations, please e-mail booktranslations@springernature.com; for reprint, paperback, or audio rights, please e-mail bookpermissions@springernature.com.

Apress titles may be purchased in bulk for academic, corporate, or promotional use. eBook versions and licenses are also available for most titles. For more information, reference our Print and eBook Bulk Sales web page at http://www.apress.com/bulk-sales.

Any source code or other supplementary material referenced by the author in this book is available to readers on GitHub via the book's product page, located at www.apress.com/9781484271032. For more detailed information, please visit http://www.apress.com/source-code.

Printed on acid-free paper

This book is dedicated to my wife, Neisha Ong. This Mixed Reality journey would have been impossible without her unrelenting support, encouragement, and involvement.

—Sean

Table of Contents

About the Authors... xiii

About the Technical Reviewer xv

Acknowledgments xvii

Introduction: The Mixed Reality Future xix

Part I: Getting Started 1

Chapter 1: Gear Up: The Necessary Hardware and Software Tools 3

Making Sure Your PC Is Ready 3

Understanding the HoloLens and Other Windows Mixed Reality Hardware................................ 5

    Inside-Out Tracking and Spatial Mapping.. 6

    Spatial Sound 8

    Transparent vs. Immersive Headsets 8

Downloading and Installing the Required and Optional Software Tools.................................. 10

    Installing Visual Studio 11

    Installing Unity 15

    Downloading the Mixed Reality Toolkit... 24

Summary.. 27

Chapter 2: Unity Crash Course.. 29

What Is Unity?.. 29

Free vs. Paid Tiers of Unity... 30

Your First Unity App.. 30

    Step 1: Create a New Unity Project.. 31

    Step 2: Save Your Scene.. 34

    Step 3: Create a Ground Plane... 35

    Step 4: Rename Your Plane 37

Step 5: Reset Ground Plane Position 38

Step 6: Zoom to Your Ground Plane 38

Step 7: Scale Your Ground Plane 39

Step 8: Create the Ball 40

Step 9: Rename Your Ball 41

Step 10: Reset the Ball's Position 41

Step 11: Zoom to Your Ball 42

Step 12: Raise the Ball's Position 42

Step 13: Color the Ground Blue 42

Step 14: Add Physics to the Ball 47

Step 15: Enable Keyboard Control 48

Step 16: Testing Your App 53

Summary 54

Part II: Building Holographic Experiences 55

Chapter 3: Creating Your First Hologram 57

Getting Unity Ready for Mixed Reality Development 57

Step 1: Import Mixed Reality Toolkit to a New Unity Project 58

Step 2: Use Mixed Reality Toolkit to Prepare Your Scene for
Mixed Reality Development 61

Your First Hologram 68

Step 1: Create a Cube 69

Step 2: Zoom to Your Cube 70

Step 3: Move the Cube Away from the Camera 70

Step 4: Resize the Cube 71

Step 5. Test Your App 72

Step 6: Install Your App on the HoloLens 73

Summary 84

Chapter 4: Introduction to the Mixed Reality Toolkit 85

What Is the Mixed Reality Toolkit? 85

The Three MRTK Repositories 86

Mixed Reality Toolkit Setup 86

    1. Importing MRTK Asset Files 86

    2. Unity Package Manager 89

Mixed Reality Toolkit Components 92

    MRTK: Input System 94

    MRTK: Hand Tracking 97

    MRTK: Solvers 98

    MRTK: Multi-scene Manager 100

    MRTK: Spatial Awareness 102

    MRTK: Diagnostic Tool 103

    MRTK: Boundary System 103

    MRTK: UX Controls 104

    MRTK: Camera System 105

    MRTK: Profiles 106

    MRTK: Standard Shader 109

MRTK Online 109

    What Is GitHub? 109

    MRTK Help and Documentation 109

Summary 110

Chapter 5: Interacting with Holograms 111

Input Methods 111

Gaze Tutorial 112

    Step 1: Set Up Unity Scene 113

    Step 2: Add Scenes to the Build Menu 114

    Step 3: Try the Scene! 114

    Step 4: Understanding the Scene 116

    Step 5: Use Gaze in Your Project 120

Gestures Tutorial 120

    Step 1. Load Test Scene 120

    Step 2. Try It Out! 121

    Step 3. Bounds Control 122

Step 4: Press and Touch Interactions 126

Step 5: Object Manipulator 128

Step 6: Implementing Gestures in Your Application 131

Voice Command Tutorial 131

Step 1: Load the Example Scene 132

Step 2. Try It Out! 133

Step 3: Understanding the Scene 134

Step 4: Add Your Own Voice Command 137

Step 5: Using Voice Commands in Your Own Project 140

Best Practices for Voice Commands 141

Other Hardware Input 142

Summary 143

Chapter 6: Using Spatial Awareness 145

What Is Spatial Awareness? 145

Spatial Awareness Tutorial 146

Step 1: Set Up Unity Scene 146

Step 2. Try It Out! 147

Step 3. Understanding the Scene 148

Step 4. Using Spatial Mapping in Your Application 150

Occlusion 152

Step 1: Apply Occlusion 152

Step 2: Try It Out! 153

Scene Understanding 154

Summary 155

Chapter 7: Spatial Sound 157

Spatial Sound Tutorial 158

Step 1: Set Up Unity Scene 158

Step 2: Try It Out! 159

Step 3: Understanding the Scene 161

Step 4: Enabling Spatial Sound in Your Application 165

Spatial Sound Design Considerations 170

    When to Use Spatial Sound 170

    What to Avoid When Using Spatial Sound... 171

Summary.. 171

Part III: Growing As a Holographic Developer 173

Chapter 8: Azure Spatial Anchors... 175

What Is Azure Spatial Anchors? 175

Azure Spatial Anchors Tutorial 176

    Step 1: Creating new Unity Scene 176

    Step 2: Installing Inbuilt Unity Packages 176

    Step 3: Download and Import Tutorial Assets 177

    Step 4: Preparing the Scene... 178

    Step 5: Configuring the Buttons to Operate the Scene..................... 179

    Step 6: Connecting the Scene to the Azure Resource 186

    Step 7: Test the Application in Device... 187

Summary.. 188

Chapter 9: Shared Experiences 189

What Are Shared Experiences?.. 189

Multiuser Capabilities Tutorial... 189

Setting Up Photon Unity Networking... 189

    Step 1: Creating New Unity Scene.. 190

    Step 2: Enabling Additional Capabilities 190

    Step 3: Installing Inbuilt Unity Packages 191

    Step 4: Importing the Tutorial Assets... 192

    Step 5: Importing the PUN Assets.. 193

    Step 6: Creating the PUN Application 195

    Step 7: Connecting the Unity Project to the PUN Application 196

Connecting Multiple Users 199

    Step 1: Preparing the Scene... 199

    Step 2: Create and Configure the User 201

Step 3: Create the Avatar 203

Step 4: Create the Prefab 204

Step 5: Configuring PUN to Instantiate the User Prefab 206

Sharing Object Movements with Multiple Users 207

Step 1: Preparing the Scene 207

Step 2: Configuring PUN to Instantiate the Objects 207

Integrating Azure Spatial Anchors into a Shared Experience 209

Step 1: Preparing the Scene 210

Step 2: Configuring the Buttons to Operate the Scene 210

Step 3: Connecting the Scene to the Azure Resource 214

Trying the Experience with Spatial Alignment 217

Summary 218

Chapter 10: Awe-Inspiring Experiences **219**

What Makes an App Awe Inspiring? 219

Optimization and Performance 220

How to Monitor for Performance 222

Best Practices for Performance 224

Simplygon 232

Stabilization Plane 233

Design and Magic 236

Best Practices for Design 237

Adding Magic: Vuforia 243

Summary 247

Chapter 11: Turning Holograms into Money **249**

Publishing Your App to the Microsoft Store 250

Freelancing and Contracts 251

Where to Find Mixed Reality Freelance Opportunities 252

Increasing Your Chances of Winning a Contract 253

Future Opportunities Today 254

Summary 254

Chapter 12: Community Resources **257**

HoloDevelopers Slack Team.. 257

    What Is Slack?.. 257

    What Is the HoloDevelopers Slack Team 258

    How to Join the HoloDevelopers Slack Team 259

    Participating in the HoloDevelopers Slack Team 260

Other Online Communities and Resources 260

    HoloLens Developers Facebook Group 261

    Unity and Unity HoloLens Forum 262

    HoloLens Subreddit 263

    Next Reality News 264

    YouTube 265

Local Events and Meetups 265

    Europe Meetups 266

    North America Meetups.. 267

    Asia Pacific Meetups 268

Hackathons 269

Notable Industry Events 270

Summary.. 271

Index **273**

About the Authors

Sean Ong is an author, engineer, entrepreneur, and tech influencer who has written on topics ranging from renewable energy to augmented reality. Sean and his wife Neisha Ong founded the Mixed Reality development company, Ong Innovations, in 2014. Sean and his team at Ong Innovations actively work with clients and partners around the globe to push the boundaries of Mixed Reality and spatial computing. Sean is also co-founder of the VR telepresence robotics platform company, Laborbot; founder of the AR/VR venue-based entertainment company, Manuvr Entertainment Inc.; co-founder of the AR/VR app creation platform company, Inflexion Point Inc.; and serves as partner and shareholder at numerous other AR/VR startup companies around the globe. He resides in Seattle, WA, with his wife and three kids, where he and his family relentlessly build the holographic future of tomorrow using today's XR devices.

Varun Kumar Siddaraju is an entrepreneur with limitless intellectual energy who isn't afraid to try out new and inventive ideas, regardless of how challenging they may be in terms of technology. He is founder of VeeRuby Technologies, a rapidly expanding Mysore-based Mixed Reality firm that caters to a wide range of enterprises. At VeeRuby, Varun is in charge of the organization's strategy, project and innovation management, thought leadership, and the development of new alliances. He is also employed as project manager and Mixed Reality engineer at Ong Innovations in Seattle, WA. At Ong Innovations, Varun oversees the creation of

Mixed Reality apps for platforms such as Android, iOS, Windows UWP, and VR headsets. He earned a Master of Science in Engineering (MS) with a concentration in electrical engineering from Texas State University. He worked as a graduate research assistant at this university for more than two years. He received an engineering degree in Electronics and Communication from Visvesvaraya Technological University.

About the Technical Reviewer

Alexander Meijers is a professional who inspires, motivates, and supports others and helps them to innovate. His goal is to help organizations achieve more by creating, improving, and working smarter, this with the aim of shortening business processes and improving the environment for employees. As a Cloud and XR architect, he is able to understand business issues and translate them into logical solutions using technology. Additionally, he supports companies in applying emerging experiences during their journey in digital transition. He uses technologies such as Virtual, Augmented, and Mixed Reality in combination with cloud services from the Microsoft Azure platform and Office 365. He has a strong background in SharePoint, Office 365, and Azure and works a lot with web services, machine learning and AI, and Mixed Reality services. His primary focus is in the manufacturing, construction, logistics, and maritime sectors. However, he certainly does not stay away from other sectors. He engages in speaking, blogging, and is an organizer of events such as the Mixed Reality User Group, GlobalXR.Community, Tech Daily Chronicles, and the Global XR Bootcamp.

Acknowledgments

I'd like to thank Alexander Meijers for his thorough technical review of this book. I also thank Jesse McCulloch for his unparalleled support of the independent Mixed Reality developer community and for establishing an amazing HoloLens community from which I attribute most of the Mixed Reality knowledge I have gained. Special appreciation goes out to my friends and valued team members at VeeRuby Technologies who contributed heavily to the updates needed for the second edition of this book. Finally, I want to thank Jonathan Gennick and Jill Balzano for their friendship, persistence, and editorial support in making this book possible.

Introduction: The Mixed Reality Future

Congratulations! If you are reading this, it means that you are on your way to becoming a pioneer responsible for building the Mixed Reality future that will dominate the next era of computing. For decades, science fiction has promised us a future filled with holograms and virtual experiences. We are finally on the verge of a technological revolution where our digital world intertwines with physical reality. This is known as *Mixed Reality.*

Let us imagine a future scenario where no screens exist. Instead, when you sit down to watch TV, a holographic screen appears on your wall. Because the screen is virtual, you can resize it to be as big as you wish. You could also move the screen to any other room, or have it follow you around the house. You sit down at an empty desk and several holographic computer monitors appear, along with virtual photos, a calendar, and a notepad. You are now ready to check your email, work on a spreadsheet, and get started on a good day's work. You will no longer need to carry around a physical smartphone. Instead, a holographic screen appears in your palm when needed. Holographic computing has the potential to replace every screen, and there is no reason to believe that it won't.

Note   The holograms referred to in this book are digital holograms and do not operate on the same optical principles of traditional holography.

Does this sound like sci-fi technology that's still several years away? You may be surprised to know that everything I just mentioned in this "future" scenario is completely possible (and available) today with devices like HoloLens 2. In fact, some Mixed Reality developers have been immersed in this technology for several years with an array of Mixed Reality headsets. Figure 1 illustrates how I use the HoloLens as a virtual desk.

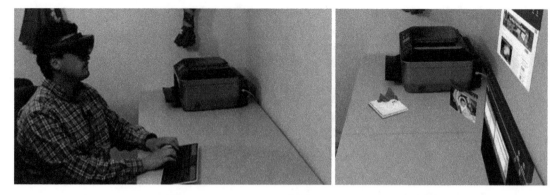

Figure 1. *The HoloLens enables an empty desk (left image) to be filled with holographic computer monitors and desk decorations (right image)*

In my previous "future scenario" example, you'll notice that I only give examples of holographic 2D screens. To some, my examples may have sounded amazing or revolutionary. They are, in fact, dull examples that don't adequately capture what the HoloLens and other holographic headsets can achieve. Think of holograms of co-workers in your office for remote meetings, advance training simulations for factory workers, collaborative engineering on complex 3D models, and using the power of cloud-based artificial intelligence to analyze and augment the world around you with helpful information. These are only a few of the possibilities that Mixed Reality technology can offer.

The challenge and opportunity of building experiences for these headsets is unlike anything that the technology industry has faced to date. Until now, the vast majority of software experiences have been designed for flat, 2D screens. Think of televisions, smartphones, tablets, laptops – or even the flat page or screen upon which you are reading this book. Video games, 3D movies, and other so-called "3D" advances over the past few years are nothing more than a glorified 2D experience we view on our flat, rectangular screens. The Windows Mixed Reality platform breaks this status quo by allowing us to develop true 3D applications in our real world. Early applications that have emerged for the HoloLens suffer from developers "thinking inside the box" by creating 2D experiences such as floating holographic screens or 2D menus and buttons for navigation. Many in the industry believe that a functional and intuitive 3D user experience has yet to be discovered and developed. As you are guided through the tutorials and example projects in this book, we will pay particular attention to 3D design elements while discussing ways to think outside the box and move beyond the 2D status quo.

It is a very exciting time to be a Mixed Reality developer. The devices are capable, the computing paradigm is new, and ideas for good applications seem to be endless. We, Mixed Reality developers, are the engineers, architects, and builders that will build the forthcoming Mixed Reality world.

The Mixed Reality future is inevitable. As with all high-tech gadgets, devices like the HoloLens will only become smaller and more powerful over time. It's not hard to imagine a near future where many (if not most) people will wear a pair of Mixed Reality glasses, whether or not they require prescription eyewear. Being equipped with these headsets will enable us to augment physical reality with relevant information, have more immersive digital experiences, and free us from the unnecessary screens that fill up our desks, walls, pockets, and purses.

How important will holographic devices be in daily life? One could speculate that most people in the near future might not be able to participate fully in society without a pair of holographic glasses. At first, this might sound like a dystopian prediction of our future. But think about how we use computers and smartphones today. It's very difficult to participate fully in today's modern society if you don't own or know how to use a computer. A vast majority of jobs in the United States require the use of a computer. We use email and online messages as primary forms of communication. Surely, if you told someone 50 years ago that they would not be able to fully participate in a future society without owning or knowing how to use a computer, they may have hesitated about such a future. Yet many of us today probably can't imagine daily life without our trusty PC or smartphone. Likewise, in 20 years, I think we'll look back and wonder how we ever lived without our trusty Mixed Reality glasses.

Perhaps I've given you a glimpse of the future. More importantly, I hope to have inspired you to start thinking about the holographic apps and experiences that will fill the world around us. All of us are relying on people like you to build our holographic future. My motivation for writing this book is to get as many people started on Mixed Reality development as possible. It is written to be easily accessible, whether you're an experienced software developer or new to the world of programming. This book is intended to get you started with everything you need to begin developing amazing Mixed Reality experiences on the HoloLens 2 and other Mixed Reality headsets!

This book is organized into 12 chapters spread across three parts. In Part I, which contains Chapters 1 and 2, you will be guided through the installation and explanation of all the necessary software and tools for developing Windows Mixed Reality applications.

Everything you need to get started is contained in Chapter 1. You can begin developing Mixed Reality apps with HoloLens and by emulation on a PC!

Things we'll cover in Chapter 1 include

- Making sure your PC is ready for Mixed Reality development

- Using a HoloLens 2 and other Windows Mixed Reality hardware

- Downloading and installing the required and optional software tools

- Understanding the HoloLens 2 and other Windows Mixed Reality hardware

In Chapter 2, we'll dive into the basics of Unity. Unity is a popular software platform for developing Windows Mixed Reality experiences. Things we'll cover in Chapter 2 include

- Understanding Unity

- Creating your first application in Unity

- Unity and Windows Mixed Reality

In Part II, we'll start building holographic experiences. Part II contains Chapters 3-9. This is where you will be guided through the fundamentals of creating a full-featured Mixed Reality application.

We'll learn how to make digital holograms in Chapter 3. You'll be guided through the creation of basic holograms which can be viewed in the HoloLens 2.

Here's what we'll cover in Chapter 3:

- Preparing Unity for Windows Mixed Reality development

- Creating a cube in Unity

- Building and deploying the Unity application to the HoloLens 2

- Finding and creating 3D objects

We discuss the Mixed Reality Toolkit (MRTK) in Chapter 4. Manually preparing Unity for HoloLens development can be cumbersome and error prone. This chapter introduces the MRTK and how you can leverage this community resource. Chapter 4 covers

- Understanding the MRTK

- Downloading and using the MRTK

In Chapter 5, we start interacting with holograms. We'll discuss the use of gestures, voice commands, eye tracking, and other ways of interacting with holographic content. Here's what we'll cover in Chapter 5:

- Voice commands

- Gestures and hand tracking

- Controllers and input accessories

- Eye tracking

Things start getting interesting in Chapters 6 and 7, where we begin to leverage the power of the HoloLens 2 by learning about using spatial mapping and spatial sound. I'll walk you through the technology, concept, and utilization of spatial mapping and spatial sound in the context of Mixed Reality applications.

Chapter 6 covers

- What is spatial mapping?

- How to use spatial mapping in projects

- Taking spatial mapping to the next level: scene understanding

Chapter 7 covers

- What is spatial sound and how is it different from "regular" sound?

- How to use spatial sound in projects

- Best practices for spatial sound

- Additional sound resources

In Chapter 8, we focus on Azure Spatial Anchors (ASA). Azure Spatial Anchors utilizes cloud services that form an effective amalgamation for a perfect application when integrated with Mixed Reality applications. It allows users to anchor the location of an object and save it.

Chapter 8 covers

- What is Azure Spatial Anchors?

- How to include Azure Spatial Anchors in projects

- Connecting to the scene to the Azure resources

- Additional Azure Spatial Anchors resources

In Chapter 9, we discuss shared experiences. Shared experiences are the epitome of Mixed Reality experiences. They allow people to come together, both locally and remotely, to experience and interact with virtual objects together. Chapter 9 covers

- Introduction to shared experiences
- Setting up Photon for shared experiences
- Building a shared Mixed Reality application
- Spatial alignment and shared spatial anchors
- Further considerations for shared experiences

Part III is about growing as a holographic developer. At this point in the book, you will be familiar with the basics of creating a Mixed Reality application. The next three chapters (Chapters 10–12) introduce ways you can optimize and enhance your experiences, publish and monetize your apps, and join the broader holographic community for support and visibility.

In Chapter 10, we'll discuss tips and tricks for awe-inspiring experiences. This chapter provides you with a primer on elements that give holographic experiences additional flair and magic, such as color choice, ambient elements, music, size, and more. Here's what we'll cover in Chapter 10:

- Optimization and performance
- Design
- Magic

Let's make some money! In Chapter 11, we'll cover the details of publishing and monetizing your applications. You'll be presented with strategies for monetization, from publishing your app in the Windows Store to freelancing as an independent Mixed Reality developer. Here's what we'll cover in Chapter 11:

- Monetization with the Windows Store
- Freelancing
- Thinking big: revolutionary opportunities

In the 12th and final chapter, we'll discuss community resources and additional information for holographic developers. This chapter introduces resources that are available to you, including relevant community forums and online groups, notable events, and other information that will help during the development process. Here's what we'll cover:

- Why are community resources important?

- Online communities

- The HoloDevelopers Slack Channel

- Events and local groups

- More information

As you embark on your journey to becoming a pioneering Mixed Reality developer, I encourage you to keep two things in mind. First, always think outside the box or outside the "2D rectangle" that has dominated computing up until this point in time. Second, understand that you are responsible for building a new industry and the Mixed Reality world of tomorrow. You are a technological pioneer. Understanding this will inspire you to reach new heights and explore new ways of creating amazing experiences!

PART I

Getting Started

CHAPTER 1

Gear Up: The Necessary Hardware and Software Tools

In this chapter, you'll learn everything you need to be equipped for Mixed Reality development. We'll make sure your PC is ready for development and walk through some recommended PC specifications. I provide a brief discussion on how your computer hardware impacts Mixed Reality development and performance. We'll also go over your hardware and emulator options for testing your app during development. We provide an overview of the HoloLens and some key features that you'll want to be familiar with before you start developing apps. Finally, you'll be guided through installing all the necessary software tools needed to dive into the world of making Mixed Reality experiences!

Tip   You don't need a HoloLens or Mixed Reality device to get started with development! You are good to go with your PC and some required software.

Making Sure Your PC Is Ready

Before getting started, you need to make sure you have a capable computer to handle Mixed Reality development. This section outlines the recommended system requirements and provides some additional context around these requirements. Fortunately, you don't need a high-end PC setup to make HoloLens apps. Unsurprisingly, Microsoft recommends Windows 10 as the operating system of choice.

© Sean Ong and Varun Kumar Siddaraju 2021
S. Ong and V. K. Siddaraju, *Beginning Windows Mixed Reality Programming*,
https://doi.org/10.1007/978-1-4842-7104-9_1

Other operating systems also work, including Windows 8.1, Windows 8, Windows 7, and more. Several HoloLens developers also have reported success developing on their Mac devices when running Windows virtually.

Here are my recommended system specs for Mixed Reality development:

- 64-bit Windows 10

- 8 GB Ram or 16 GB Ram for PCs using emulator

- 30 GB of available hard drive space

That's intended to be a fairly small list to illustrate how you don't need much to get started. You can technically get away with even lower system specs, but then you'll have a very painful and slow experience, and I would recommend against it.

If getting a capable device is of particular interest to you, I've included a deeper discussion here of the various spec categories and what it means for your development experience:

- **RAM** (random access memory) is your computer's way of storing memory that's quickly accessible. If you have a lot of open windows, websites, and applications, then you'll want to have more RAM to speed up multitasking on your computer. I recommend a minimum RAM size of 6 GB. For an optimal experience, you should aim for 12 GB to 16 GB of RAM. This allows you to have multiple (20+) browser tabs open, multiple windows open, Unity, Visual Studio, your music application, and background PC tasks running without slowing down your system.

- The **processor** or CPU is responsible for doing all the computational work. When the processor starts working hard, you'll immediately notice the difference between a slow processor and a fast processor. These crucial times include *compiling* your app (which is essentially the computer's way of converting the code you've written into something your HoloLens can install and understand), loading and working with complex 3D objects in Unity, and any other processing work that involves many objects in your Unity scene. I recommend the Intel Core i5 or Core i7 processors (or another processor with similar speed).

- The **operating system** or OS of your computer is typically Windows, Mac OS, or Linux. As mentioned earlier, you can develop under a range of Windows versions (and even Windows on a Mac), but the recommended OS for Mixed Reality development is Windows 10. Microsoft is heavily promoting the use of 3D in Windows via the "Windows 10 Creators Update." Tethered Windows Mixed Reality headsets will also rely on Windows 10 to work. Based on this, I consider it worthwhile to get a Windows 10 computer for Mixed Reality development.

- The **graphics processing unit** or GPU is often poorly understood and gets less attention than the other items I've listed earlier. Many laptops and low- to mid-end PCs don't include a dedicated graphics card, but rather rely on graphics capabilities that are built into the processor (also known as integrated graphics). When developing Mixed Reality applications, having a GPU is not required but can boost editing performance especially when using Unity's holographic emulation features, especially when dealing with complex scenes and textures. That said, any Unity application struggling to run on an integrated desktop GPU is probably going to fare worse on the HoloLens itself, due to the limited graphics capabilities of the headset.

Understanding the HoloLens and Other Windows Mixed Reality Hardware

In this section, we'll cover some basics of the way the HoloLens works. There could be an entire book written on the technological miracle of the HoloLens and the science behind it, but I'll cover just enough so that we can design the best app experiences for this and other Mixed Reality headsets.

Inside-Out Tracking and Spatial Mapping

What sets the HoloLens and other Windows Mixed Reality headsets apart from other popular headsets (as of this writing) is the ability to perform *inside-out tracking*, which is the ability for the headset to track its environment without the need for external sensors. Outside-in tracking headsets require the user to set up a few sensors around a room or area, which allows the headset to know where it is as the user moves around. Inside-out tracking avoids the cumbersome need to set up external sensors and can work in nearly all environments. Some basic Virtual Reality headsets that you may have heard about (e.g., Google Cardboard, Samsung Gear VR) have no positional tracking, with only the ability to "look around." Figure 1-1 shows a diagram of the HoloLens cameras, several of which are used for inside-out spatial tracking.

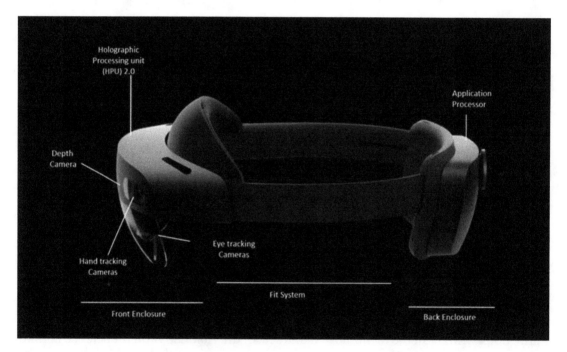

Figure 1-1. *Diagram of HoloLens 2 cameras and their functions*

The HoloLens 2 has eight cameras on the headset, five of which are used to track its environment (four environment tracking cameras, one depth camera), two eye tracking cameras, and one regular camera for recording video or taking pictures. The HoloLens is constantly tracking its environment and building a 3D model of the area that it's in.

This is called *spatial mapping*. Figure 1-2 illustrates how the HoloLens uses a mesh made of triangles to recreate a digital version of the user's surroundings. Spatial mapping is important for several reasons:

- It tells the HoloLens which holograms to hide from view. For example, if you place a hologram in your hallway and then walk into another room, the spatial map of that room's walls will prevent you from seeing the hologram in your hallway. This feature of HoloLens is referred to as occlusion. This simple feature has a significant impact on the comprehended naturalism of holograms. If there were no spatial map, you would see the hologram as if it were visible through your walls, causing an unrealistic experience.

- It allows users to interact with the spatial map – for example, pin items to your walls, allow characters to sit on your sofa (as seen in Microsoft's "Fragments" app!), or automatically decorate your surroundings.

- It allows for *hologram persistence*, which is the ability for holograms to stay where the user left them – even after turning off your device. Your HoloLens will (remarkably) be able to remember your space and restore any holograms that you had placed in that space.

Figure 1-2. *Illustration of the HoloLens using spatial mapping to track its environment*

Spatial Sound

We rely heavily on our ears to precisely locate objects around us. In the context of Mixed Reality, this is called *spatial sound*. The HoloLens has the ability to send spatial sound to the user's ears using a sound wave phase-shift approach. This increases the feeling of immersion. Users will still be able to hear objects (if the objects are intended to make noise) around them, even if they can't see those objects. This increases the user's perception of these objects and makes the holograms feel like they are actually in the user's area.

Transparent vs. Immersive Headsets

Some Windows Mixed Reality devices like the HoloLens uses transparent displays that allow you to see holograms placed in your real world. Other devices, such as Lenovo's Windows Mixed Reality headset, are occluded, meaning that you are unable to see your surroundings. Instead, these headsets immerse you in a virtual world. Immersive headsets still boast inside-out tracking, which is helpful for making the user aware of walls or other obstructions while wearing the headset. Some immersive headsets may also utilize spatial mapping, allowing the user to see a virtual representation of their surroundings. Figure 1-3 shows several examples of Windows Mixed Reality headsets.

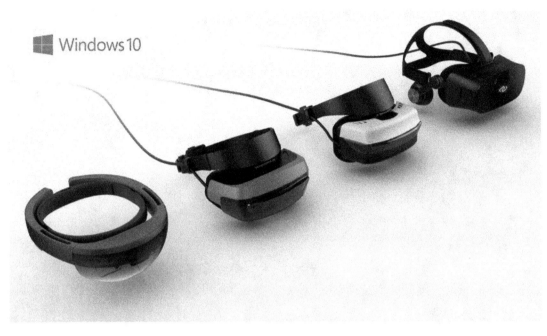

Figure 1-3. *Examples of Windows Mixed Reality devices include both transparent headsets such as the HoloLens and occluded headsets (Source: Microsoft)*

All existing devices as of this writing have a *field-of-view* (FOV) limitation, which means that you are unable to see holograms in all of your peripheral vision. As shown in Figure 1-4, the HoloLens FOV limitation causes holograms to be limited to a small "window" through which they can be viewed. As headset display technology improves, we can expect resolution to increase and FOV limitations to reduce over time. The FOV limitation in today's devices means that you'll need to be creative when designing your app to be as immersive as possible. Using spatial sound is one key element to increasing the user's perception of holograms. Other visual cues (such as arrows pointing to holograms outside of the FOV) are also strategies for helping the user. We'll discuss these in more detail in Part III.

Figure 1-4. *Example of the HoloLens field-of-view limitation, photographed from behind the device*

Downloading and Installing the Required and Optional Software Tools

In this section, you will be guided through the installation of all the necessary software and tools for developing Windows Mixed Reality applications. There are only two applications needed to get started with Mixed Reality development: Unity and Visual Studio. In this book, we'll define and frame everything in the context of Mixed Reality development. However, both these applications are widely used in the software and gaming industries and have been around for many years. Here's a brief description of each:

- **Unity** is the preferred software platform for developing Windows Mixed Reality experiences. All your app development happens within Unity. It is where you will program holograms to do things. Outside of the Mixed Reality world, Unity is widely used for game development. This is excellent news, because it means that there are years of tutorials, resources, and forum discussions to help answer almost any question you may have as you are developing your Mixed Reality applications.

- **Visual Studio** is primarily responsible for editing the code of your app and is also used to *deploy* your app to your Mixed Reality headset for testing and debugging. Deploying simply means installing the app to your headset. When your app is complete, you may also use Visual Studio to deploy your app to the Windows Store. As of this writing, you cannot deploy apps to your HoloLens directly from Unity (as mentioned previously, however, you can stream apps to your HoloLens). It's possible that Unity will soon allow users to deploy directly to the HoloLens without needing to go through Visual Studio.

Note   The tools shown in this book are updated regularly, and screenshots may not look exactly like the most current versions of these applications. Keep that in mind as you follow the instructions in the following. The versions used in this book are as follows, Unity Hub version 2.4.2 and Visual Studio 2019 version 16.8.

In addition to installing Unity and Visual Studio, you will also need to download the Mixed Reality Toolkit. The Mixed Reality Toolkit is not an application, but rather a collection of useful Mixed Reality scripts and features to import into Unity. Rest assured, I have an entire chapter dedicated to the Mixed Reality Toolkit and all it has to offer!

Installing Visual Studio

In this section, we'll walk through how to download and set up Visual Studio for Mixed Reality development. As of this writing, the version required for Mixed Reality development is Visual Studio 2019; the versions are updated regularly, but the installation process will be very similar between versions.

To check the latest version of Visual Studio for Mixed Reality development, use Microsoft's Installation Checklist, located at

```
https://developer.microsoft.com/en-us/windows/Mixed-Reality/install_the_tools
```

You will see a table similar to the one shown in Figure 1-5.

Installation checklist

Tool	Notes
  Windows 10 (Manual install link) ⬈ Install the most recent version of Windows 10 so your PC's operating system matches the platform for which you're building mixed reality applications.	**Installing Windows 10** You can install the most recent version of Windows 10 via Windows Update in Settings or by creating installation media, using the link in the left column. See current release notes for information about the newest mixed reality features available with each release of Windows 10. **Enable developer mode on your PC at Settings > Update & Security > For developers.** **Note for enterprise and corporate-managed PCs** If your PC is managed by an your organization's IT department, you might need to contact them in order to update. **'N' versions of Windows** Windows Mixed Reality immersive (VR) headsets are not supported on 'N' versions of Windows.
 Visual Studio 2019 (16.8 or higher) (Install link) ⬈ Fully-featured integrated development environment (IDE) for Windows and more. You'll use Visual Studio to write code, debug, test, and deploy.	**Installing Visual Studio 2019** Be sure you install the following workloads: • *Desktop development with C++* • *Universal Windows Platform (UWP) development* • *Game development with Unity (if planning to use Unity)* Within the UWP workload, make sure the following components are included for installation: • *Windows 10 SDK version 10.0.19041.0 or 10.0.18362.0* • *USB Device Connectivity (required to deploy/debug to HoloLens over USB)* • *C++ (v142) Universal Windows Platform tools (required when using Unity)* **Note about HoloLens (1st gen) and desktop Windows Mixed Reality headsets** If you are only developing applications for desktop Windows Mixed Reality headsets or HoloLens (1st gen), you can use Visual Studio 2017 and use the Windows SDK installed by it. **Known issues** There are some known issues with debugging mixed reality apps in Visual Studio 2019 version 16.0. Please ensure that you update to Visual Studio 2019 version 16.8 or higher.

Figure 1-5. *Be sure to check Microsoft's Installation Checklist for the most recent versions of tools to install. To download Visual Studio, click the corresponding title (circled in red)*

You can also download Visual Studio from the following link:

`https://developer.microsoft.com/en-us/windows/downloads`

If you don't already have a Visual Studio subscription, you can download the free version of Visual Studio, also known as "Visual Studio Community." Figure 1-6 shows what the download button may look like.

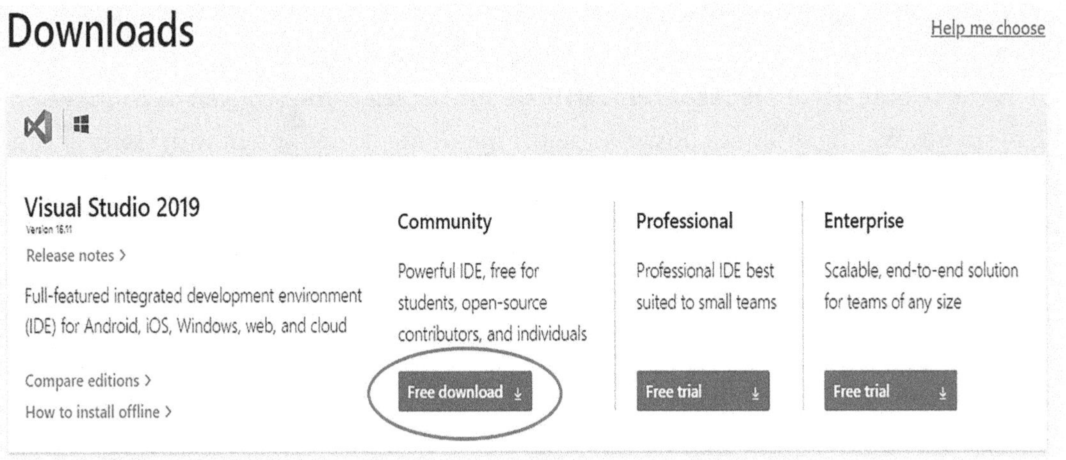

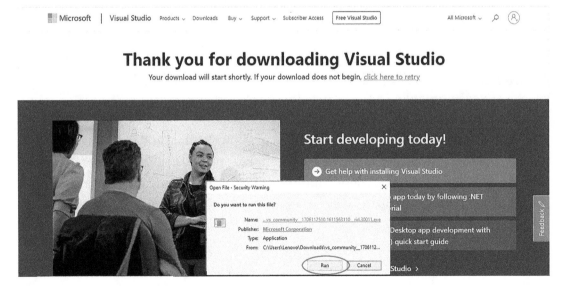

Figure 1-6. *Click the "Free Download" button for Visual Studio Community to begin your download*

Save the Visual Studio installer to a location of your choice. After the download is complete, you may run the Visual Studio installer to begin the installation process. Figure 1-7 shows how running the installer appears in the Microsoft Edge browser.

Figure 1-7. *Run the Visual Studio installer to your PC*

When you launch the Visual Studio installer, you will encounter a few seconds of initialization followed by the option to select features, as shown in Figure 1-8.

In the feature list of **Visual Studio 2019**, be sure to select the "Universal Windows Platform development" check box. Also select the Game development with Unity check box. You may deselect the Unity Editor check box in the right panel, since you will be installing the most current version of Unity later in this chapter. Click "Next" or "Install" after making the appropriate selections.

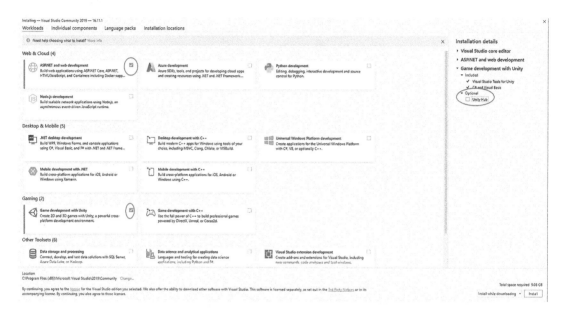

Figure 1-8. *For Visual Studio 2019, be sure you select Universal Windows Platform development and Game development with Unity*

After clicking "Install," Visual Studio will begin downloading and installing your selected features. Visual Studio is a very large application and could take several hours to download and install, depending on your Internet connection. Prepare for the installation process to take a while! After the installation has completed, you may be prompted to restart your PC. After restarting, you may verify that the installation completed successfully by opening Visual Studio. When you first open Visual Studio, it should look similar to the welcome page shown in Figure 1-9, depending on your edition of Visual Studio.

Figure 1-9. *You may optionally verify that Visual Studio installed correctly by launching it after setup is complete*

Congratulations! You have successfully installed Visual Studio. You don't need to do anything with Visual Studio for now. Later, when we deploy apps to our HoloLens via Visual Studio, we will go through an initial pairing process. If you haven't already, you may need to log into Visual Studio with your Microsoft account. Visual Studio may also apply a "license" to your account to use Visual Studio. All the licenses on Visual Studio are per user based. A licensed user can access their account on any number of devices to design and develop. Multiple user accounts can be accessed inside Visual Studio, thus increasing its flexibility further. Next, we will install Unity.

Installing Unity

In this section, we'll walk through how to download and set up Unity for Mixed Reality development. As of this writing, the version required for Mixed Reality development is Unity 2019. Versions are updated regularly, but the installation process will be very similar between versions.

To check the latest version of Unity for Mixed Reality development, use Microsoft's Installation Checklist, located at

https://developer.microsoft.com/en-us/windows/Mixed-Reality/install_the_tools

You can also download Unity from the following link:

https://store.unity.com/download

Once you arrive at Unity's download page, you will see a download button similar to the one shown in Figure 1-10. Run the "Unity Hub" installer to your PC once the download has completed (Figure 1-11).

Figure 1-10. *Download the latest version of Unity Hub from the Unity website*

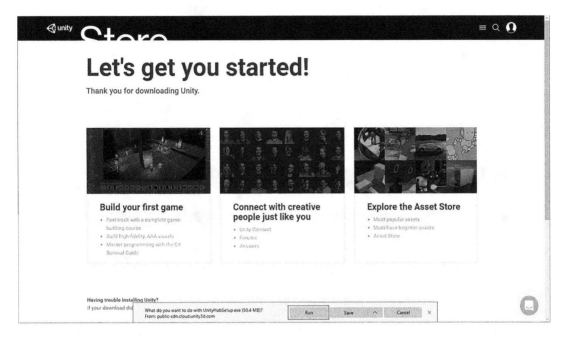

Figure 1-11. *After the download is complete, run the Unity installer*

After launching the Unity Hub installer, you will be greeted with the Download assistant, as shown in Figure 1-12. Click "Agree" to begin the installation process.

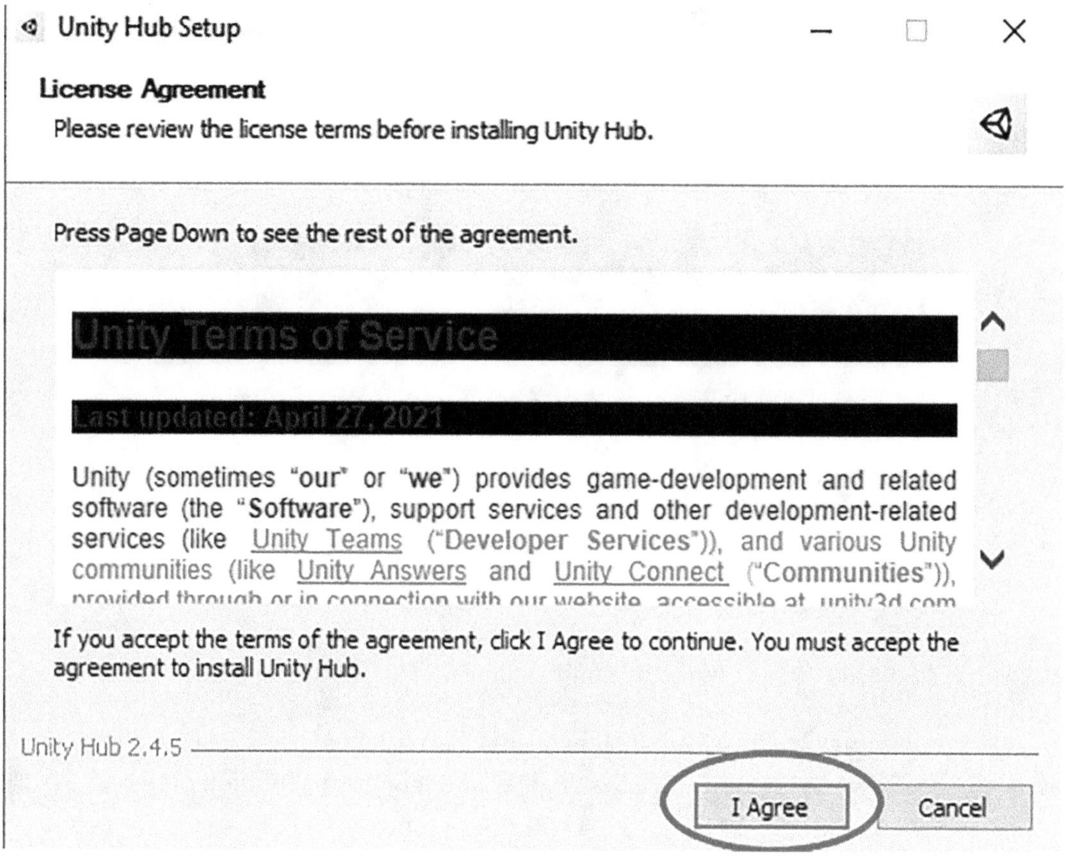

Figure 1-12. *Accept the license agreement*

After accepting the agreement, please select the preferred location where you want the Unity Hub to be installed. By default, program files will be selected as the destination folder.

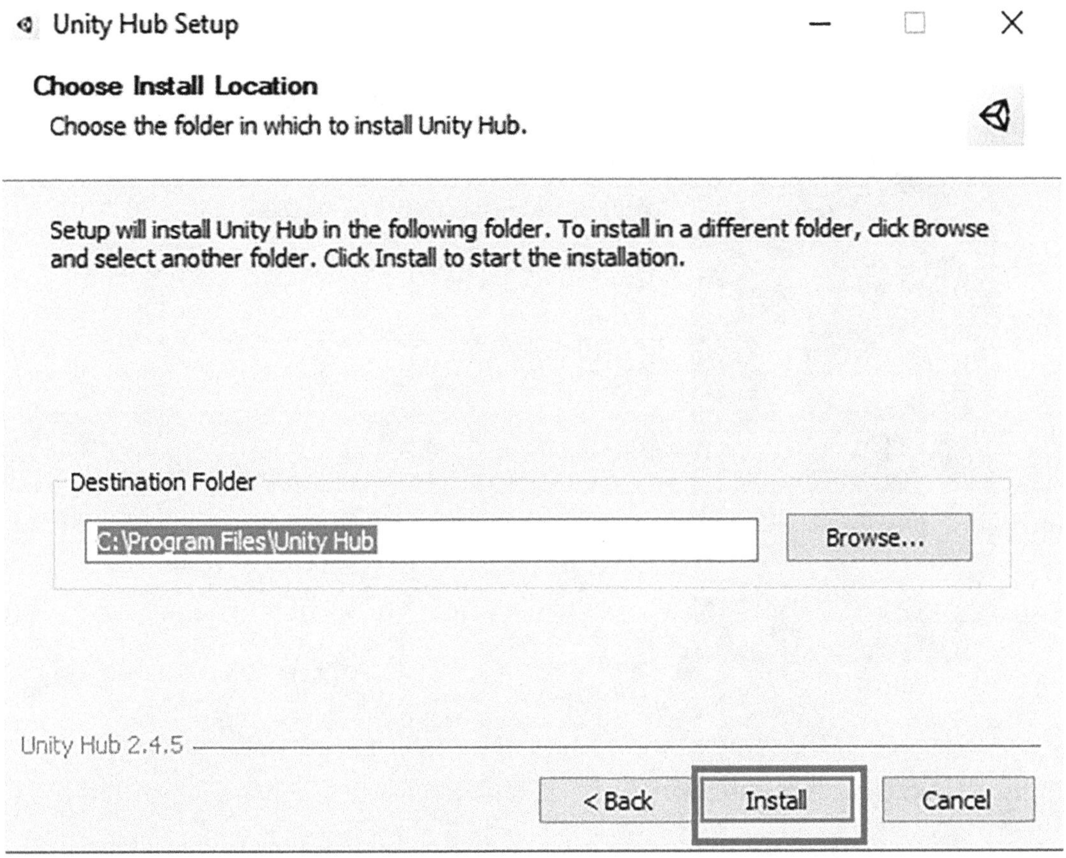

Figure 1-13. *Install Unity Hub in the destination folder*

After installing Unity Hub successfully in the destination folder, complete the installation by clicking Finish in the "Completing Unity Hub Setup" menu.

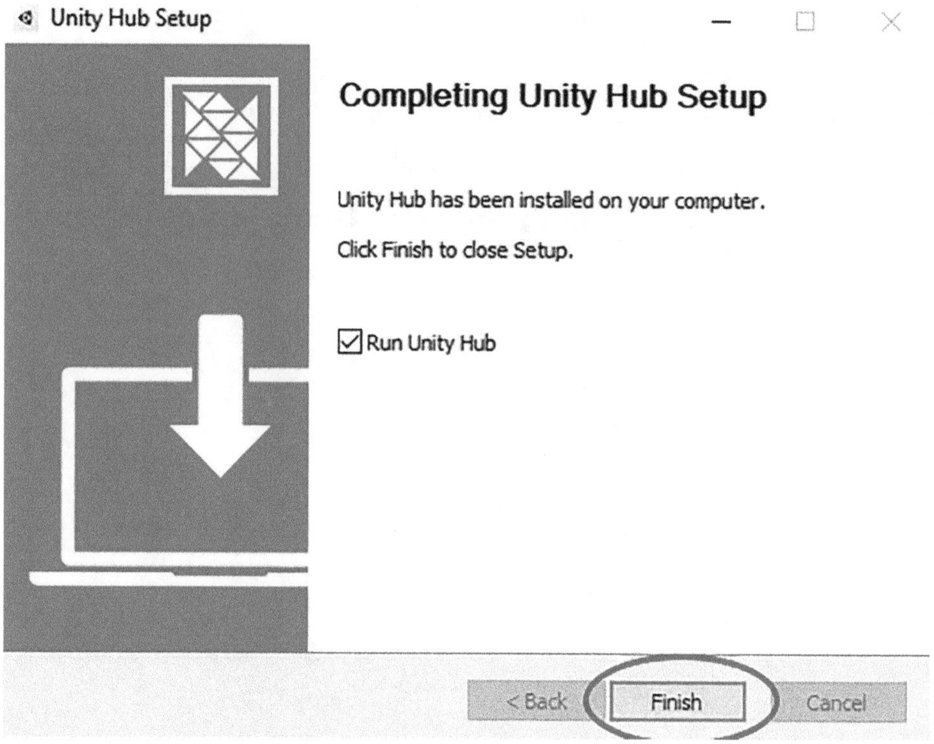

Figure 1-14. *Finish installation*

Open the Unity Hub software, and you will be asked to log in to your existing Unity account or to create a new one. Log in if you already have your Unity account created or else create a new Unity account.

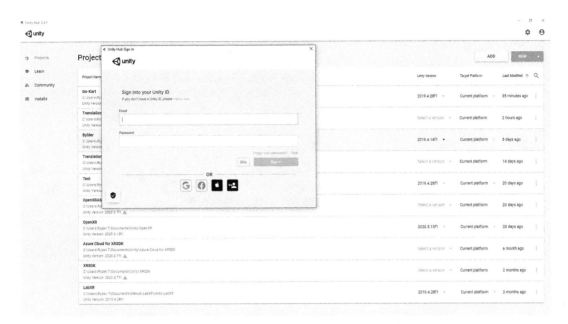

Figure 1-15. *Log in to your existing Unity account or create a new one, if you don't have an account*

When you select to create a new Unity account, a new web page will open asking you to enter your account details. Fill in all the details, and create your Unity account. We obtain a free license on choosing Unity for personal use. Unity personal is an impressive place for beginners to get started. It is integrated with all the crucial game features, engine features, continuous updates, beta releases, and all publishing platforms.

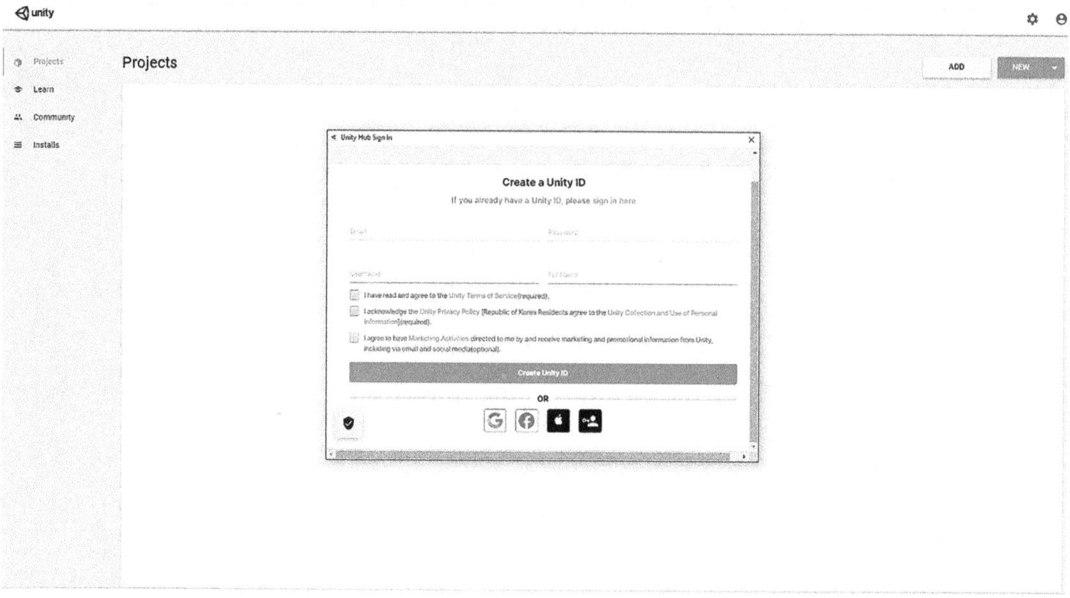

Figure 1-16. *Unity will open a web page where you can sign up for a new Unity account*

Once you create a new account or log in using your existing account, go to the Installs section in Unity Hub, and select "Add." A new menu will pop with various Unity versions. Please select the latest version, and click Next to start the Unity installation process.

Note   You can also visit the Unity download archive to download specific versions of Unity. On clicking the download option, you will be redirected to Unity Hub for further steps. We are using Unity 2019.4.16 throughout this book.

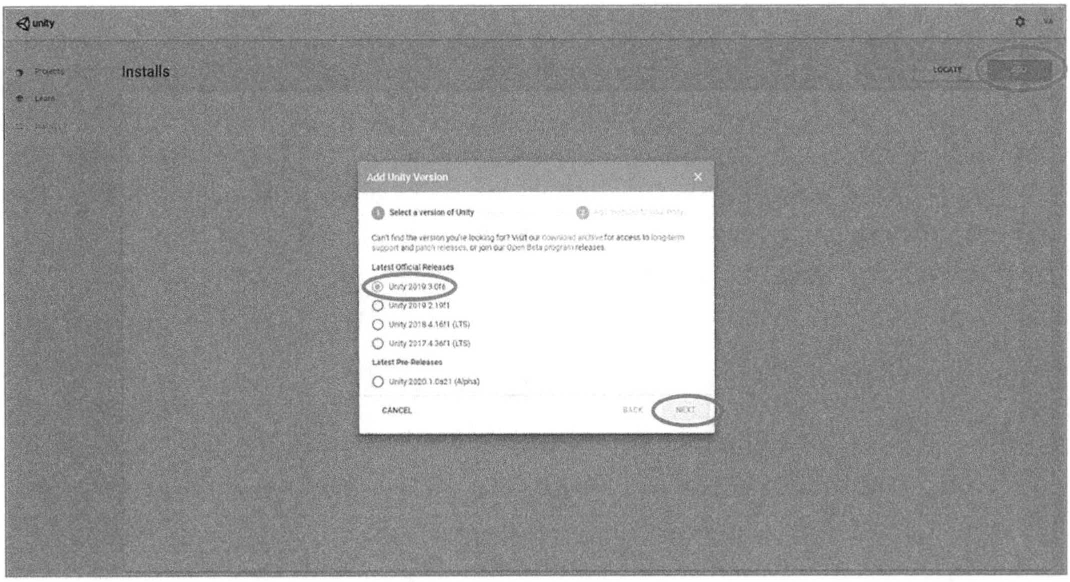

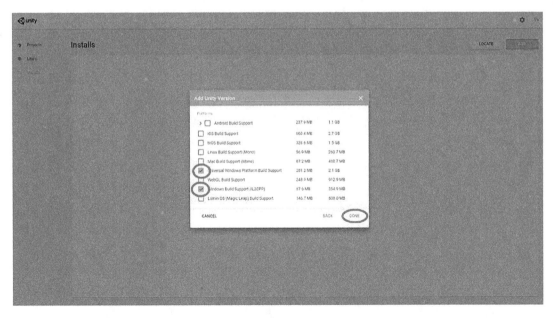

Figure 1-17. *Be sure to select the required components shown in this figure. Click "Next" to continue*

Figure 1-18. *The downloading and installation of Unity components may take a long time*

As shown in Figure 1-18, Unity will begin to download and install the selected components. This may take several hours, depending on the speed of your Internet connection. Be prepared for a long wait. Once the installation is complete, click the "Finish" button.

Congratulations! You now have Unity installed on your PC. You can access the newly installed Unity and create new projects by opening Unity Hub. How to create a new Unity project will be discussed in the next lesson.

Downloading the Mixed Reality Toolkit

In this section, I'll walk you through downloading the Mixed Reality Toolkit, which isn't a program but rather a collection of useful scripts and features to import into Unity. To download the Mixed Reality Toolkit Unity package, go to the following URL:

https://github.com/microsoft/MixedRealityToolkit-Unity/releases/

Make sure that you download the latest release of the Mixed Reality Toolkit, typically located near the top of the page. The Mixed Reality Toolkit version used in this book is 2.5.3. Be sure that the Mixed Reality Toolkit version you download is compatible with the version of Unity that you downloaded. Typically, compatibility is announced in the title of the Mixed Reality Toolkit version, as shown in Figure 1-19. To download the Mixed Reality Toolkit Unity package, click the download link that has the extension ".unitypackage." For example, in Figure 1-19, the appropriate download link (circled in red) is named "Microsoft.MixedReality.Toolkit.Unity.Foundations.2.5.3.unitypackge."

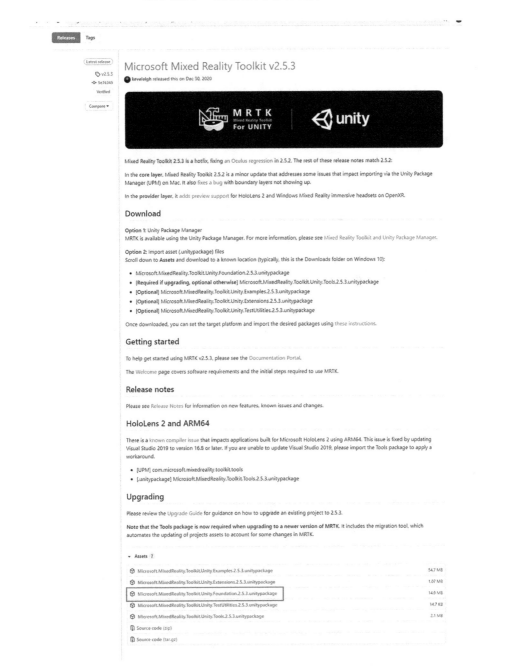

Figure 1-19. *Browse to the Mixed Reality Toolkit download page, and download the Mixed Reality Toolkit Unity package, circled in red*

In Figure 1-19, you observe five different ".unitypackage" files. These packages serve different purposes and can be included in your Unity project. Let's understand the needs of these packages:

1. Foundation package: Foundation package, as the name suggests, lays an understructure for Mixed Reality development. It comprises codes that allow you to support standard functionalities in your application across various Mixed Reality platforms. Since it is a significant package to build your application, you must download and import it.

2. Extensions package: Extensions package is an optional package that assists us in extending the functionalities by adding additional services. This package requires the foundation package to function.

3. Tools package: Tools package is also an optional package that comprises helpful tools that strengthen the development experience. These tools can be found in the Mixed Reality Toolkit ➤ Utilities menu in Unity editor. Tools package is dependent on the foundation package. Therefore, it requires the foundation package to operate normally.

4. Test utilities package: The optional test utilities package includes helper scripts that allow the user to create play mode tests comfortably. Play mode tests are the tests that can check how features respond to different input sources like hands or eyes. This package is handy to developers who are creating Mixed Reality Toolkit components.

5. Examples package: Examples package is another optional package that is highly beneficial if you are a beginner. It showcases various features of the Mixed Reality Toolkit. This package consists of demos, sample scenes, and sample codes that employ functionalities in the foundation package. Examples package requires foundation package to function precisely.

You are free to download any optional packages as stated earlier based on your requirements. Save the Mixed Reality Toolkit to your PC. We will import this package into Unity later.

Summary

You now have everything you need to get started with Mixed Reality development! In the upcoming chapters, we'll learn some basics of Unity, we'll make our very first Mixed Reality application, and then we'll start diving into the details of making amazing Mixed Reality experiences. Let's recap what we've learned in this chapter:

- We've discussed the recommended PC hardware specifications for developing Mixed Reality experiences.

- We took a brief hardware tour of the HoloLens and other Windows Mixed Reality headsets and what makes them unique.

- Finally, we went through step-by-step installation instructions for Visual Studio, Unity, and the Mixed Reality Toolkit.

CHAPTER 2

Unity Crash Course

In this chapter, we'll dive into the world of Unity. Unity is the preferred software platform for developing Mixed Reality applications. If you want to master Mixed Reality development, it means that you first need to master Unity! We'll take a tour of Unity and understand what Unity is used for. I'll also walk you through building your very first Unity app.

What Is Unity?

Before we begin, you might be wondering what Unity is and how people use it. *Unity is a powerful program for building both 2D and 3D games and apps.* It is very popular among game developers, especially mobile game developers. Unity also supports a wide range of platforms. A few examples include iOS, Android, PlayStation, Nintendo, Xbox One, Windows, Mac, HoloLens, Oculus, and many more!

A very basic Mixed Reality workflow in Unity looks like this:

1. Import your 3D objects and other items (called *assets*) into Unity.

2. Program how you will interact with the objects and how the objects will interact with you, other objects, and the world.

3. Test your app.

4. Export your app so that you can install it on your device.

Unity is a very large, nuanced platform. In this book, we'll only cover the essential parts of Unity needed for Mixed Reality development. As you continue to grow as a Windows Mixed Reality developer, you'll invest much of your time into mastering Unity and programming for Unity.

© Sean Ong and Varun Kumar Siddaraju 2021
S. Ong and V. K. Siddaraju, *Beginning Windows Mixed Reality Programming*,
https://doi.org/10.1007/978-1-4842-7104-9_2

Free vs. Paid Tiers of Unity

There are several pricing tiers of Unity available for developers. Most individuals looking to learn Unity can get started with a personal (free) account. However, there are restrictions and benefits to be aware of for the various pricing levels. In Table 2-1, I provide a discussion that explains these tiers.

Table 2-1. *Unity pricing tiers*

Pricing Tier	Restrictions and Benefits
Unity Personal (free)	You can only use this tier if your company makes less than $100k (including investor funding)
	Your app is forced to have Unity's logo when launched (splash screen)
Unity Plus ($40/person monthly)	You can only use this tier if your company makes less than $200k (including investor funding)
	You can use a custom (or no) splash screen
	Additional Plus services
Unity Pro ($150/person monthly)	No revenue/finding cap
	You can use a custom (or no) splash screen
	Additional Pro services

Your First Unity App

In this section, we'll build our very first Unity application! We will create a game to control a rolling ball with your keyboard. As we walk through creating your first Unity app, we will also familiarize ourselves with some basic Unity components and learn about the Unity interface. Because this tutorial is intended to familiarize yourself with Unity, we will not be making a Mixed Reality application yet (we'll do that in the next chapter.) Before we begin, be sure that you have already installed Unity and set up your Unity account per the instructions in Chapter 1.

Tip   This basic Unity tutorial is known as the *Roll-A-Ball Tutorial*. It is recommended for all Unity beginners.

Step 1: Create a New Unity Project

Every Unity (and Mixed Reality) project begins with creating a new Unity project. To start a new project, launch Unity Hub, and select the "NEW" icon as shown in Figure 2-1. If you haven't already, you may need to enter in your account information (created in Chapter 1) prior to seeing the screen shown in Figure 2-1.

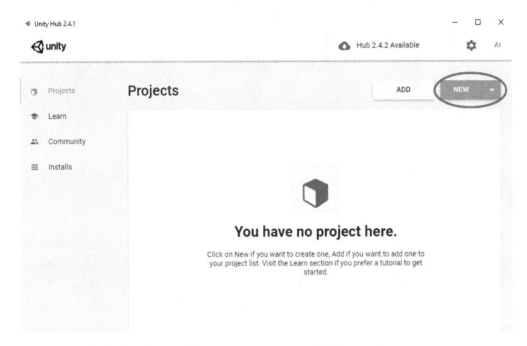

Figure 2-1. *Click the "NEW" icon to start a new Unity project*

Alternatively, if you are already within a Unity project, you can create a new project by going to File ➤ New Project as shown in Figure 2-2.

Figure 2-2. *You can also start a new Unity project by going to File ➤ New Project*

Unity will then open a pop-up window where you can set up your new project. As shown in Figure 2-3, give your new project a name. I choose "FirstApp." If you wish, you can also select a different location for your project to be stored. The project should already be a "3D" project, but if not, be sure to select the "3D" option button. When done, click the "Create" button.

Warning   Avoid storing your Unity project on an SD card or MicroSD card. Visual Studio will not be able to properly build your project if it's on an SD card due to an unknown bug. You may store your Unity project on an external hard drive.

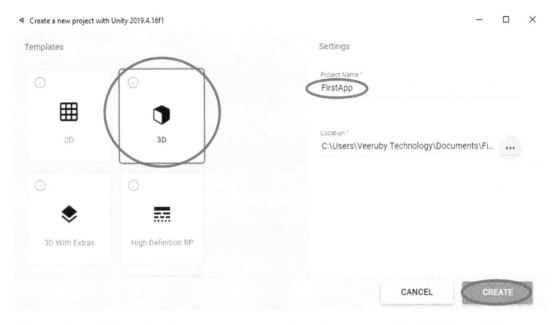

Figure 2-3. *Tell Unity about your new project. Be sure to select "3D" and give your new project a name*

You will now see a new empty project! You should see something similar to Figure 2-4. This is called the Unity editor, and it is where most of your project editing will take place. In Figure 2-4, I also provide brief descriptions for important panels contained within the editor.

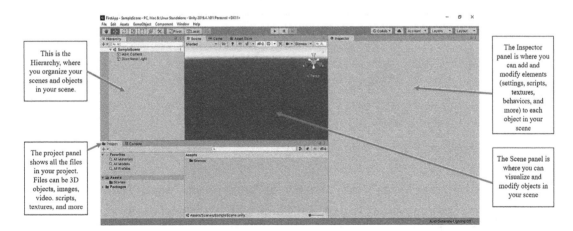

Figure 2-4. *The Unity editor window contains several important panels. This is where most Unity project editing occurs*

In your scene panel, you will see something that resembles a blue sky and a brown or gray ground. This is your empty *scene*. Right now, it only contains some light (the sun icon) to illuminate the scene and the camera through which you see the world when operating the game (the camera icon.)

Step 2: Save Your Scene

Before we begin editing this empty scene, let's save the scene. Right-click scene and select Save Scene As. Figure 2-5 shows where to find the save scene option. A dialog box will pop up, allowing you to name your scene and choose a location to save it. Name your scene "MiniGame," and feel free to use the default location. You can name your scene with any name, but I recommend using the same name I use so that it will be easier for you to follow along as we go through this tutorial.

Figure 2-5. *Save your scene before editing it*

The scene is now saved as MiniGame in your Assets folder. In your Hierarchy panel, you should now see your scene named MiniGame with two objects under it (Main Camera and Directional Light.)

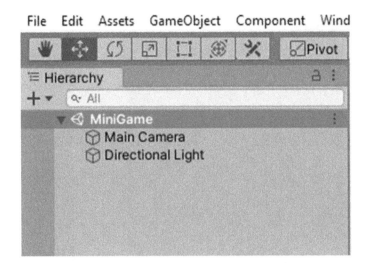

Figure 2-6. *Your new scene should have two default objects under it in the Hierarchy panel*

Step 3: Create a Ground Plane

We can now start building out our game scene. First, we'll need to create the ground plane for the ball to roll on. Click the MiniGame scene in the Hierarchy so that it's highlighted (to ensure that you are not highlighting the Main Camera or Directional Light). Go to GameObject ➤ 3D Object ➤ Plane. See Figure 2-7 for where to access the Plane object. A Plane object is a large, flat surface.

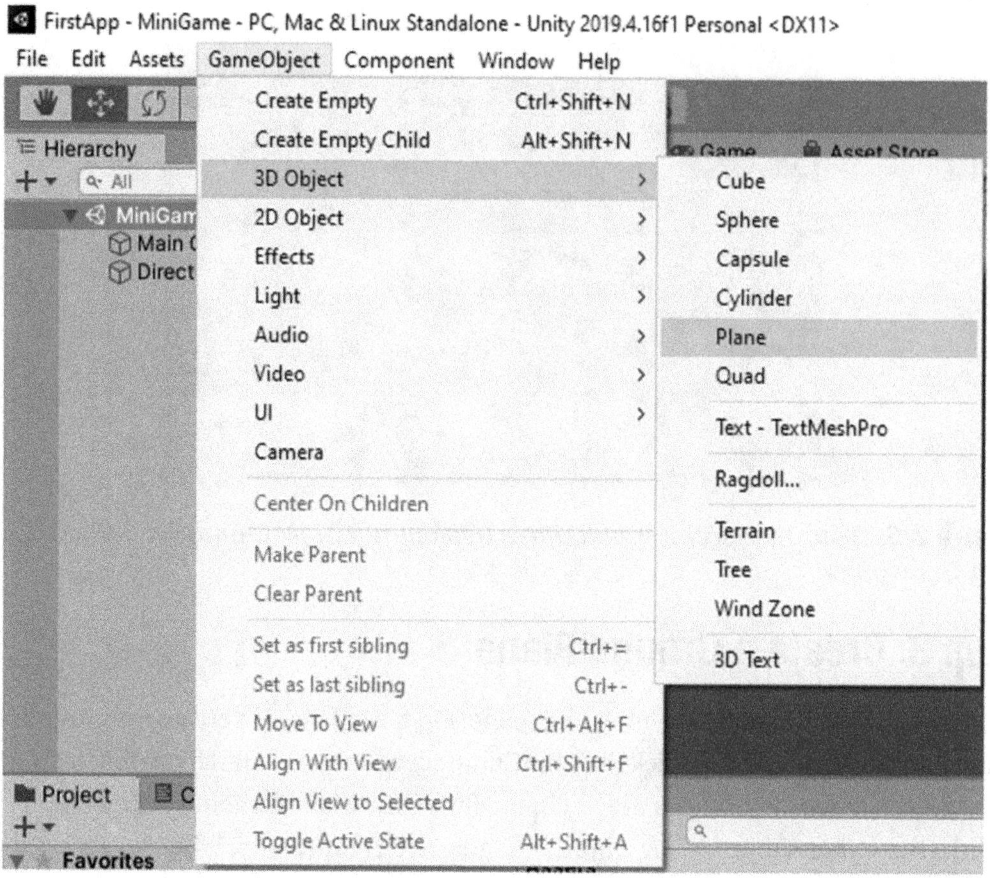

Figure 2-7. *Create a new Plane for the ground*

The Plane you just created will appear in your scene panel as a gray plane on the ground. It will also appear in your Hierarchy panel, as shown in Figure 2-8. Objects in the Hierarchy are referred to as *game objects*.

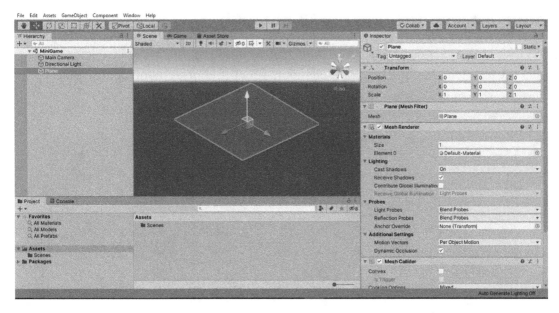

Figure 2-8. *Illustration of what the Plane object looks like after it is created*

Step 4: Rename Your Plane

Let's rename our Plane game object to "Ground." To do this, highlight (click) the Plane game object in the Hierarchy once. After waiting for a second, click the Plane game object again. You will now be able to edit the name of the game object. You may also rename the object by right-clicking and selecting "Rename." Rename it to "Ground" as it is shown in Figure 2-9.

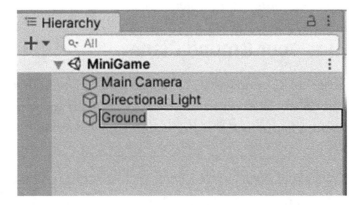

Figure 2-9. *Rename the "Plane" game object to "Ground"*

37

Step 5: Reset Ground Plane Position

Next, let's reset the position of our Ground game object to 0,0,0. In the Inspector panel, click the gear icon for the Transform element. After the context menu opens, select Reset, as shown in Figure 2-10.

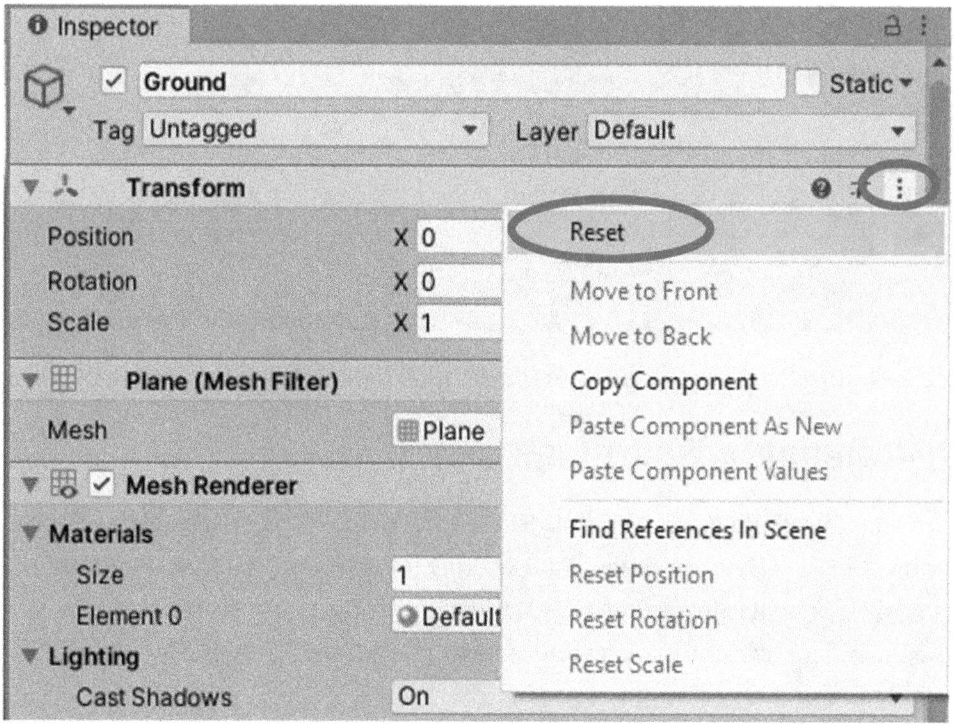

Figure 2-10. Reset the Ground game object's position

Step 6: Zoom to Your Ground Plane

In the Hierarchy, select the Ground game object, and press "F" on your keyboard. Doing this activates the *Frame Selected* command, which causes the scene window to zoom in or zoom out so that the game object you selected fills your scene window.

Tip   If you can't find your object in the scene, just select the game object's name in the Hierarchy and type "F" to automatically zoom to your object. This command is also helpful for quickly zooming to very large or very small objects in your scene.

Step 7: Scale Your Ground Plane

Next, we'll learn how to *scale* game objects by scaling the ground plane. To scale an object means to resize it. There are several different ways to scale game objects. I've listed some common methods here:

- Click the scale icon, and then click and drag one of the colored axes on the game object. Dragging the red axis scales in the X direction, green for the Y direction, and blue for the Z direction.

- Press "R" on your keyboard as a shortcut to clicking the scale icon.

- Click and drag the X, Y, or Z titles of the scale fields.

- Directly type in the scale of your choice in the scale fields.

Figure 2-11 illustrates where to find these scaling commands.

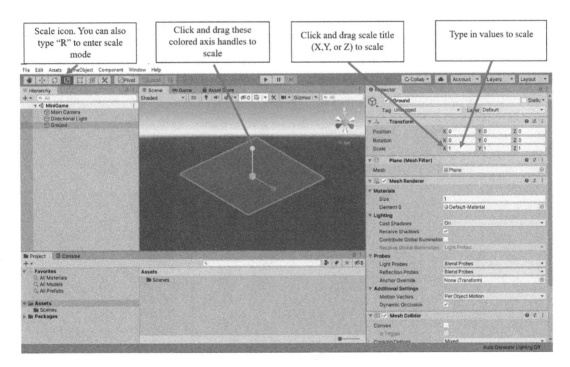

Figure 2-11. *There are many ways you can scale your game object*

Scale your object so that the X, Y, and Z axes are all set to a scale of 1.

Note   The Plane object is an exception toward other objects as it appears to be ten times bigger than other objects. It was just an arbitrary decision to make the plane unique compared to others, as many people use this object as floors or walls. Therefore, when you set the values of X, Y, and Z to 1, it considers ten meters with the plane.

Step 8: Create the Ball

Remember, we're creating a game called roll a ball. You will be controlling a rolling ball on a flat surface. To create a ball, we need to add a sphere to our scene. Adding a sphere is similar to adding a plane. Click our scene, MiniGame (to make sure we've not selected another game object), and then go to GameObject ➤ 3D Object ➤ Sphere. Figure 2-12 illustrates where to find this command.

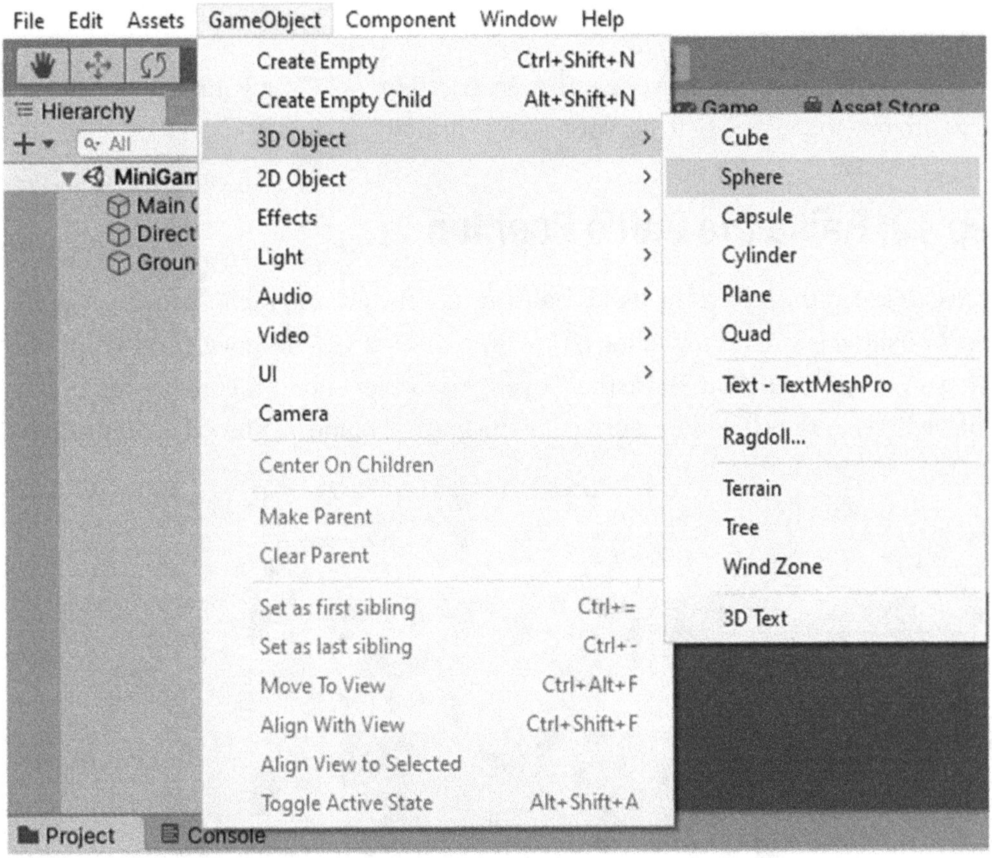

Figure 2-12. *Create a Sphere game object for your ball*

Step 9: Rename Your Ball

Rename your ball by selecting the "Sphere" game object in the Hierarchy, and clicking it again after one second, just like you renamed your Plane in Step 4. Name your sphere "Player."

Step 10: Reset the Ball's Position

Next, let's reset the position of our Player game object (our ball) to 0,0,0. In the Inspector panel, click the gear icon for the Transform element. After the context menu opens, select Reset, just like we did in Step 5 (see Figure 2-10.)

Step 11: Zoom to Your Ball

In the Hierarchy, select the Player game object, and press "F" on your keyboard to zoom in or zoom out so that the ball fills your scene window.

Step 12: Raise the Ball's Position

As you can see in the scene, the ball is halfway into the ground plane. Moving a game object's position is similar to scaling it (see Step 7). Figure 2-13 shows several options for moving an object's position. Raise the Player game object up to 0.5 units. After doing so, the ball will rest perfectly on the surface of the ground plane, as shown in Figure 2-13.

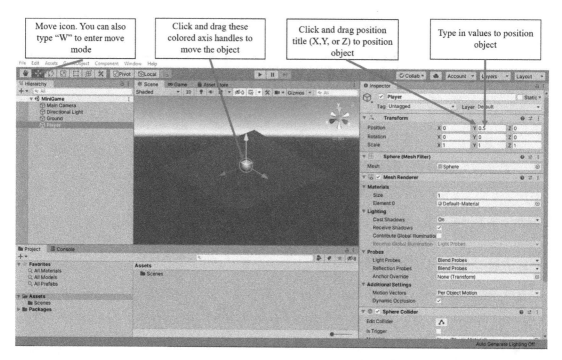

Figure 2-13. *There are a variety of ways to position game objects within Unity*

Step 13: Color the Ground Blue

So far, you've created the ground plane and a ball. The default color of the objects you've created is gray. Let's change some colors so that we can distinguish better between the Player ball and the ground plane. Within Unity, there are many options for modifying the appearance of your object. There's an intricate world of textures, materials, and shaders, which will be discussed in Chapter 4. For now, let's apply a simple material to our ground plane. First, let's create a folder to organize our materials. It's always a good practice to keep your project files organized, which will help avoid confusion and speed up development work, especially in very large and complex projects. To create a folder, click the "create" drop-down list in the Project panel, and select "Folder," as shown in Figure 2-14.

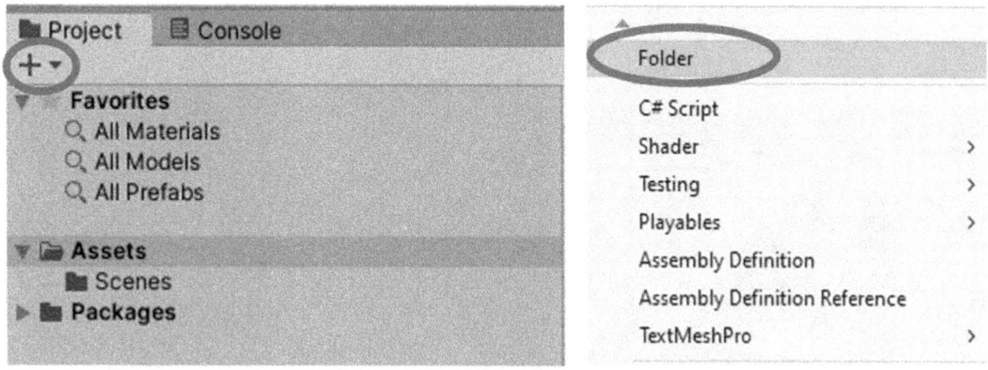

Figure 2-14. *Illustration of how to create a new folder in Unity*

Once the folder is created, rename the folder to "Materials," as shown in Figure 2-15.

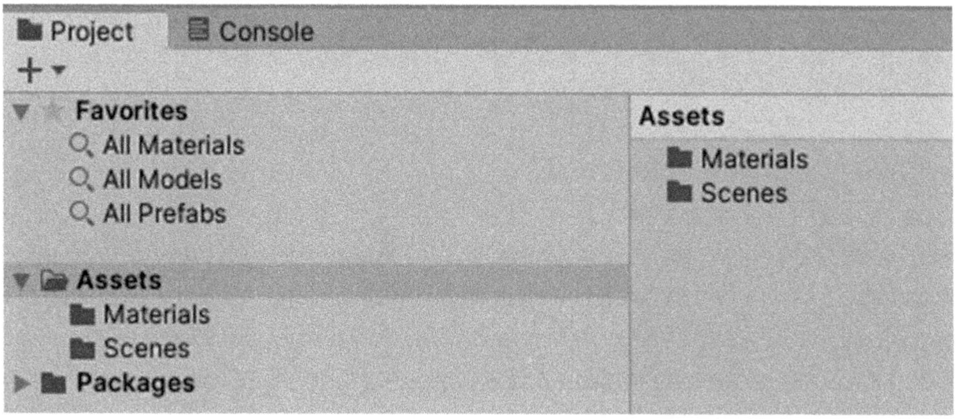

Figure 2-15. *After renaming, you will now have a "Materials" folder in your project list*

Next, we will create the material. Select the Materials folder that you just created so that it is highlighted. Using the same "create" drop-down menu that you used to create the Materials folder, create a new material as shown in Figure 2-16. The new material you created should now be inside the Materials folder (because the Materials folder was selected when you created the new material.) Rename the Material to "Background" in the same way you have renamed other items during this tutorial.

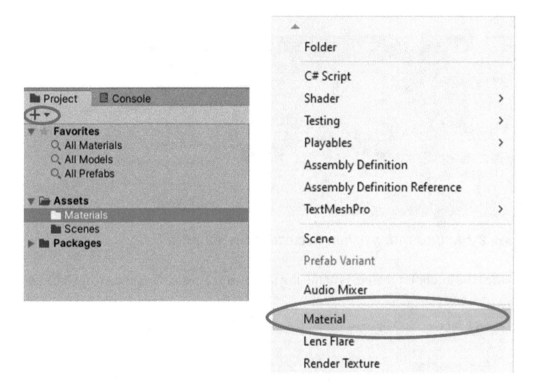

Figure 2-16. *Create a new material*

Next, select your new Background material, and open the Albedo setting in the Inspector, as shown in Figure 2-17. To open the Albedo setting, click the colored box (the default color is white) to the right of the word "Albedo." Do not click the eye-drop icon or the gray box on the left side of "Albedo." A pop-up window will open, where you can select various color options for your material, as shown in Figure 2-17.

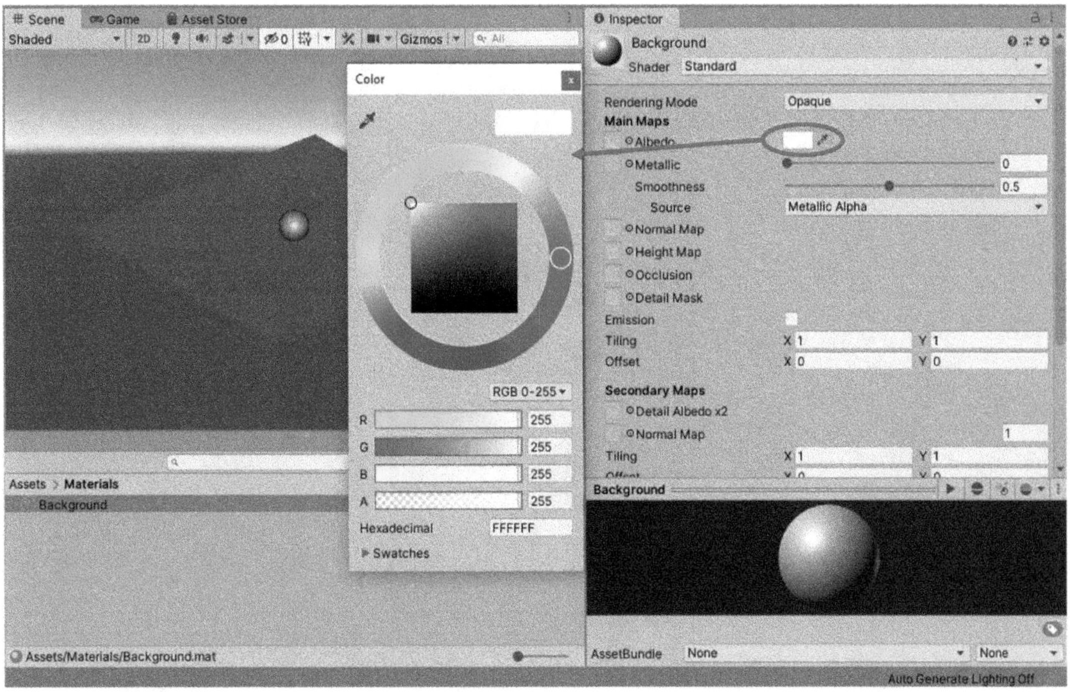

Figure 2-17. *Select the Background material's Albedo setting to change its color*

Within the pop-up color window, choose a dark blue color. You may need to drag the "Hue" bar to blue and then select a color within the square color box, as shown in Figure 2-18. Of course, you may choose any color you wish.

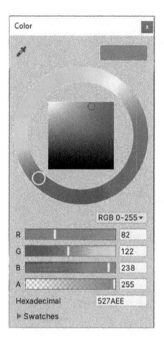

Figure 2-18. *Choose a dark blue color by changing the Hue and Brightness/ Saturation settings. You may also type in the specific numerical values shown*

Next, apply the blue Background material to the ground plane by dragging the material from the Project window to the ground plane, as shown in Figure 2-19. The ground plane should become blue, allowing the ball to stand out better.

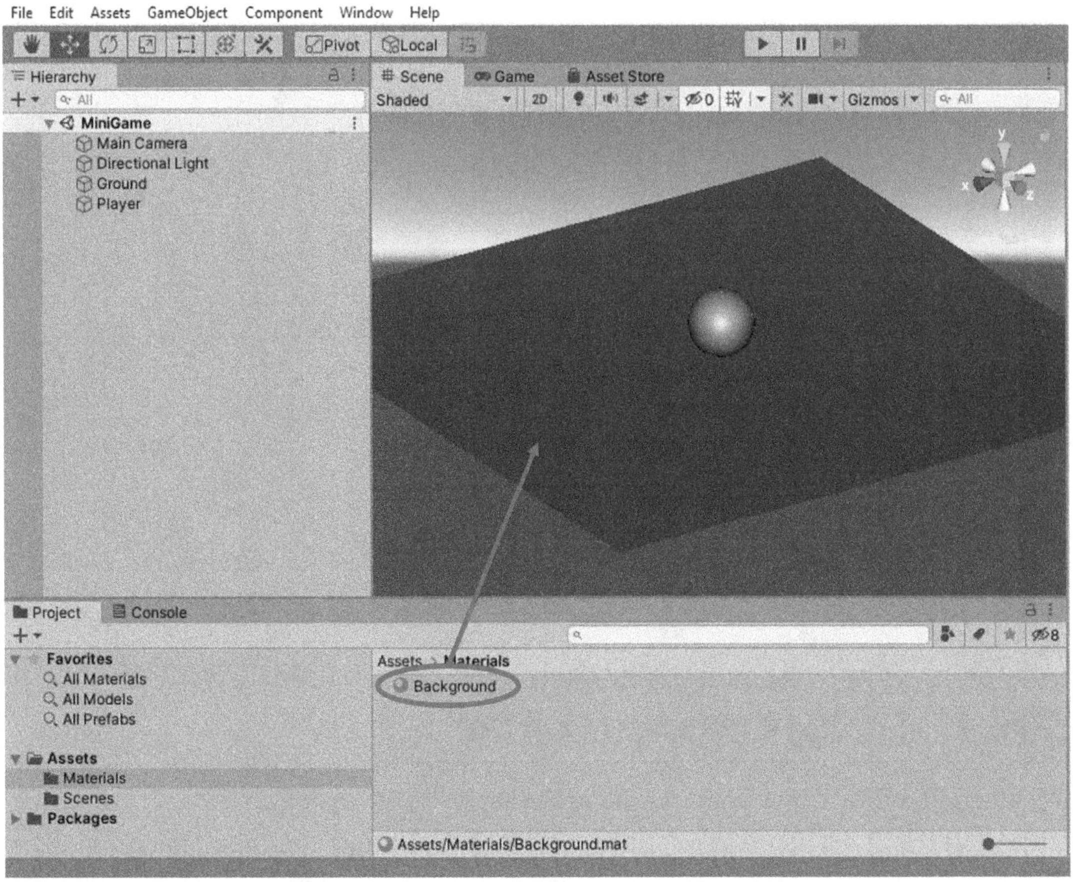

Figure 2-19. *Drag and drop your blue Background material from the Project panel to the ground plane. The ground plane will turn blue!*

Step 14: Add Physics to the Ball

Since this game will involve rolling our ball on our ground plane, we want our ball to behave somewhat like a ball would in the real world. This means that we want to use Physics. To use Physics, select our ball (which is the Player game object) in the Hierarchy, then click the "Add Component" button in the Inspector, and select Physics ➤ Rigidbody. See Figure 2-20 for the location of these menu items. *Rigid bodies* are a fundamental component of the Unity physics engine and is responsible for storing various state variables needed for the equations of motion.

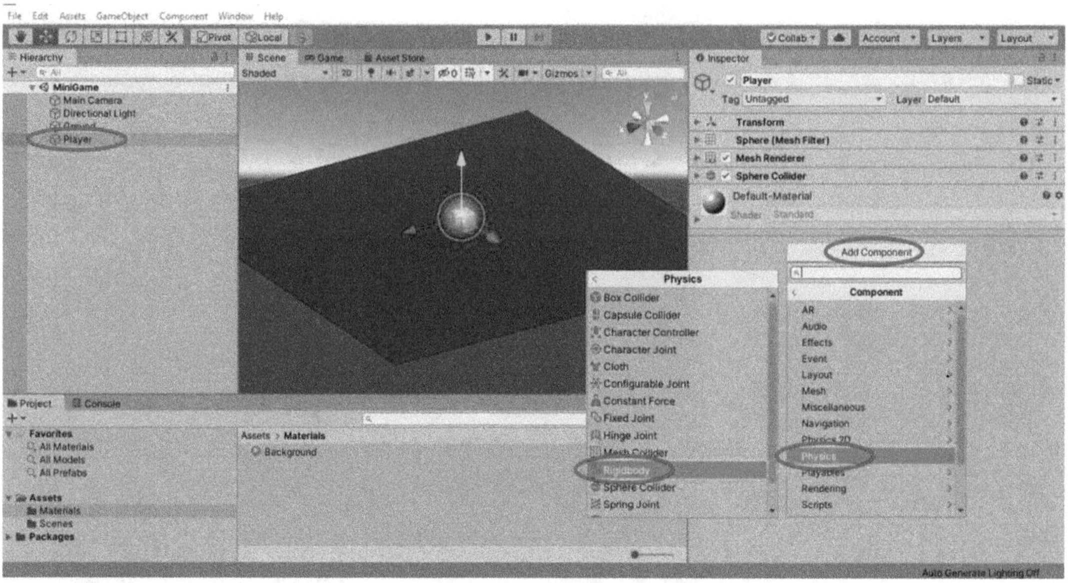

Figure 2-20. *Add the Rigidbody component to the Player game object to apply Physics to our ball*

Step 15: Enable Keyboard Control

We want to be able to move our ball using our keyboard as a game controller. To achieve this, we will need to apply some code to our ball! In Unity, our code documents are called *scripts*. Let's stay organized by creating a new folder to store our scripts, just like we created a new folder to store our materials in Step 13.

1. To create our new folder, go to your Project panel, and click Create
   ➤ Folder. Be sure that the Scripts folder is created in the Assets
   folder and not inside the Materials folder.

2. Rename your new folder "Scripts." Next, we want to add a new
   script to our ball.

3. Select the Player game object.

4. Click the "Add Component" button in the Inspector.

5. Scroll to the bottom of the list, and select "New Script."

6. In the next window that opens, be sure that the language of the
   script is set to C sharp (or sometimes referred to as C#).

7. Name your script "PlayerController."

8. Click the "Create and Add" button.

Figure 2-21 illustrates how to add and name your new script.

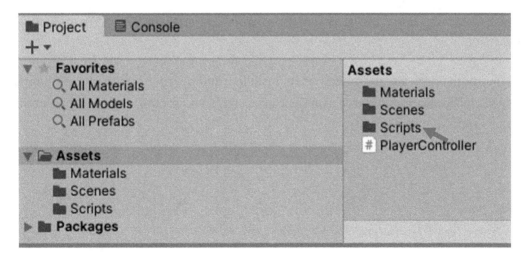

Figure 2-21. *Create a new script for your Player game object called "PlayerController"*

You'll notice in your Project panel that the new script you just created was not placed inside your Scripts folder. Drag and drop the PlayerController script inside your Scripts folder, as shown in Figure 2-22. Getting into the habit of staying organized is important!

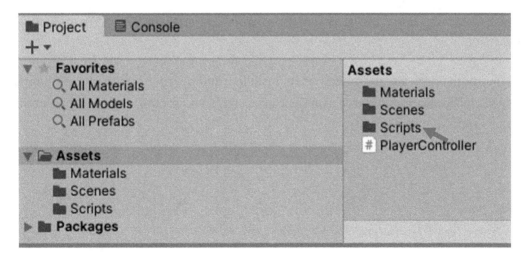

Figure 2-22. *Drag and drop the PlayerController script inside your Scripts folder to stay organized*

Next, we'll program our Player game object to respond to keyboard control:

1. Select the Player game object in the Hierarchy.

2. Double-click the PlayerController script in the Inspector, as shown in Figure 2-23. Visual Studio should now launch, so that you can start editing your script.

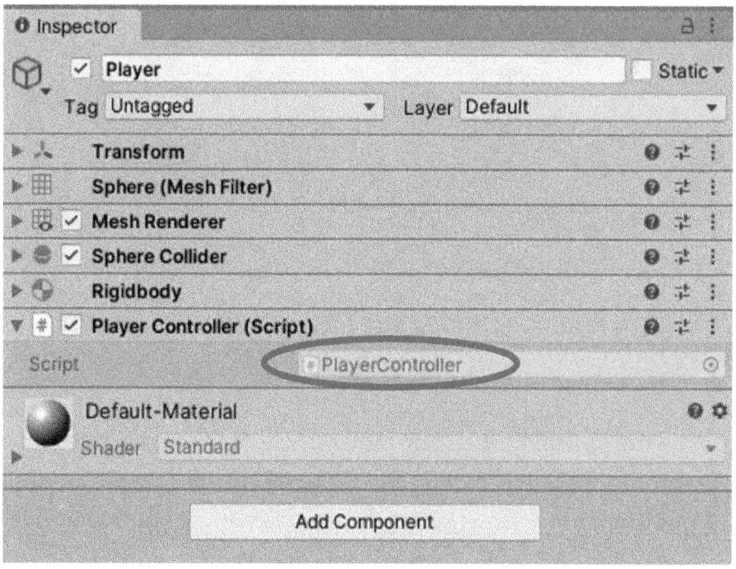

Figure 2-23. *Double-click the PlayerController script to open it in Visual Studio for editing*

You should have already downloaded, installed, and set up Visual Studio in Chapter 1. Once Visual Studio opens your PlayerController script, you should see a window similar to what is shown in Figure 2-24.

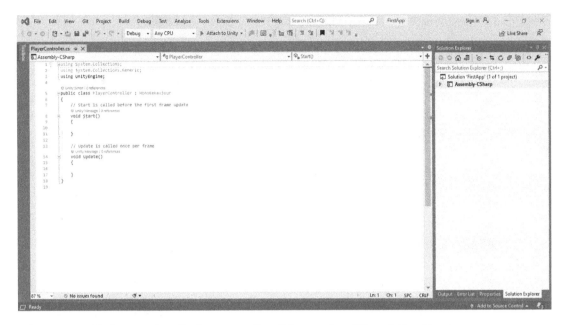

Figure 2-24. *Example of what you should see after Visual Studio opens your PlayerController script*

In Visual Studio, go ahead and erase all the code you see and replace it with the code provided in Listing 2-1.

Listing 2-1. The PlayerController script allows you to roll the ball by using your keyboard controls

```
using UnityEngine;
using System.Collections;

public class PlayerController : MonoBehaviour {

    public float speed;

    private Rigidbody rb;

    void Start ()
    {
        rb = GetComponent<Rigidbody>();
    }
```

```
void FixedUpdate ()
{
    float moveHorizontal = Input.GetAxis ("Horizontal");
    float moveVertical = Input.GetAxis ("Vertical");

    Vector3 movement = new Vector3 (moveHorizontal, 0.0f,
    moveVertical);

    rb.AddForce (movement * speed);
}
}
```

Your Visual Studio window should now look like Figure 2-25. Save your code by clicking the "Save All" icon, circled in red in Figure 2-25.

Figure 2-25. *Replace all the default code in PlayerController with the code provided. Save your script by clicking the "Save All" icon, circled in red*

We won't go into the explanation of this code in this tutorial, since this chapter is primarily intended to familiarize yourself with Unity's workflow. As we begin developing Mixed Reality applications, I will walk through scripts in detail so that you understand how the code works.

Step 16: Testing Your App

Next, we'll test our new app to ensure everything works as designed. Go back into the Unity editor, and select the Player game object in the Hierarchy. You'll notice a new field has appeared under the Player Controller in the Inspector, as shown in Figure 2-26. This is due to the new script that we programmed. For this to show up in the Inspector panel, you will need to save your script and allow Unity a few seconds to process the saved changes and update the Inspector panel. Change the value of "Speed" to 10, and click the play button (located above the scene panel), as shown in Figure 2-26.

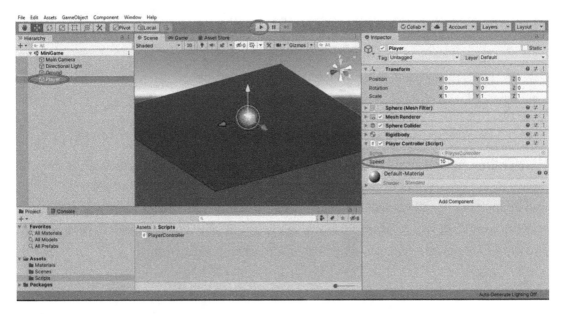

Figure 2-26. *Set the Player's speed to 10 in the Inspector, and then click the play button (top) to test your new app*

After clicking play, you will enter "Game" mode, where you will view the game through the scene's camera. Go ahead and try pressing the left, right, up, and down arrows on your keyboard and watch the ball move! If you fall off the edge of the ground plane, you can always reset the game by clicking play again to stop the game and then clicking play once more to enter the game. Feel free to explore how changing the speed of your Player impacts gameplay.

Summary

Congratulations! You have successfully completed your very first Unity application. Here are some things we've learned in this chapter:

- We discussed some basic information about what Unity is.

- We looked at Unity's pricing tiers.

- We learned about the Unity's editor interface.

- We learned how to create new game objects.

- We learned how to scale and move game objects.

- We learned how to apply materials to game objects.

- We learned how to apply physics to game objects.

- We learned how to create and apply scripts to game objects.

- We created and tested our first Unity app!

Now that you are familiar with the basics of Unity, we can start exploring how to create Mixed Reality experiences with this powerful platform. Unity is a very large and nuanced tool, and you will spend much of your time as a Mixed Reality developer refining your Unity skills. As we walk through Mixed Reality development in the subsequent chapters, we'll also dive deeper into various Unity topics.

PART II

Building Holographic Experiences

CHAPTER 3

Creating Your First Hologram

In this chapter, we'll build our very first holographic experience! We'll begin by setting up Unity for holographic development using the Mixed Reality Toolkit. After creating our first hologram, we'll test our app by deploying directly to our HoloLens using Visual Studio. In this chapter, I will also discuss ways to create or find your own holograms (3D models) for your project.

Getting Unity Ready for Mixed Reality Development

Before we begin creating our first hologram, we first need to make sure Unity is ready for Mixed Reality development. There are several settings in Unity that need to be changed for our apps to work on the HoloLens and other Mixed Reality devices. For example, in Chapter 2's Unity tutorial, you may have noticed a gray/brown floor and blue sky in the scene. We usually won't want this digital floor and sky to appear in all our Mixed Reality experiences, so we need to black out our background so that it does not appear on our device; having a black background helps you acquire a transparent background in HoloLens. We also need to adjust our camera settings, so that each eye sees a slightly different perspective of our scene, which will allow users to perceive depth when wearing the headset. These are just a few examples of settings that need to change to prepare Unity for Mixed Reality development. All these settings can be changed manually, but it would be very tedious and time consuming to do this each time you create a new Mixed Reality project.

Fortunately, Microsoft has provided a community resource called the Mixed Reality Toolkit, which will help us automatically set up Unity for making Mixed Reality apps. I have an entire chapter on the Mixed Reality Toolkit in this book, so we won't cover all

© Sean Ong and Varun Kumar Siddaraju 2021
S. Ong and V. K. Siddaraju, *Beginning Windows Mixed Reality Programming*,
https://doi.org/10.1007/978-1-4842-7104-9_3

it has to offer in this chapter. The following steps will walk you through preparing your scene for Mixed Reality development.

Note   The Mixed Reality Toolkit is updated regularly, and some elements may have changed since these instructions were written. Be sure to check the Mixed Reality Toolkit documentation for updated instructions if you are unable to find the objects I refer to in this tutorial. You can find the Mixed Reality Toolkit instructions at this URL: `https://microsoft.github.io/MixedRealityToolkit-Unity/Documentation/GettingStartedWithTheMRTK.html`

Step 1: Import Mixed Reality Toolkit to a New Unity Project

Before proceeding, be sure that you have already downloaded and saved the Mixed Reality Toolkit Unity package as per the instructions in Chapter 1:

1. Create a new Unity project (see Chapter 2, if you need a reminder on how to do this), and name it "Holo World."

Important   [OBJ] Save your scene, and give it a name that you wish. If you do not save your scene, you will not be able to apply HoloLens settings in Step 2. How to save your scene is explained in Chapter 2. Revisit to know more.

---

2. From the menu bar, go to Assets ➤ Import Package ➤ Custom Package. In the pop-up window that appears, browse to the Mixed Reality Toolkit that you downloaded in Chapter 1. See Figure 3-1 for an illustration of these menu items.

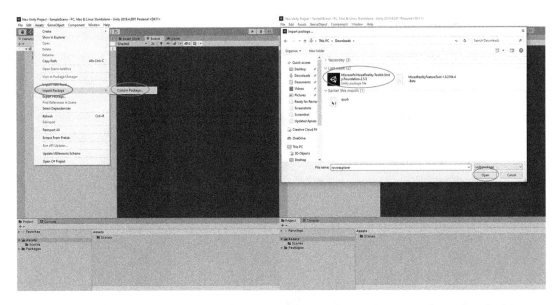

Figure 3-1. *Import the Mixed Reality Toolkit package that you downloaded in Chapter 1*

3. Unity will take a minute to prepare the package you selected and then show you another pop-up window where you can select or deselect package items. Go ahead and leave everything checked (everything should be checked by default), and click the Import button, as shown in Figure 3-2.

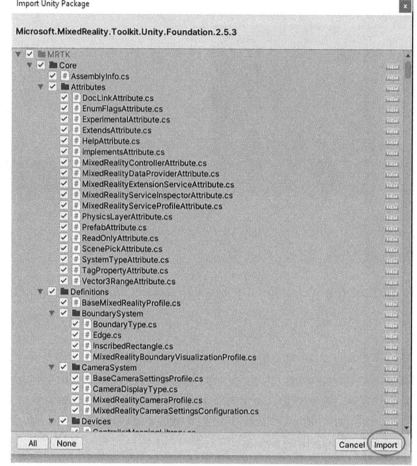

Figure 3-2. *Click the Import button to import the Mixed Reality Toolkit package*

4. After importing, you will get the MRTK project configurator window in that click Apply. Refer to Figure 3-3 (left). After clicking Apply, your final Unity environment should look similar to Figure 3-3 (right).

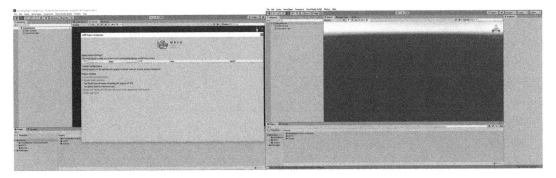

Figure 3-3. Click the Apply button to apply the settings (left). After importing, your Unity environment will look like this (right)

Step 2: Use Mixed Reality Toolkit to Prepare Your Scene for Mixed Reality Development

After completing Step 1, you should now see a "Mixed Reality Toolkit" menu item in your menu bar, as shown in Figure 3-4:

1. From the menu bar, select Mixed Reality Toolkit ➤ Add to scene and configure settings. Do not forget to save your scene as when you proceed.

2. From the menu bar, select Mixed Reality Toolkit ➤ Utilities ➤ Configure Unity Project. This will convert the Unity project to a Windows Direct 3D (D3D) project, optimize quality, and enable Virtual Reality support. Unity will require you to reload your project. *If you did not save your scene from the previous step, you will lose all changes to the scene and need to apply scene settings again.*

Tip   After choosing to apply settings from the Mixed Reality Toolkit menu, a pop-up window appears showing settings to apply. Click each item to learn more about each item.

---

3. Remove the "Main Camera" and "Directional Light" game objects from the Hierarchy by right-clicking each item and choosing "Delete" from the context menu.

4. Save your scene.

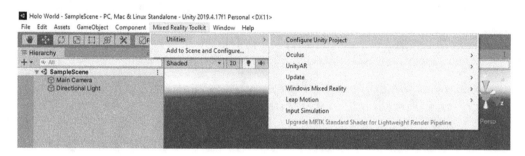

Figure 3-4. *You now have a shiny, new Mixed Reality Toolkit menu item!*

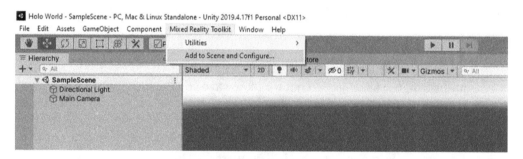

Figure 3-5. *After deleting the "Main Camera" and "Directional Light" objects, insert the HoloLensCamera to scene*

- In order to develop the application for HoloLens 2, we need to switch platform to UWP (Universal Windows Platform). In the Unity menu, select File ➤ Build Settings to open the Build Settings window, and click UWP and then Switch Platform as shown in Figure 3-6.

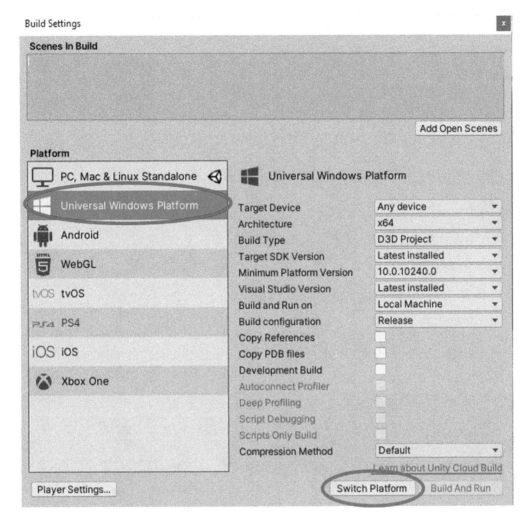

Figure 3-6. *Switch platform to UWP*

- Also we need to install XR Plugin Management. XR Plugin
  Management initializes automatically and starts your XR
  environment when the application loads. In the Unity menu, select
  Edit ➤ Project Settings, and in Project Settings, click XR Plugin
  Management on the left side and click Install XR Plugin Management
  as shown in Figure 3-7.

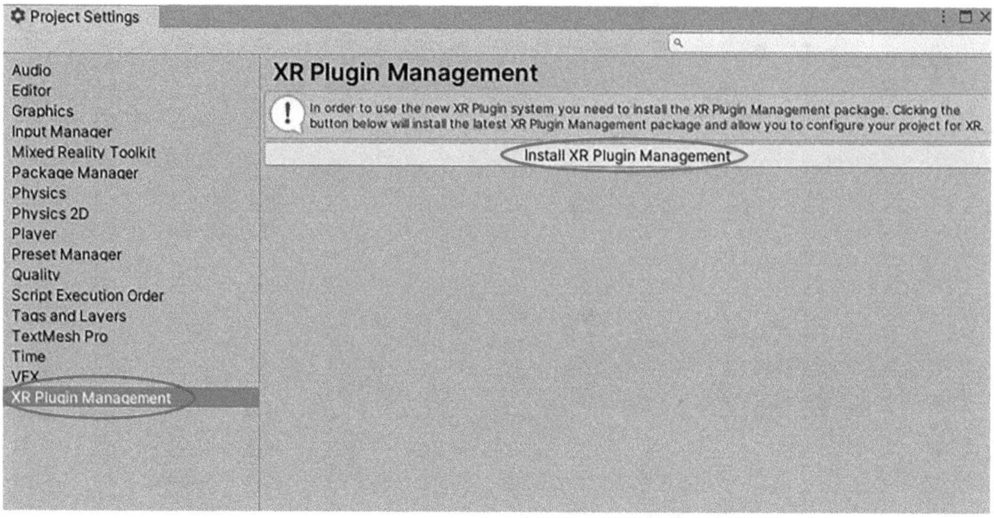

Figure 3-7.   *Install XR Plugin Management*

- Ensure that you are in Universal Windows Platform settings, and check the Initialize XR on Startup check box as shown in Figure 3-8.

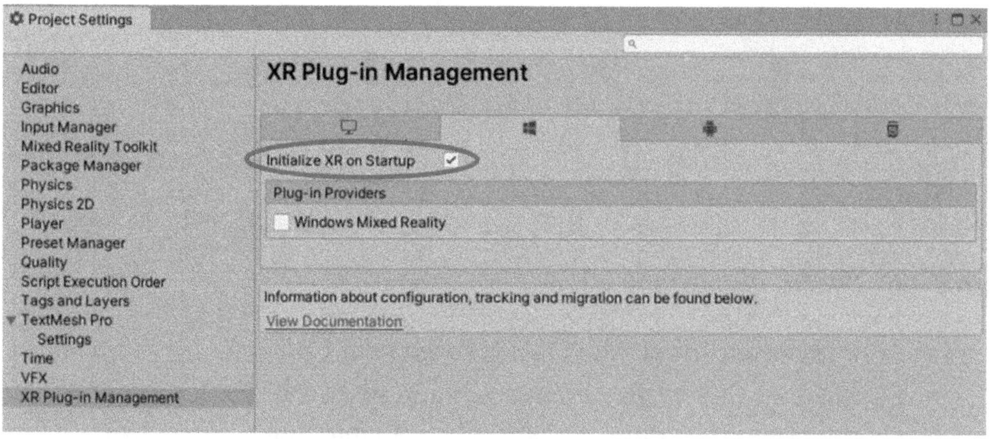

Figure 3-8.   *Initialize XR on Startup check box*

- In the Project Settings window, select Player ➤ XR Settings, and ensure Virtual Reality supported is checked. Click the + icon, and select Windows Mixed Reality to add the Windows Mixed Reality SDK.

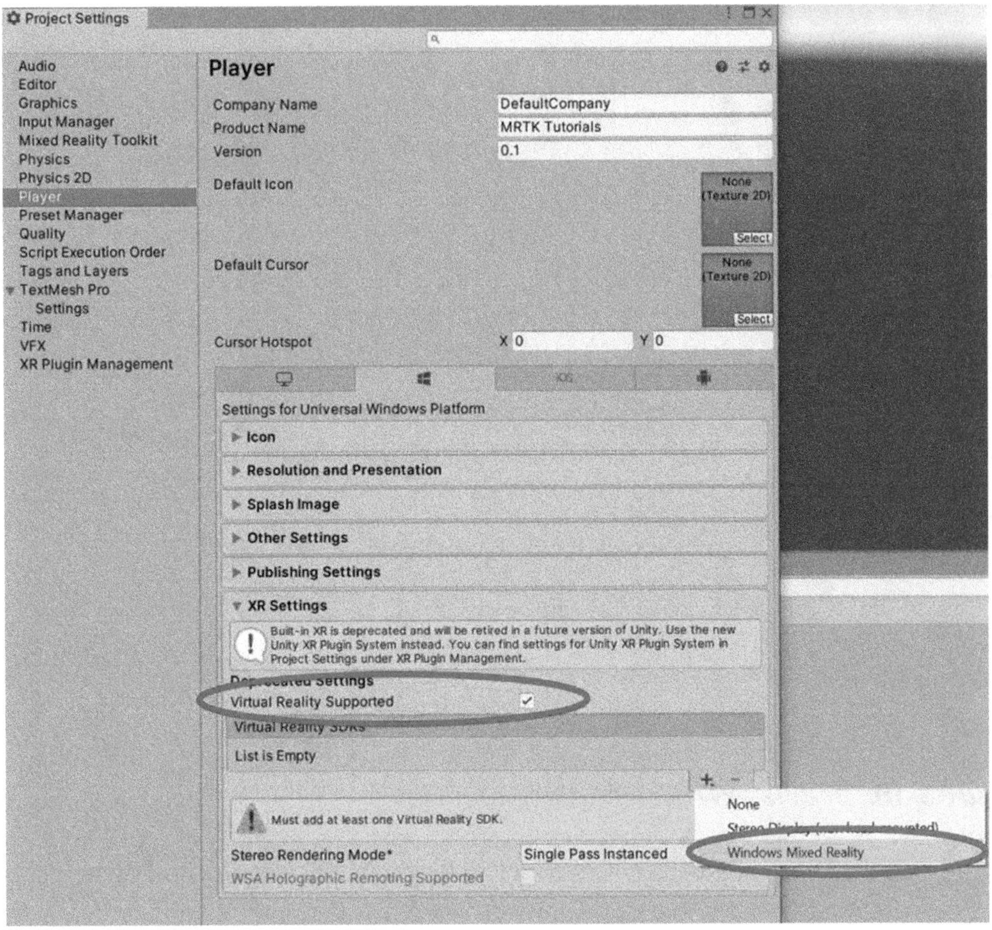

Figure 3-9. *Virtual Reality Supported is checked and add Windows Mixed Reality SDK*

- In the MRTK project configurator window, use the Audio Spatializer drop-down to select the MS HRTF Spatializer, and then click the Apply button to apply the setting as shown in Figure 3-10. Setting the Audio Spatializer property is optional but may improve the audio experience in your project. If you set it to MS HRTF Spatializer, this Spatializer plug-in will be used when Unity's AudioSource.spatialize property is enabled.

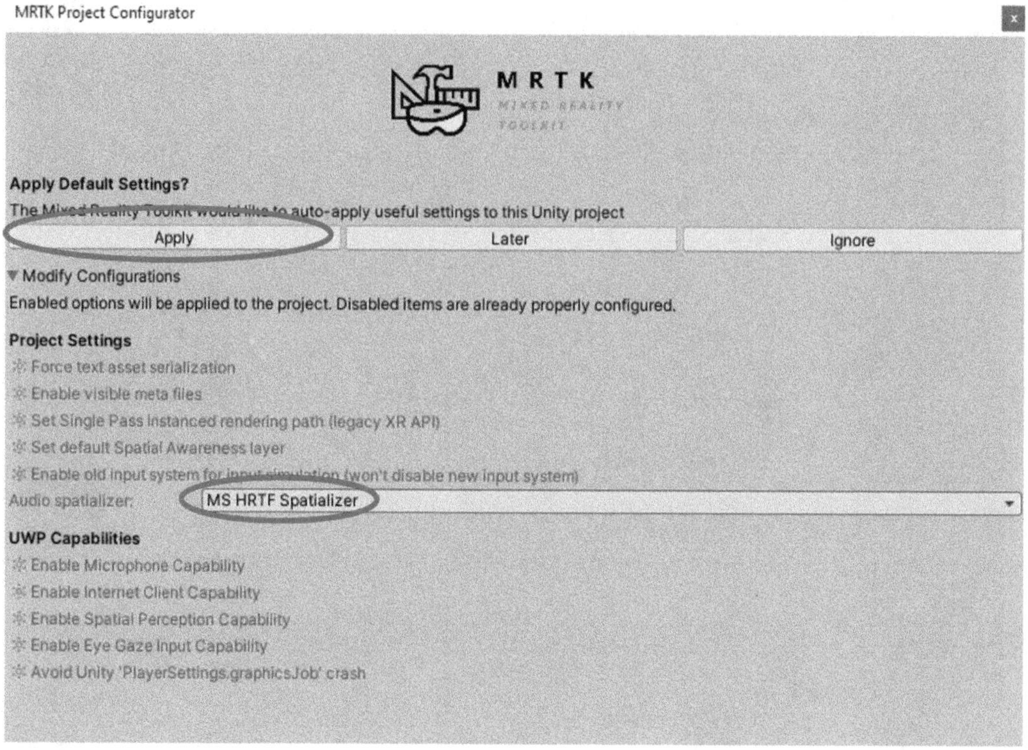

Figure 3-10. *Enable MS HRTF Audio Spatializer*

- In the Project Settings window, select Player ➤ XR Settings, and then use the Depth Format drop-down to select 16-bit depth. Reducing the Depth Format to 16 bits is optional but may help improve graphics performance in your project.

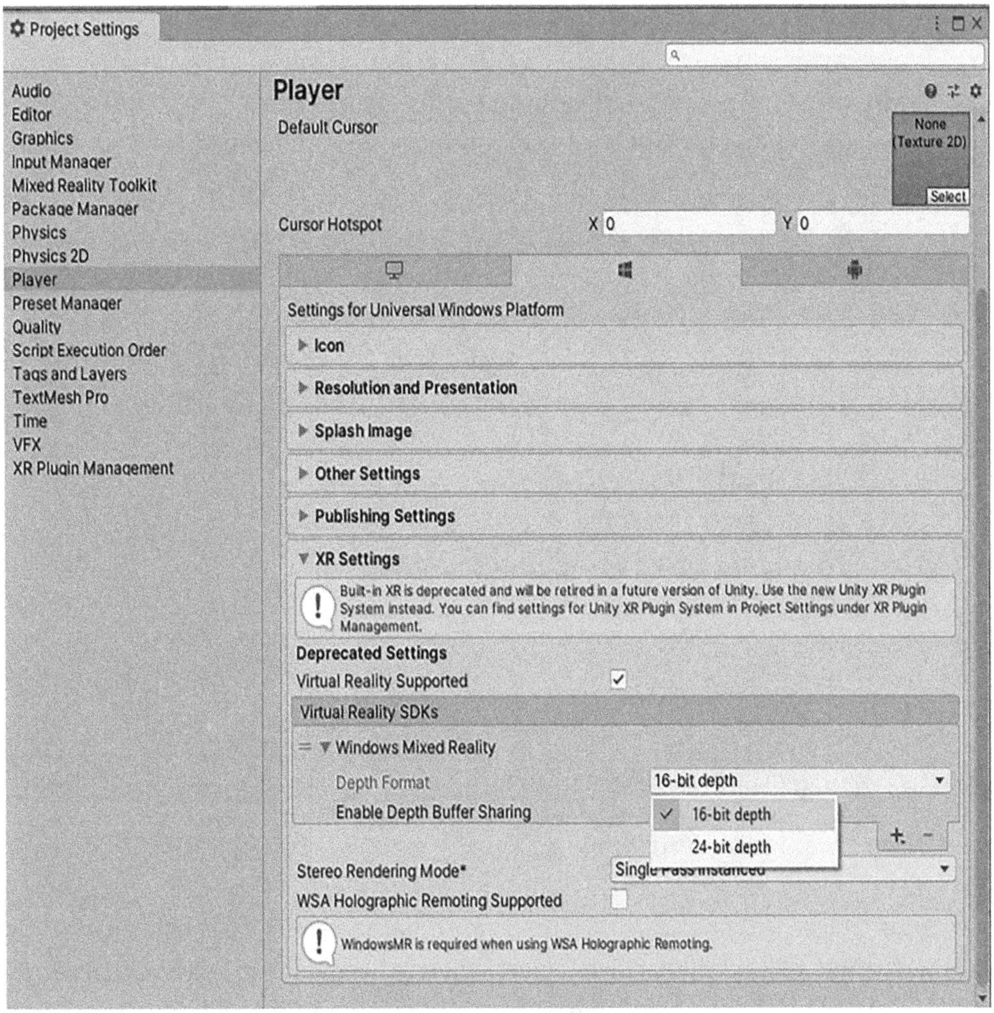

Figure 3-11. *Set Depth Format to 16 bits*

- The Mixed Reality Toolkit centralizes as much of the configuration required to manage the toolkit as possible (except for true runtime "things"). The MRTK profile is a tree of nested profiles that make up the configuration information for how the MRTK systems and features should be initialized.

- • In the Hierarchy window, select the MixedRealityToolkit object; then in the Inspector window, verify that the MixedRealityToolkit Configuration Profile is set to the DefaultHoloLens2ConfigurationProfile as shown in Figure 3-12.

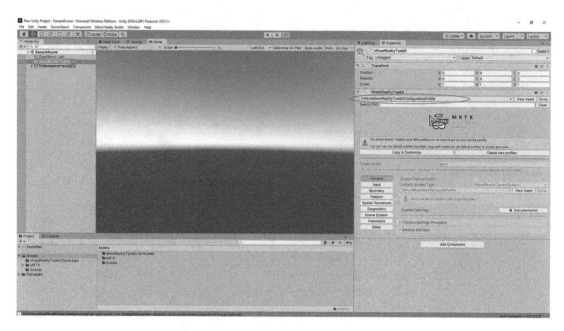

Figure 3-12. *Enable DefaultHoloLens2ConfigurationProfile*

Congratulations, your scene is now ready for holograms! Before starting each new Mixed Reality project in the future, you'll want to repeat these basic preparation instructions. While you can keep using the same Mixed Reality Toolkit package that you downloaded, it's always a good idea to regularly check for updates to the Mixed Reality Toolkit. New features are added all the time, and bugs are constantly being fixed. You can explore the Mixed Reality Toolkit at this URL: *https://github.com/Microsoft/Mixed Reality Toolkit-Unity*. Be sure to look around this page for reports of bugs, recent fixes, updates, and more.

Your First Hologram

You will still be able to see a floor grid and horizon when in the scene view. If you were to deploy this "app" to your HoloLens, you would see nothing. In this section, we'll create a simple cube object, which will serve as our first hologram.

Note   In the context of Windows Mixed Reality, a "hologram" is any visible game object. To stay consistent with Microsoft's naming conventions, I generally call any visible game object or 3D model a hologram but may use these terms interchangeably throughout this book.

Step 1: Create a Cube

In Chapter 2, you created a plane and a sphere within Unity. Use the same approach to create a cube game object in your scene. In addition to the approach you learned in Chapter 2, you can also create a cube by right-clicking an empty place in the Hierarchy, and in the pop-up context menu, select "3D Object" ➤ "Cube" as shown in Figure 3-13.

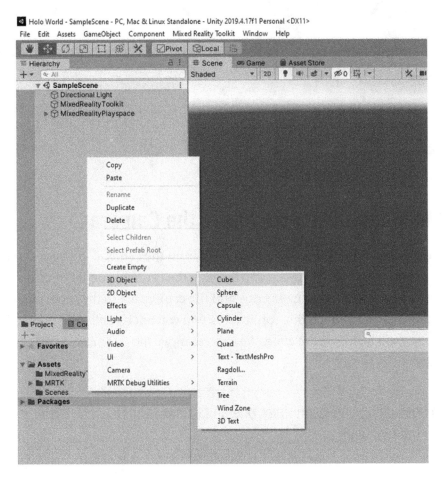

Figure 3-13. *Create a cube in the Hierarchy*

Step 2: Zoom to Your Cube

If you haven't already, be sure to switch to the scene view so that you can view objects in your scene. You can switch between views by clicking the tabs that are above the visualization window, as shown in Figure 3-14. Zoom to your cube by selecting the cube game object in your Hierarchy and pressing the F key. Your scene should look similar to Figure 3-14.

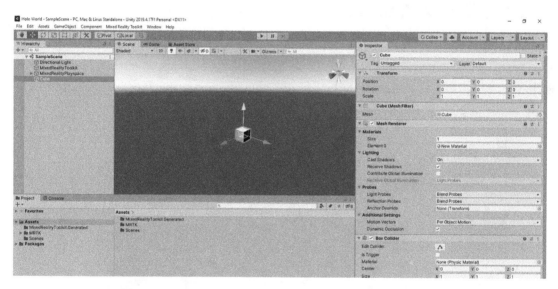

Figure 3-14. *Zoom to your cube*

Step 3: Move the Cube Away from the Camera

Next, we'll want to move the cube game object away from the camera. *In Unity, think of the camera as your eyes.* You view your app through the camera. You'll notice in the scene (see Figure 3-10) that both the cube and the camera are in the same place. This means that when you launch this application, you will not be able to see the cube because your eyes will be inside the cube! We need to move the cube a short distance in front of our face.

Tip   When positioning objects in Unity, one unit is approximately one meter (over three feet) in the real world.

Let's move the cube about two units in front of our face, which is about two meters in the real world:

- Select the Cube in the Hierarchy.

- In the Inspector, change the Position to "2" as shown in Figure 3-15.

As you can see in Figure 3-15, the cube is now two units in front of the camera.

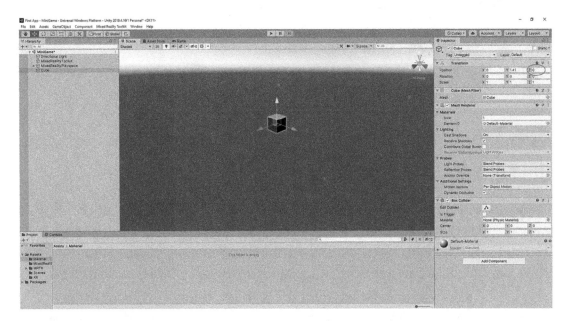

Figure 3-15. *Move the cube two units in front of the camera*

Step 4: Resize the Cube

Currently, our cube has a scale of 1 by 1 by 1, meaning that it's a cube that's approximately one meter on each side. Let's make our cube smaller so that we can view the entire cube within our field of view.

Use the approach in Step 7 of Chapter 2 to scale (resize) your cube down to 0.2 by 0.2 by 0.2, as shown in Figure 3-16.

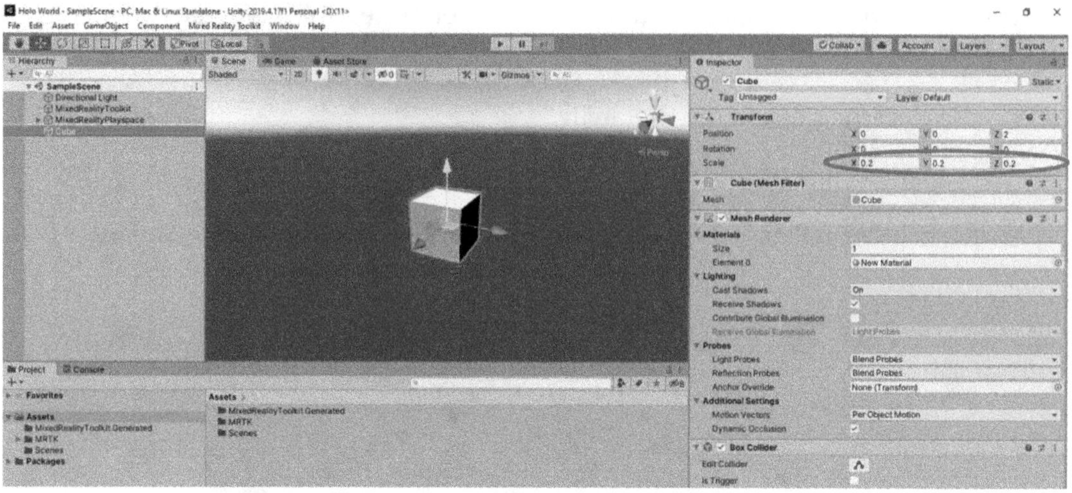

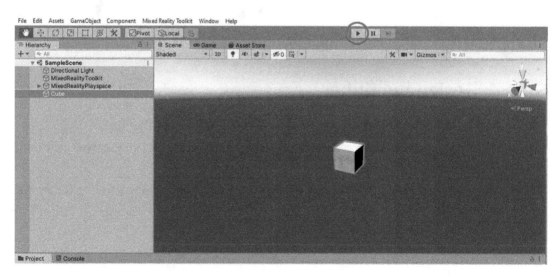

Figure 3-16. *Scale the cube down in size to make it easier to see*

Step 5. Test Your App

It's important to regularly test your app as you develop it to ensure that it is behaving as you intend. Unity provides a very quick way of testing your app. To begin, simply click the play button that is located near the top of the Unity editor, as shown in Figure 3-17. When you click play, you should see your cube surrounded by a black background.

Figure 3-17. *Click the play button to quickly test your app*

The MRTK also includes the ability to "move around" in your scene. Try it by pressing the left/right/up/down arrows on your keyboard while in Game mode (you may need to click the Game window before the keys work.) You can also right-click your mouse to drag the camera's view. Be careful when pressing keys, as the movement can be very fast and you may lose sight of your cube! If that happens, just restart your app test.

Click the play button again to exit Game mode. This was a very quick and easy way to test your app.

Step 6: Install Your App on the HoloLens

Now that we have tested our Cube app, let's install it on our HoloLens to experience our first hologram in person! Here's what to do:

1. Be sure that you have exited out of Game mode from the previous step. The play button should be black when you are not in Game mode. It is blue when you are in Game mode.

2. In your menu bar, go to File ➤ Build Settings.

3. A pop-up window will appear, as shown in Figure 3-18.

4. Be sure to click the "Add Open Scenes" button to add your current scene to the list of scenes to build.

5. If you applied all the HoloLens projects settings at the beginning of this chapter correctly, then the remaining settings should not need to be modified. Review to make sure the Platform is set to Windows Store, the SDK is set to Windows 10, the Target Device is set to HoloLens, the UWP Build Type is set to D3D, and that "Build and Run on" is set to Local Machine. See Figure 3-18 for how these settings should appear.

6. Click the "Build" button.

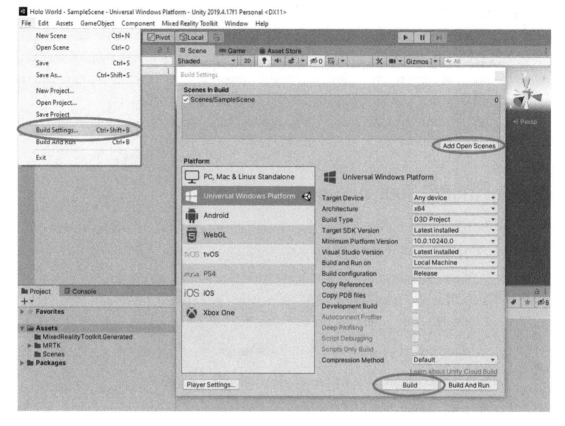

Figure 3-18. *Export your first Mixed Reality app using the Build Settings window in Unity*

- After you click the Build button, another pop-up window will appear. Create a new folder and name it. I typically name my folder "App." Click your newly created folder, and click "Select Folder" as shown in Figure 3-19.

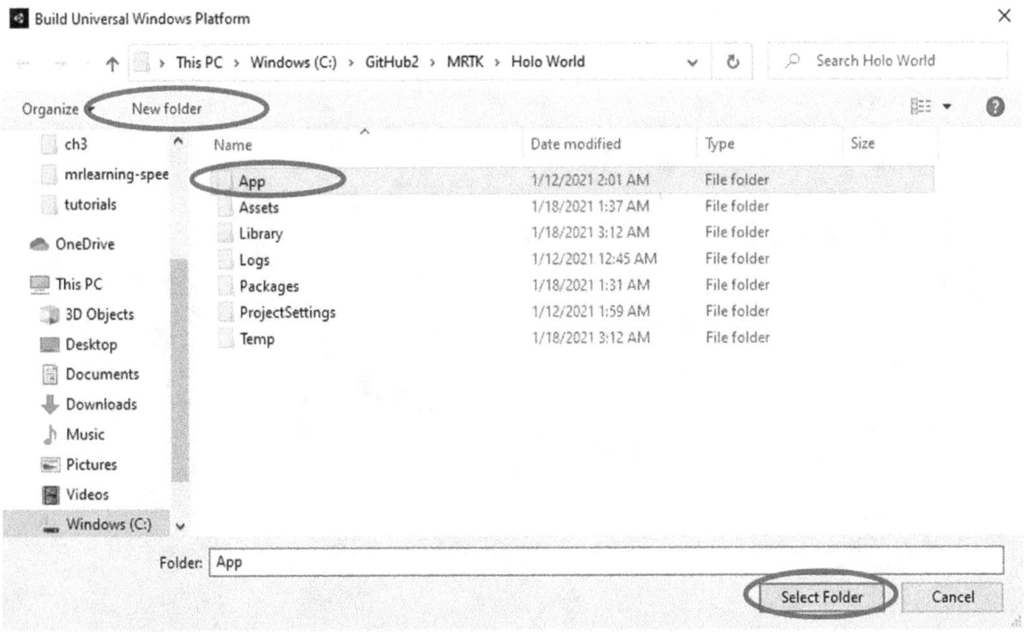

Figure 3-19. *Create a new folder to contain your app*

- Unity will spend a few minutes building your new app and placing project files in the new folder you created. After Unity has completed building you app, a pop-up window will appear, showing the new folder you created. Open this folder.

- Double-click "Holo World.sln" to open your project in Visual Studio. Your file may be named differently if you did not name your project "Holo World."

- We will use Visual Studio to deploy (install) our app to our HoloLens. Before we can do this, we need to enable *Developer Mode* on the HoloLens. Turn on your HoloLens, and open the *Settings* app. Select the *Update & Security* menu item, as shown in Figure 3-20.

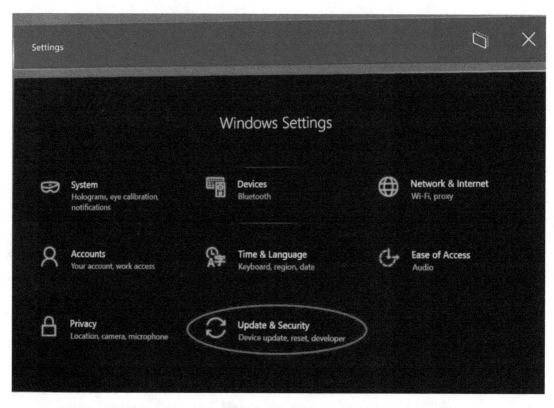

Figure 3-20. *In the Settings app, go to the Update & Security menu item*

- Once in the Update & Security menu, navigate to the "For developers" section, and ensure that Developer Mode is turned on, as shown in Figure 3-21.

Figure 3-21. *Navigate to the "For developers" section and enable Developer Mode*

- Make sure that your HoloLens is connected to the same Wi-Fi network as your development PC.

- On your PC, set your configuration to *Release or Master* and your platform to *ARM64*, as shown in Figure 3-22.

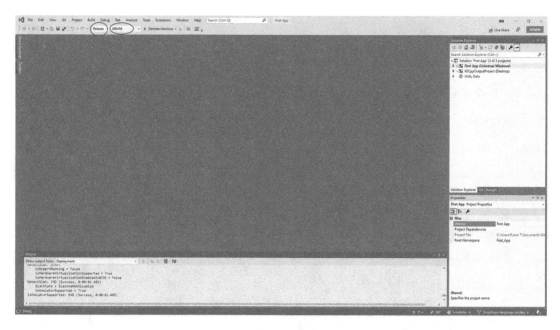

Figure 3-22. *Set your configuration to "Release" and your platform to "ARM64"*

- Set your Target Device to Remote Machine, as shown in Figure 3-23.

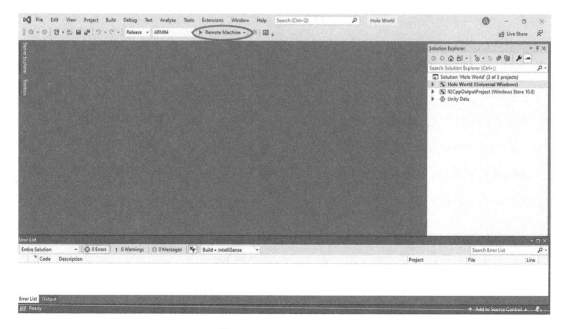

Figure 3-23. *Set your target to "Remote Machine"*

- Go to Settings ➤ Network & Internet ➤ Advanced options. See
  Figure 3-24 for guidance on where to find the IP address in your
  HoloLens' Settings app.

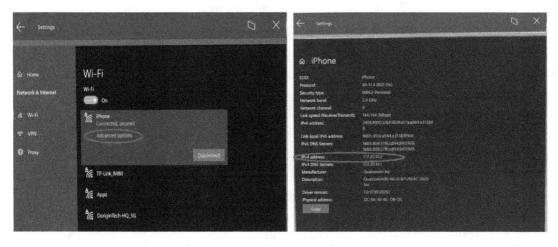

Figure 3-24. Illustration of where to find your HoloLens IP address in the Settings app

- Once you know your HoloLens IP address, ensure that the Universal
  Windows project in the solution is selected, and go to Project ➤
  Properties ➤ Debugging, and enter the IP address under machine
  name in Visual Studio, and click the "OK" button, as shown in
  Figure 3-25.

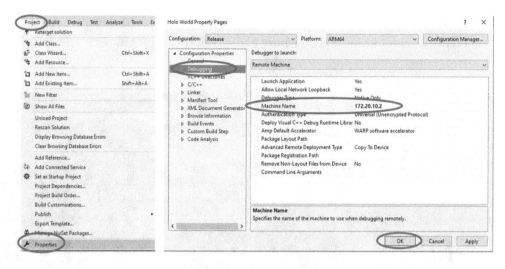

Figure 3-25. *Enter your HoloLens IP address into Visual Studio*

- You are now ready to deploy your app to your HoloLens. In the Debug menu, select "Start Without Debugging" as shown in Figure 3-26.

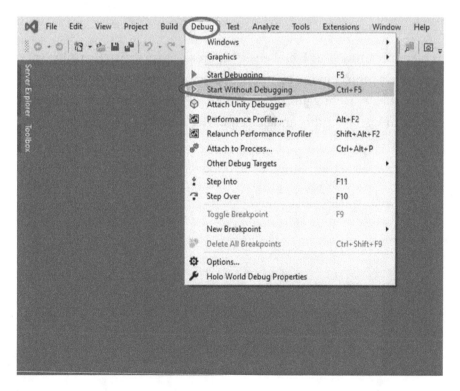

Figure 3-26. *Start the app deployment process by going to Debug ➤ Start Without Debugging*

- If this is your first time deploying to your HoloLens from this PC, you will be prompted to pair your HoloLens with Visual Studio, as shown in Figure 3-27. To pair your HoloLens, go back to the "For developers" section of your HoloLens Settings app, and click the "Pair" button as can be seen in Figure 3-21. You will see numbers appear on your HoloLens (see Figure 3-28 for an illustration of this), which you can then type into the pop-up window in Visual Studio.

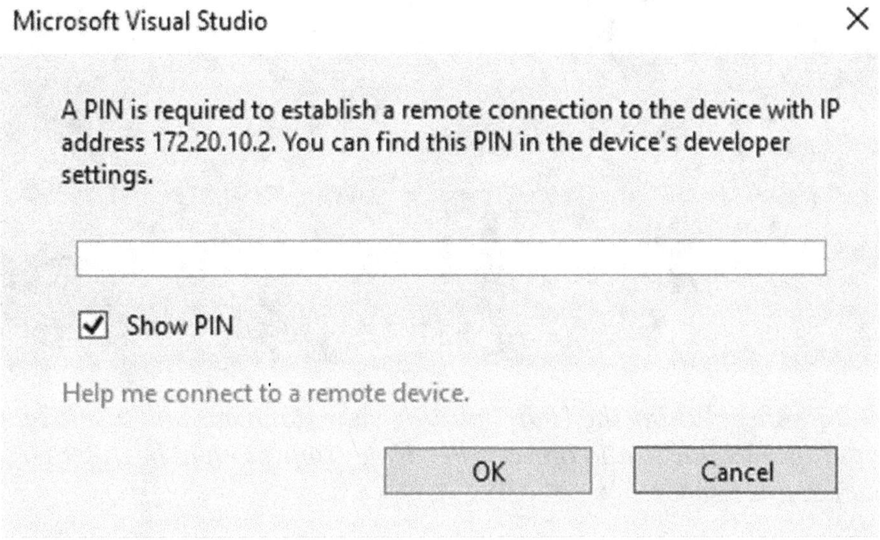

Figure 3-27. *Visual Studio will prompt you for a pin if this is the first time you are deploying to your HoloLens from this PC*

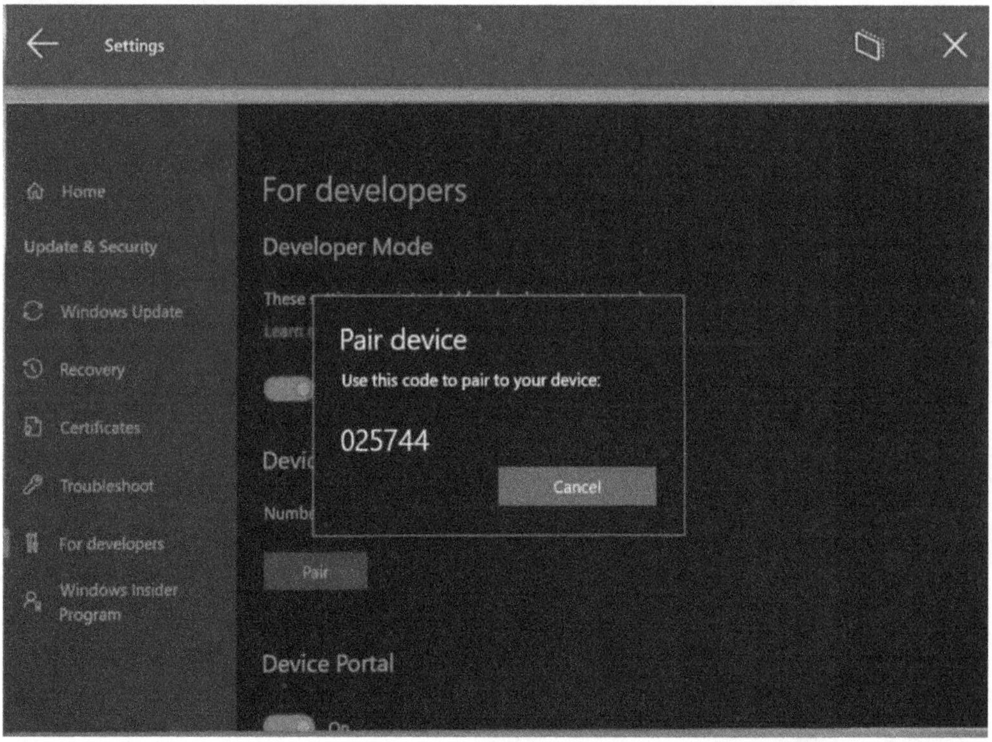

Figure 3-28. *After clicking the "Pair" button, your HoloLens will display a pin for you to enter into Visual Studio on your PC. Note: Your pin will be different than the one shown in this figure*

- After entering your HoloLens PIN into Visual Studio on your PC, you may dismiss the PIN pop-up on your HoloLens by clicking the "Done" button.

- Visual Studio will begin deploying your app to the HoloLens! You should see some output text in Visual Studio indicating that your app was successfully deployed to the HoloLens, similar to Figure 3-29. If you receive any error messages and a failed deployment, please check the output to see what the error messages are. Check to make sure you followed all the steps in this tutorial. Even if you followed all the steps correctly, there may be other reasons why a deployment may fail. For example, if you run out of disk space on your drive, or if Visual Studio was not installed correctly. If a mysterious error is preventing a successful deployment, I've found that restarting your computer and HoloLens often helps resolve the issue. Other potential solutions include rebuilding your app folder (deleting all contents and rebuilding from Unity) or reentering your HoloLens' IP address into Visual Studio.

Figure 3-29. *Example of text displayed by Visual Studio if deployment to the HoloLens is successful*

- You should now be experiencing your very first Mixed Reality app. Congratulations! Feel free to walk around your hologram (cube) and look at it from various angles. What happens when you try to touch it? Is your hologram behind your computer monitor or wall? If so, restart your app while facing an open area.

- Your app is now installed on your HoloLens – which means you will see it appear in your apps list as "Holo World" (if you named it Holo World, as I did in this tutorial).

Summary

Congratulations! Having created your very first hologram, you are well on your way to becoming a Mixed Reality developer. Creating and seeing your first hologram is a very satisfying experience! Let's recap what we've learned in this chapter:

- You learned how to prepare Unity for holographic development using the Mixed Reality Toolkit.

- You learned how to place a hologram into a scene.

- You learned how to install your app on a HoloLens by deploying it using Visual Studio.

The tutorials in this chapter serve as the building blocks for all Mixed Reality development workflows.

CHAPTER 4

Introduction to the Mixed Reality Toolkit

In this chapter, we'll learn more about the Mixed Reality Toolkit and its importance for Mixed Reality development. We'll learn about the various components and example scenes included with the Mixed Reality Toolkit and how we can leverage this community resource for development.

What Is the Mixed Reality Toolkit?

You might think that Mixed Reality Toolkit is an optional toolkit for enhancing your development experience. In fact, the Mixed Reality Toolkit is an essential part of Mixed Reality development. The Mixed Reality Toolkit provides developers with all the tools needed to get started with developing Mixed Reality applications. We will refer to Mixed Reality Toolkit as MRTK throughout this chapter. MRTK provides multiple platform input systems, fundamental components, and common constituents for spatial interactions to develop Mixed Reality-based applications.

The MRTK is a community resource that is overseen by Microsoft and other trusted individuals/groups. It aims on removing barriers by allowing all to develop Mixed Reality applications and contributing to the community. Anyone, including you, can contribute content to the MRTK (it will first need to be vetted before being incorporated). As such, the MRTK is constantly being updated and improved. In fact, it has already vastly improved from the time I started writing this book until the moment you are reading this chapter. After learning of some of the useful MRTK features in this chapter, I recommend exploring the MRTK repository online to learn about any additional changes. Toward the end of this chapter, I will walk you through navigating the online MRTK repository.

© Sean Ong and Varun Kumar Siddaraju 2021
S. Ong and V. K. Siddaraju, *Beginning Windows Mixed Reality Programming*,
https://doi.org/10.1007/978-1-4842-7104-9_4

The Three MRTK Repositories

There are actually three MRTK repositories online. The first is called
"MixedRealityToolkit," the second is called "MixedRealityToolkit-Unity," and the third
being "MixedRealityToolkit-Unreal." You can check them at the following links:

> MixedRealityToolkit: *https://github.com/microsoft/*
> *MixedRealityToolkit*

> MixedRealityToolkit-Unity: *https://github.com/microsoft/*
> *MixedRealityToolkit-Unity*

> MixedRealityToolkit-Unreal: *https://github.com/microsoft/*
> *MixedRealityToolkit-Unreal*

MixedRealityToolkit-Unity repository possesses Unity-specific components and
will be what we focus on throughout this book. The "regular" MixedRealityToolkit is
a generalized version of the MixedRealityToolkit that contains the core C++ code and
HTML code base that many of the Unity toolkit features are built atop of or are merely
wrappers around. MixedRealityToolkit-Unreal provides a set of features and options to
enhance the development procedure with Unreal. We will learn more about GitHub at
the end of this chapter.

Mixed Reality Toolkit Setup

In this section, I'll walk you through downloading and installing the MRTK. There are
two ways in which you can import Mixed Reality Toolkit onto your Unity project:

- By importing the Mixed Reality Toolkit asset files

- Through Unity Package Manager

1. Importing MRTK Asset Files

To download the MRTK Unity package, go to the following URL:

> https://github.com/microsoft/MixedRealityToolkit-Unity/releases

Make sure that you download the latest release of the MRTK, typically located near
the top of the page. Be sure that the MRTK version you download is compatible with

the version of Unity that you downloaded. Scroll down to the Assets section of the page. To download the MRTK Unity package, click the download link that has the extension ".unitypackage." For example, in Figure 4-1, the appropriate download link (circled in red) is named "Microsoft.MixedReality.Toolkit.Unity.Foundation.2.5.3.unitypackge."

Figure 4-1. *Browse to the MRTK download page and download the MRTK Unity package, circled in red*

Save the MRTK to your PC. Start a new project with an appropriate name; refer to the previous chapter for some heads up. In your Unity project's menu bar, go to Assets ➤ Import Package ➤ Custom Package. In the pop-up window that appears, browse to the MRTK that you just downloaded. See Figure 4-2 for an illustration of these menu items.

Unity will take a minute to prepare the package you selected and then show you another pop-up window where you can select or deselect package items. Go ahead and leave everything checked (everything should be checked by default), and click the Import button, as shown in Figure 4-3.

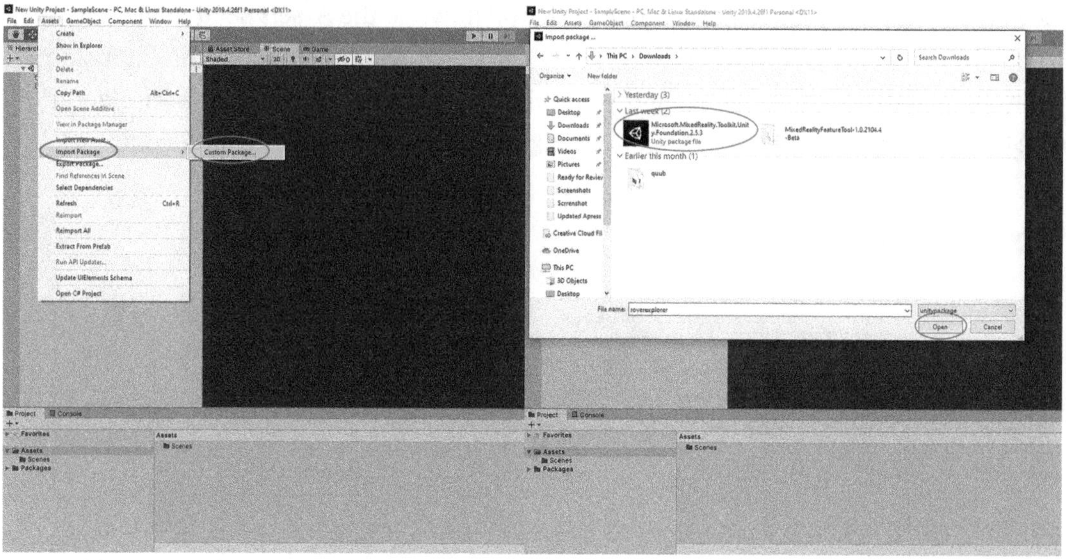

Figure 4-2. *Import the MRTK package that you downloaded in Chapter 1*

After completing these steps, the MRTK will now be installed to your project.

Figure 4-3. *Click the Import button to import the MRTK package*

2. Unity Package Manager

Another way in which you can install the Mixed Reality Toolkit is through the Unity Package Manager. The Unity Package Manager uses a manifest file (manifest.json) to control which packages to install and the servers from where they have to be installed. For each Unity project that uses MRTK, ensure that the manifest.json file has a Mixed Reality scoped registry added to it. In order to add the Mixed Reality scoped registry, follow the succeeding instructions.

Start by creating a new Unity project with an appropriate name. Open your Project folder, and navigate to the "Packages" folder. In the Packages folder, open the "manifest" file in any text editor, such as Visual Studio 2019. At the beginning of the manifest file, add the code given in Listing 4-1 to include Mixed Reality Server to the scoped registry (it is essential to have the server before including the packages). See Figure 4-4 for an illustration of these items.

Listing 4-1. Code to add Mixed Reality Server to the scoped registry

```
{
  "scopedRegistries": [
    {
      "name": "Microsoft Mixed Reality",
      "url": "https://pkgs.dev.azure.com/aipmr/
      MixedReality-Unity-Packages/_packaging/Unity-packages/npm/registry/",
      "scopes": [
        "com.microsoft.mixedreality",
        "com.microsoft.spatialaudio"
      ]
    }
  ],
```

After adding the following code, your file should look something similar to Figure 4-4. Adding the Mixed Reality Server to your scoped registries is an essential step as you can add the required packages only after including the Mixed Reality Server.

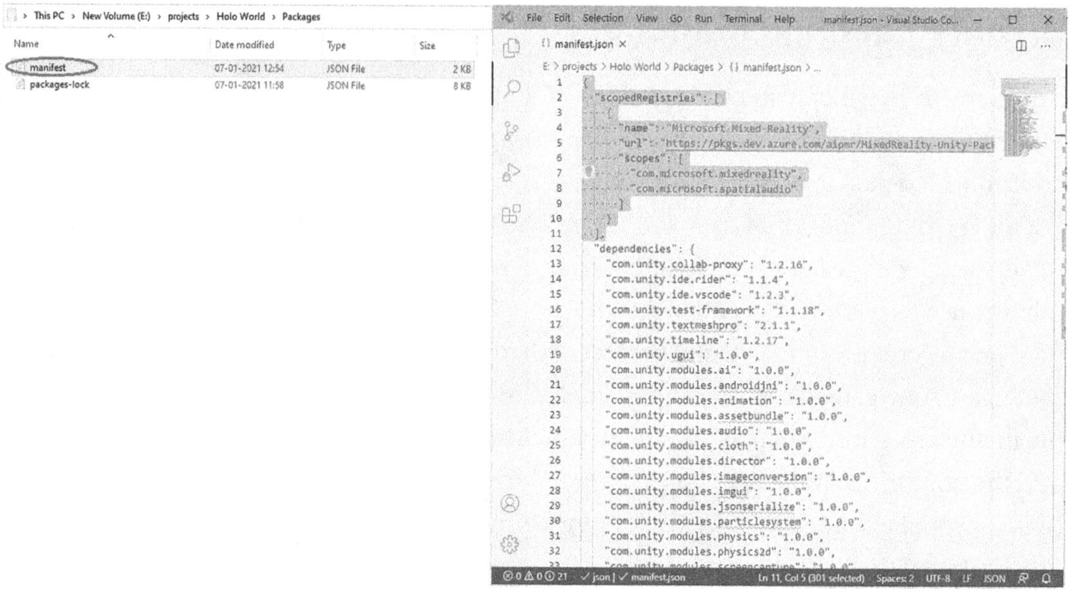

Figure 4-4. *Open the manifest file and add the code given at the beginning of the file*

Once the Mixed Reality Server has been added to the file, you can start adding the desired packages. To add an MRTK package to your project, you need to modify the "manifest" file's dependencies section. The code in Listing 4-2 allows you to add the foundation, examples, and tools packages to your Unity project. Standard asset package is added automatically as a dependency of the foundation. Figure 4-5 shows an illustration of the code.

Listing 4-2. Code to add the required packages to your Unity project

```
"dependencies": {
    "com.microsoft.mixedreality.toolkit.foundation": "2.5.3",
    "com.microsoft.mixedreality.toolkit.tools": "2.5.3",
    "com.microsoft.mixedreality.toolkit.examples": "2.5.3",
```

Note   Do not forget to save your manifest file after adding the code.

Figure 4-5. *Illustration of the code*

When you return to your project, you will encounter an MRTK configurator window pop-up; you can click Apply to save the settings to your project. You have now successfully added the packages to your Unity project; you can manage them through the Unity Package Manager user interface. To open Unity Package Manager, click the "Windows" option on your Unity project menu bar, and select "Package Manager." A window pops up, as shown in Figure 4-6.

Note   You can also observe the "Up to date" become active when newer versions on MRTK packages are available. Feel free to work on the newer versions by clicking the "Up to date" button if activated.

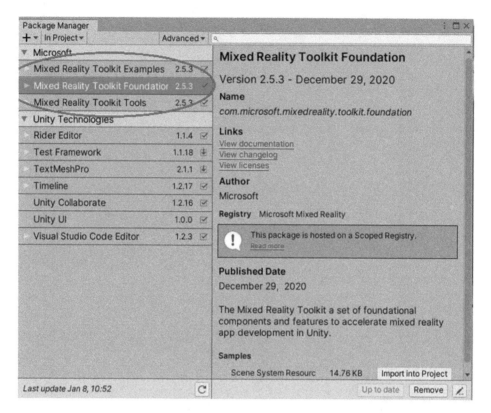

Figure 4-6. *Unity Package Manager shows the packages installed through the manifest.json file*

After you have saved the manifest file with required dependencies, MRTK will now be installed in your project. Feel free to follow any one of the two methods that are mentioned previously to install MRTK.

Note   You will need to import the MRTK every time you start a new Unity project.

Mixed Reality Toolkit Components

We're now at the exciting part of the chapter where I'll walk you through the various components of the MRTK. The MRTK includes several feature areas. Table 4-1 lists each feature area and provides a brief description.

Table 4-1. *Displays the list of components available on MRTK*

Feature Area	Description
Input System	Allows developers to provide inputs through a wide range of input sources like six DOF controllers, and speech, over input events
Hand Tracking	Hand Tracking component in MRTK furnishes a new sense of presence and enhances social engagement. This feature helps the user in providing a chance for more natural interactions with the environment
Eye Tracking	Eye Tracking is another outstanding feature offered by HoloLens; it enables users to interact with the holograms on the screen effortlessly. Discussed in detail in the next chapter
Solvers	Allows developers to calculate the object's position and orientation based on a prebuilt algorithm
Multi-Scene Manager	The Scene system allows the application to load multiple scenes to establish a comfortable experience for the users
Spatial Awareness	Allows your application to understand the physical environment. For example, it can differentiate between chairs, tables, and other common structures
Diagnostic Tool	Tool that runs within your application to examine application issues
In-Editor Simulation	Allows the user to test the functions of their applications through Unity editor rather than deploying it on the device
Boundary System	Boundary System allows envisioning of Virtual Reality boundaries in Mixed Reality applications
UX Controls	A collection of useful utilities, such as buttons, solvers, bounds control, sliders, pointers for configuring Unity, and more
Camera System	The camera system allows the MRTK to customize the application's camera to be included in Mixed Reality applications
Profiles	Allows the developer to configure MRTK using various profiles available in the foundation package

(*continued*)

Table 4-1. (*continued*)

Feature Area	Description
MRTK Standard Shader	The shading system utilizes a single flexible shader which successfully provides visuals similar to Unity's Standard Shader
Speech & Dictation	Allows the user to provide inputs through keywords that can raise appropriate events. Dictation provides users the opportunity to record audio clips and acquires written texts
Experimental Features	It contains features under development and those which have a high initial value

In the following subsections, I will discuss highlights for each of the ten feature categories. We'll cover some of these features in greater detail in subsequent chapters. Some features have entire chapters devoted to them!

MRTK: Input System

The Input System of the MRTK allows you to draw inputs from different input sources like gestures, six DOF controllers, hands, and speech via input events. It even allows you to include theoretical actions like menus and relate them to distinct input sources. One can set up pointers to the controllers to drive objects on the scene through pointer events.

Input Data Providers put together user inputs. Each Data Provider is unique based on the input received, such as Unity Touch, Unity Joystick, Windows Speech, Windows Mixed Reality (WMR), etc. These providers are included in your project via a Registered Service Providers Profile, which will automatically produce input events when the input source is available.

There are a wide range of example scenes, where you can test various features included in the input feature set. Example scenes are an excellent way to explore MRTK features and gain inspiration for your own projects! I often use example scenes as templates for my own project. There are dozens of example scenes across all MRTK features. Let's walk through how to explore one of these example scenes.

Tip   Example scenes are a great way to see MRTK items in action and learn how to implement them. You can also use an example scene as a template for your next project!

How to Run a Test Scene

Example scenes are typically located in a project folder called "Scenes." Within the input feature area, you can find the scenes folder by going to Assets ➤ MRTK ➤ Examples ➤ Demos, as shown in Figure 4-7. Each of the feature groups may have a slightly different folder organization. Folder organization within the MRTK is evolving over time, so be sure to explore the project folders or check the latest MRTK documentation if you are unable to find the test scenes in your version of the MRTK.

Note   Make sure to import the example Unity package to work with the example scenes provided in MRTK. Refer to the previous chapter to have some insight on how to import a Unity package.

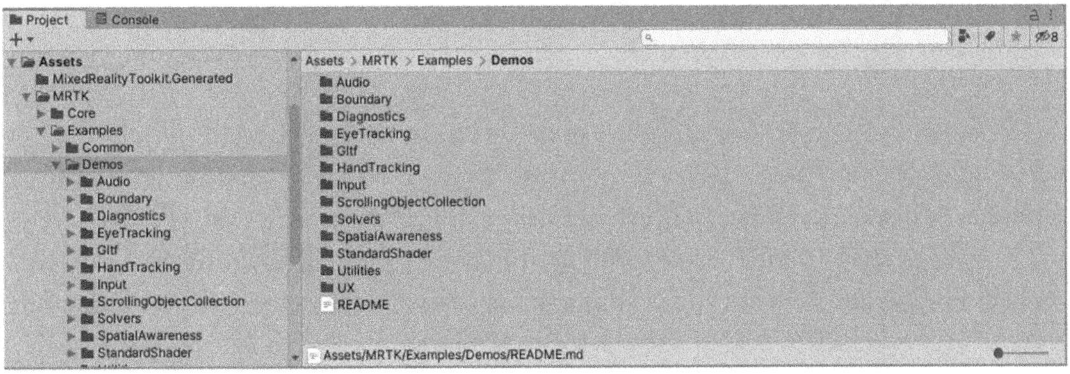

Figure 4-7. *Navigate to the Demos folder to try out various example scenes relating to different MRTK features*

Asset names in your Project panel may be shortened (a partial name will be displayed, followed by "..."). If you would like to see the full name, you may adjust the icon view by adjusting the slider, as shown at the bottom right corner of Figure 4-7.

In the Unity editor, navigate to Assets ➤ MRTK ➤ Examples ➤ Demos ➤ Input ➤ Scenes, choose the scene you are interested in trying (in our case, the InputActionExample scene), and drag it from the Project panel to an empty area in your Hierarchy, as shown in Figure 4-8.

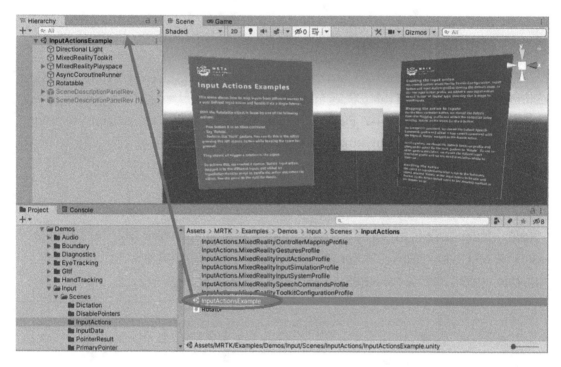

Figure 4-8. *To explore an example scene, drag it into your hierarchy*

To avoid conflicts, disable any other open scenes by right-clicking the other scenes and selecting "Unload Scene" from the context menu. Unloading a scene will temporarily disable it, making it quick and easy to toggle scenes. You may also choose to "Remove Scene" if you no longer wish to work with a scene. You can still reimport the scene from your Project panel, if you did not intend to remove the scene from your Unity project.

Now that you have your example scene loaded, feel free to try it out by clicking the play button. You may also deploy it to your HoloLens 2 or stream it to your device using holographic emulation. This is a great opportunity to explore the code being used and see how the test project works! There are many example scenes included with the MRTK. I recommend you try as many of them as possible!

MRTK: Hand Tracking

Hand Tracking provided by MRTK promises users to provide a more immersive experience where users can utilize their hands and interact with the components on the scene. The hand-tracking feature of MRTK can be customized according to the user's need by changing a few settings in the HandTrackingProfile found under the InputSystemProfile. You need to clone the InputSystemProfile and HandTrackingProfile to access some of the settings. Refer to Figure 4-9 for more information.

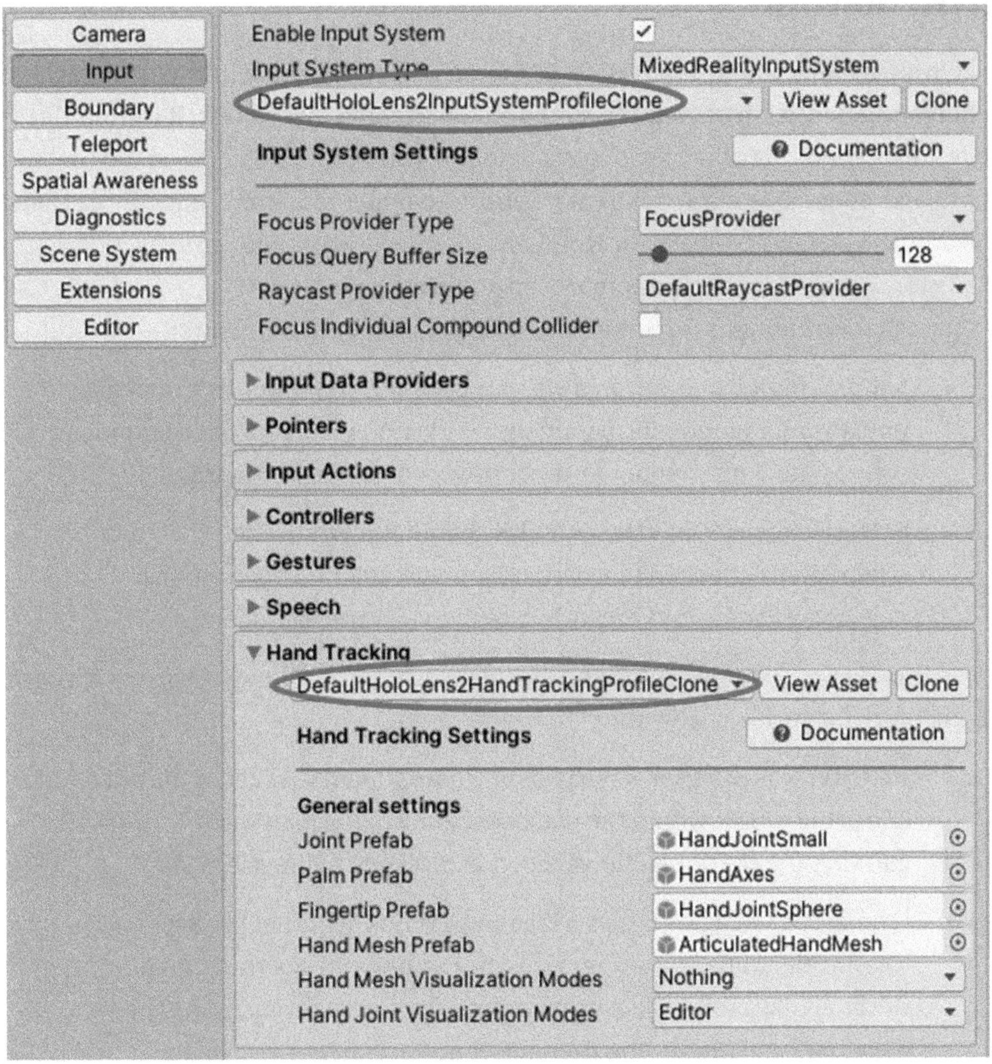

Figure 4-9. *HandTrackingProfile and its options*

Joint Prefab, Palm Prefab, Fingertip Prefab, and Hand Mesh Prefab help in the visualization of hands during interactions on the screen. You may change the prefabs if you wish, but retaining the default settings is recommended to prevent future errors. Hand Tracking can be achieved using Leap Motion (by Ultraleap). This method helps in swift prototyping your application in the editor. Leap Motion Data Providers authorizes articulated hand tracking for VR. The Data Provider can be structured to use Leap Controller attached to the headset or placed on the desk face up.

MRTK: Solvers

Solver System helps you to add positioning to an object. It helps you to calculate the position and orientation of your objects based on prebuilt algorithms. It is a family of scripts and actions that allow the objects to follow you or other objects on the screen. You can also attach objects at different positions to make your application more natural. For example, you can observe your HoloLens menu following your gaze. By doing so, it will be more convenient for a user to use an application.

Solver System contains three varieties of scripts; they are as follows:

- Solver: This is a foundational abstract class that monitors state tracking, update order, smoothing parameters and implementation, and automatic solver system integration. All other solvers derive from this class.

- SolverHandler: SolverHandler class handles all the solver components attached to a particular game object. This class also helps in updating and executing them in a proper sequence.

The third variety comprises the solvers themselves. The following solvers act as a building block for various behaviors:

- RadialView: RadialView is a tagalong component that keeps the part of a game object within the truncated zone of the user's view. Users can vary the portion of the object that is visible in the user's view.

- Orbital: Orbital class is also a tagalong component that behaves like the electrons in an atom. This class allows the users to make the attached game object orbit around the tracked transform. The developer can modify the fixed offset according to their needs. The developer can utilize this and make menus or other scene components be at eye level or waist level.

- InBetween: InBetween class keeps the attached game object between two tracked transforms. The game object has its SolverHandler properties, which define the endpoints of the two transforms.

- SurfaceMagnetism: SurfaceMagnetism emits rays to the surface and lines up the object to hit the surface accordingly. Users must be cautious about the colliders added to the game objects when using SurfaceMagnetism.

- DirectionalIndicator: DirectionalIndicator, as the name suggests, helps the user to point at the desired location in space. It is beneficial for the user as it helps in navigating the objects conveniently.

- HandConstraint: HandConstraint provides a solver which remains in safe regions. Safe regions are areas that do not overlap with the hand. There are different derived classes which carry out different solver in safe areas.

Let us try out an example scene included in the Unity examples package. Start by creating a new Unity project and give it an appropriate name. Import the foundation and examples unity packages to your project; refer to the steps provided in the previous chapter to import the Unity packages. Navigate to Assets ➤ MRTK ➤ Examples ➤ Demos ➤ Solvers ➤ Scenes as shown in Figure 4-10. Drag and drop the SolverExamples example scene to your Hierarchy window to view the scene. You may unload or remove any other scenes present in the Hierarchy window to avoid conflicts.

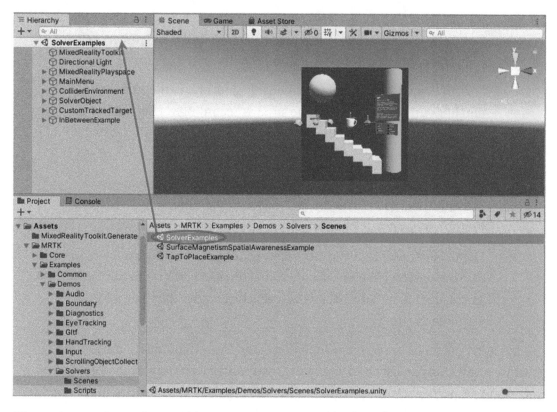

Figure 4-10. *To explore SolverExamples example scene, drag it into your hierarchy*

With the example scene being loaded, you can explore the available options by clicking the play button. This example scene provides you a brief idea of how different kinds of solvers work. You can refer to the main menu displayed on the blue plane to have a crisp idea of how the example scene works.

MRTK: Multi-scene Manager

What would you do if you want to run multiple scenes without disturbing the MixedRealityToolkit instance? MRTK provides you an option to do so without having to complicate things. It helps you to load various scenes to enhance your experience. You can monitor when the scenes are being loaded and unloaded through various properties provided by the SceneSystem. The SceneOperationInProgress will be set to 0 initially; once the scene is wholly loaded, the SceneOperationInProgress will be set to 1. These properties are affected only by content scene operations.

You can switch between scenes by including the using Unity.SceneManagement namespace in your code. After including the namespace, SceneManager.LoadScene, add scene index value. The scene index value usually starts with 0 for the first scene; you can verify the scene index value at the Build Settings window as displayed in Figure 4-11 by dragging and dropping the scenes to the Scenes In Build space in a sequence that you want as shown in Figure 4-11.

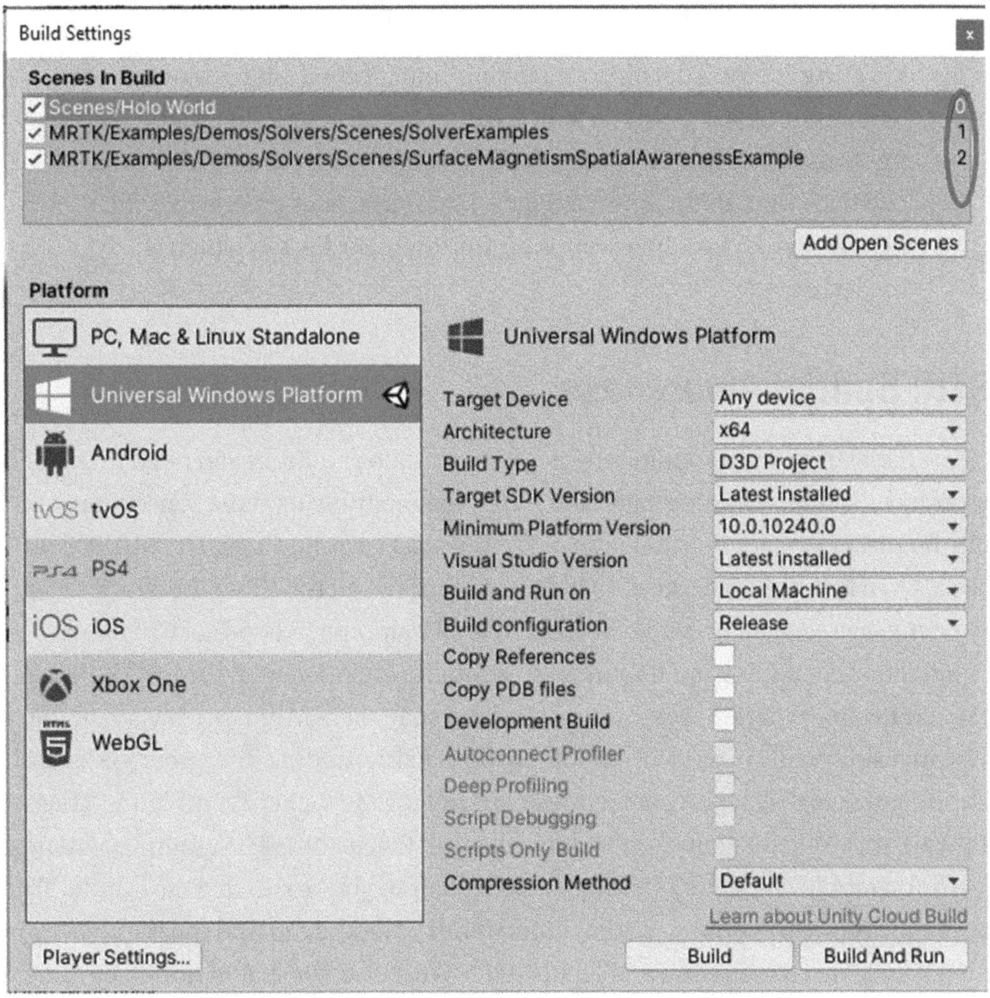

Figure 4-11. *Verify the scene index values in the Build Settings*

There are three main scenes:

- **Content scene:** Content scenes are the ordinary scenes that you deal with frequently. Any contents and objects can be loaded and unloaded.

- **Manager scene:** Manager scenes are the scenes that are created by default. It can have objects which should not be destroyed under it and act as an alternative to DontDestroyOnLoad.

- **Lighting scene:** Adjusting and maintaining the lighting settings across multiple scenes is a tedious and repetitive task. By using lighting scenes that store lighting information and lighting objects can overcome these disadvantages. Lighting scenes ensure that the lighting across multiple scenes is uniform regardless of which is loaded or unloaded.

MRTK: Spatial Awareness

MRTK's spatial mapping module provides you with the resources you need to include your project's spatial mapping capabilities. Spatial mapping uses the sensors on a Mixed Reality headset to create a virtual map of the physical surroundings. The MRTK provides resources to use this map or mesh to hide or occlude objects behind the mesh, interact with the mesh, and visualize it. We'll cover spatial mapping in depth in Chapter 6.

Spatial understanding is a remarkable capability included with the MRTK that allows our Mixed Reality experiences to understand the spatial environment. Based on the precise measurements taken with spatial mapping, this module interprets the spatial mesh and guesses which parts of the mesh are walls, tables, chairs, and more! There are many ways that Mixed Reality applications can use this feature. For example, you might have a holographic character or avatar sit on a chair in your room during a game. To achieve this, you will need the spatial understanding module to find the part of a room that is a sitting surface, as shown in Figure 4-12. We will cover spatial understanding in Chapter 6.

Figure 4-12. *Example of the spatial understanding module being used to find the sitting surface of a chair*

MRTK: Diagnostic Tool

MRTK provides an opportunity to analyze your applications through diagnostic tools which run in your application. It is highly recommended to enable the diagnostic system at the beginning of the development and disable during the deployment process. Diagnostic tools are beneficial to keep a check on the system's performance; they provide you information on the system's hard drive, RAM, CPU temp, and so on. These tools help you in identifying some problems which are affecting your system's performance.

MRTK: Boundary System

Boundaries play a significant role in immersive applications as it defines a safe area for you to move. It also helps you to avoid concealed obstacles in the scene while using your headsets. Boundary System in MRTK provides boundary visualization in Mixed Reality applications. Generally, in Virtual Reality platforms, a white line is superimposed on the virtual world to warn you about the border. MRTK's Boundary System extends this handy feature in Mixed Reality applications by displaying the tracked area's outline and other features that will provide additional data to you about your surroundings.

MRTK: UX Controls

The MRTK's utilities module provides several useful tools that can be used in your Mixed Reality applications. I recommend exploring this module in the MRTK and reading the online documentation for the most up-to-date listing of tools, as tools are added to this module regularly. In the following, I've listed and described some of the most common and useful tools included in the MRTK. This is far from an exhaustive list, but will give you a taste for the type of tools included in this module.

- **Buttons:** Buttons serve as a user interface to collect inputs from you and perform immediate actions. It is the most fundamental component in MRTK. MRTK provides a range of button prefabs that can be used by you in your applications.

    A few of them are listed for you here:

    - PressableButtonUnityUI.prefab

    - PressableButtonUnityUICircular.prefab

    - PressableButtonHoloLens2UnityUI.prefab

    - UnityUIInteractableButton.prefab

- **Hand menu:** How cool would it be to have a menu pop up every time you bring up your hand? MRTK allows you to attach frequently used UI menus to your hands. A lot of confusion can arise when you try to use other options on your application, but the hand menus keep on popping up. There are supporting options like "Require Flat Hand" and "Use Gaze Activation" to avoid false activation.

- **Slider:** Sliders are UI components present in MRTK, which allows you to change values continuously. Sliders work on both AR and VR. Currently, pinching sliders are used to change values by grabbing them directly or at a distance. You can add sliders of your length and dimensions.

- **Tooltips:** Objects on the scene would be more sensible if some information is provided along with them. To add extra details relating to any objects in the background, you can include Tooltips. Tooltips can be used to explain objects in the physical environment.

- **Slate:** Slate prefab is an exceptional alternative to display 2D contents on the screen; it provides a thin window style control to show 2D contents like texts or articles. Additional features like "Follow Me" and "Close" help you in easy operations of the prefab.

MRTK: Camera System

The Camera System in Microsoft Mixed Reality Toolkit allows you to customize and optimize its camera to be used in your Mixed Reality applications. The Camera System supports transparent (AR) and opaque (VR) applications without writing different scripts for each. The Camera System can be configured using Near Clip, Far Clip, Clear Flags, Background Color, Quality Setting, etc.

The Camera System can be accessed using the MixedRealityToolkit object present in the Hierarchy window. Navigate to the Inspector panel under the Camera tab to ensure that the Enable Camera System check box is checked, as shown in Figure 4-13. You can also customize the Camera System Type and the Profile used.

To provide platform-specific camera configurations, you can configure settings at the Camera Settings Providers. You can add and remove the Camera Settings Providers in this section. Not all applications need Camera Settings Providers. If there are no providers compatible with the platform, then the MRTK will apply default settings.

Display Settings allow the users to configure the camera during run time. They also provide an option to switch between opaque and transparent backgrounds. The quality of your graphics on the scene can be adjusted using the Quality Setting option under the Display Settings highlighted in Figure 4-13.

Note   You might have to clone a few profiles to be able to configure the earlier settings. Cloning an MRTK profile will be briefed in the next section.

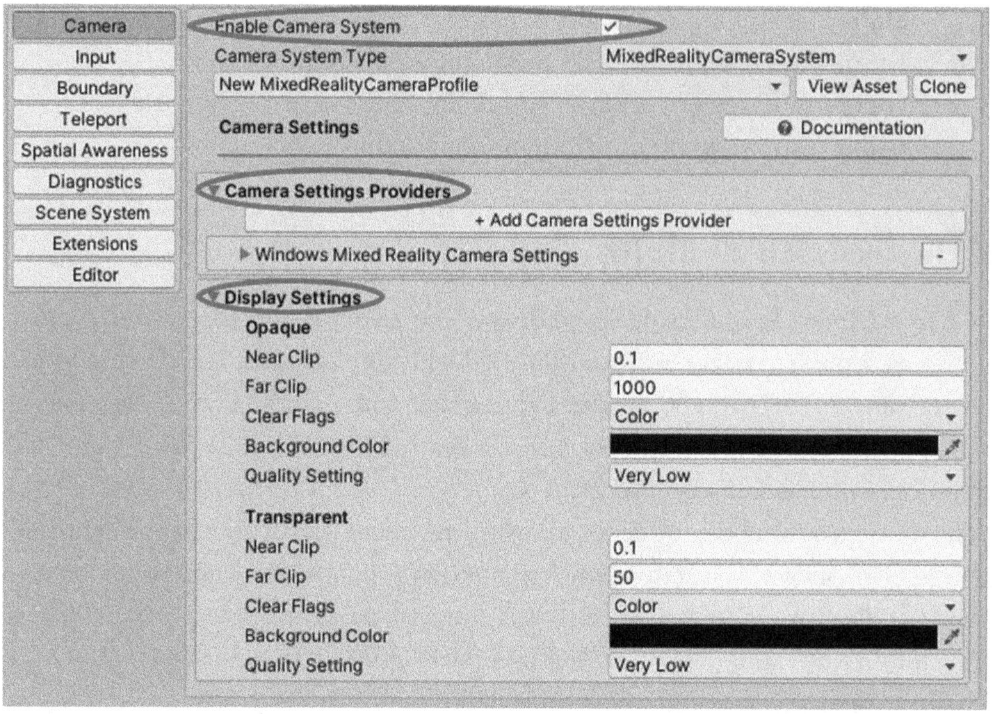

Figure 4-13. *Camera System settings provided by MRTK*

MRTK: Profiles

Profiles in MRTK allow you to configure the MRTK settings based on your project requirements. The main MixedRealityToolkit object on your Hierarchy window will have an active profile attached to it, which is scriptable. The top-level configuration file has sub-profiles that are associated with each core system. These sub-profiles are also scriptable objects and may contain references to other profiles as well. An entire connected tree of profiles states how to initialize and configure MRTK subsystems and features.

We understand that some Data Providers handle a particular framework across multiple platforms. This way, we can design an application that is machine independent or platform independent, thereby increasing the flexibility of the application. Profiles help you build your applications in the way stated earlier. MRTK provides you a set of default profiles that cover most platforms and scenarios that MRTK can cover. For example, when you select DefaultMixedRealityToolkitConfigurationProfile, you can try out scenarios on VR-supported platforms and HoloLens (1 or 2). This profile is used for general purposes and not optimized for a particular use case. If you wish to focus on a particular instance in a platform, you can choose a profile supporting those settings.

For example, DefaultHoloLens2ConfigurationProfile is another default profile that is optimized for deployment and testing on HoloLens 2. There are differences between the default profile and HoloLens 2 profile to provide better settings and options specific to the platform. To customize some options provided by different profiles, you need to create clones of them. Follow the instructions to create clones of MRTK profiles:

1. Click the MixedRealityToolkit object on the Hierarchy window.

2. Navigate to the Inspector window, and select the profile of your choice from the drop-down as shown in Figure 4-14. I have chosen the DefaultHoloLens2ConfigurationProfile.

3. Click the Copy & Customize button.

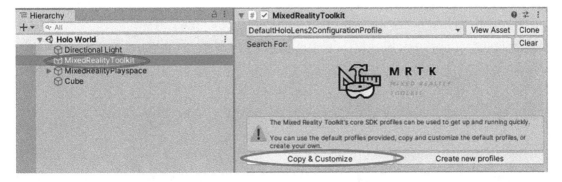

Figure 4-14. *Copy & Customize the selected profile*

4. A Clone Profile pop-up window appears on clicking the Copy & Customize button. Give an appropriate name to the new cloned profile, and click the Clone button as displayed in Figure 4-15.

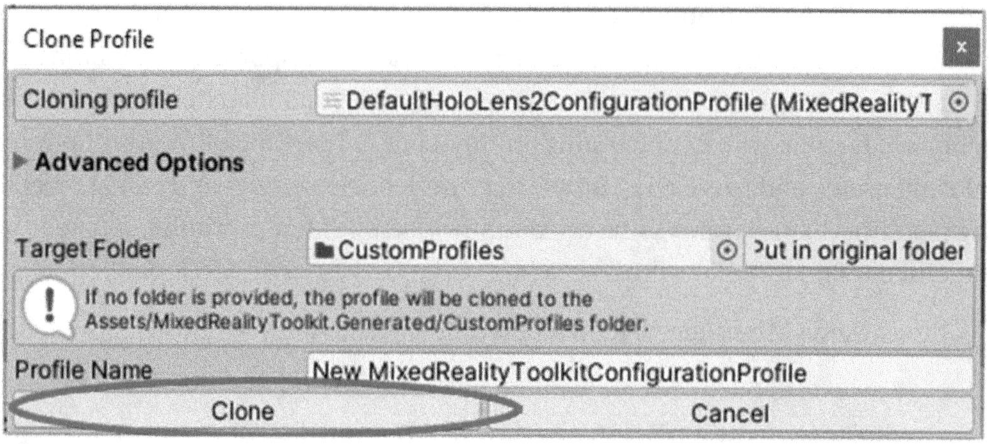

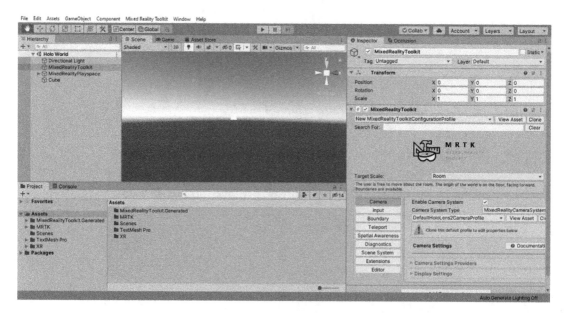

Figure 4-15. *Click the Clone button to create a clone of your profile*

After following these steps, you might observe some options being available on cloning the profile. Refer to Figure 4-16 to see your Unity environment after cloning. To further customize some of the features, you need to clone the sub-profiles as well. Click the Clone button present beside these sub-profiles to receive the Clone Profile pop-up window.

Figure 4-16. *You might observe some of the options getting activated after cloning*

MRTK: Standard Shader

MRTK Standard Shader is a single workable shader capable of producing visuals similar to Unity's Standard Shader. It allows you to autogenerate special shaders based on the material properties. MRTK Standard Shader is advantageous over Unity's Standard Shader in terms of performance. MRTK Standard Shader requires fewer computations when compared to Unity's Standard Shader to produce similar results.

MRTK Online

As mentioned previously, the MRTK is constantly being updated and improved by a community of developers that use it. In this section, we'll learn about the online MRTK repository so that you can keep updated on the latest updates, issues, and improvements.

What Is GitHub?

If you're not familiar with GitHub, it is a commonly used website among developers for storing and sharing software project files. It allows for careful monitoring and approval/rejection of changes to project files, making it an ideal platform when many developers are using and modifying a project at the same time.

MRTK Help and Documentation

As of this writing, finding all documentation for MRTK components is admittedly challenging and somewhat fragmented. I've included a few links here to help you quickly access documentation for the MRTK:

- *https://github.com/microsoft/MixedRealityToolkit-Unity/blob/mrtk_development/README.md* – The "readme" section of MixedRealityToolkit-Unity contains detailed documentation on each of the several features/modules included in the MRTK.

- *https://github.com/Microsoft/MixedRealityToolkit-Unity/wiki* – The Wiki of MixedRealityToolkit-Unity contains some additional context and background for several features. I recommend reading the material here first, before reading the detailed documentation from the readme sections. The MRTK Wiki includes some links in the home page and some additional links in the "Pages" bar on the right of the Wiki's web page.

- `https://github.com/microsoft/MixedRealityToolkit-Unity/issues` – The issues section of the MRTK is important for understanding any outstanding issues that you might experience as you are using the MRTK. If you discover any new issues, this is also the area you can use to report them.

Summary

In this chapter, we've familiarized ourselves with the seven MRTK features or modules. We learned what the MRTK is and its importance when developing Mixed Reality experiences. We learned how to download and install the MRTK, how to try test scenes that are included with the MRTK, and how to navigate the online repository.

The MRTK is an active community resource that's constantly changing and evolving. New features are added almost daily, and old features are depreciated (deleted or made obsolete). As such, I recommend you to explore the MRTK and discover any new and amazing features that may have been added. And as you continue your Mixed Reality journey, you will likely contribute new and exciting content to the MRTK that will benefit other users too!

CHAPTER 5

Interacting with Holograms

In this chapter, we'll learn about input mechanisms used with Mixed Reality development. There are several ways that users can interact with holograms and other elements within an application. These include hand gestures, voice commands, gaze, and controllers. We'll walk through each input method and learn how to use input resources found in the MRTK.

Input Methods

Each input method used with Windows Mixed Reality has its benefits and limitations. The following list provides a description for each input category:

- **Gaze:** The use of gaze in Windows Mixed Reality is the primary method by which the user focuses on holograms and objects. Gaze is as essential to Mixed Reality as the mouse is to the PC. You use the mouse to point at objects on your PC screen. In the same way, you use your gaze (the direction you look) to point to objects in 3D space. On a PC screen, the location of your mouse is represented by a cursor or arrow. The gaze cursor is typically represented by a small dot or donut-shaped object. Currently, gaze is controlled by the movements of your head and not the physical gaze of your eyes. There are many ways to use gaze in Mixed Reality, such as pointing at objects, pointing at faraway locations (for use in teleportation), and having objects follow your gaze.

© Sean Ong and Varun Kumar Siddaraju 2021
S. Ong and V. K. Siddaraju, *Beginning Windows Mixed Reality Programming*,
https://doi.org/10.1007/978-1-4842-7104-9_5

Note   Some Mixed Reality headsets may not have the sensors to support gestures and instead rely on motion controllers as their primary   form of input.

- **Voice:** Voice input is the use of voice commands to interact with your Mixed Reality experience. Voice commands are extremely useful when developing Mixed Reality applications because they allow a high level of control and customization without needing a cluttered UI. Users can say a word or series of words to select objects, activate features, and enhance their experience. Voice can also be used to dictate words and sentences (speech to text) for fast text input instead of using a keyboard. Voice recognition is more accurate when you are connected to the Internet. This is because your voice data will be sent to Microsoft cloud-based speech recognition technologies. When the online speech recognition setting is turned off, speech services are constrained to use only device-based recognition like the Windows Speech Recognition app. Voice recognition still works, but Microsoft won't collect any voice data.

- **Other hardware:** In addition to the primary input methods listed already, there are a wide range of hardware options that can be used with Windows Mixed Reality headsets. These include devices such as Bluetooth keyboards and mice, Bluetooth game pads, clickers, and other Bluetooth accessories.

In the subsequent sections of this chapter, I'll walk you through how to utilize each input method in your Mixed Reality application.

Gaze Tutorial

In this section, I'll walk you through some key elements used with the gaze input method. I'll show you how to use cursors to represent your gaze and provide an overview of how gaze is implemented in code. Gaze exists in two forms, head gaze and eye gaze. Head gaze is based on the direction that the camera/head is looking. Head gaze is used when the system does not support eye gaze or when eye gaze is not enabled. It is typically linked to HoloLens 1 style interactions. Eye gaze is based on where the user is looking. Eye gaze is enabled only in a system supporting eye tracking. Here is a simple example scene that helps you in providing a better understanding of eye gaze.

Step 1: Set Up Unity Scene

For this tutorial, we will use a test scene from the Mixed Reality Toolkit. If you haven't already, be sure to set up Unity for Mixed Reality development as described in Chapter 4. You may also refer to Chapter 4 for a refresher on how to run MRTK test scenes in Unity.

Navigate to Assets ➤ MRTK ➤ Examples ➤ Demos ➤ Eye Tracking ➤ Scenes. Drag the EyeTrackingDemo-00-RootScene into your Hierarchy, as shown in Figure 5-1. Be sure to remove all other scenes that you might have open.

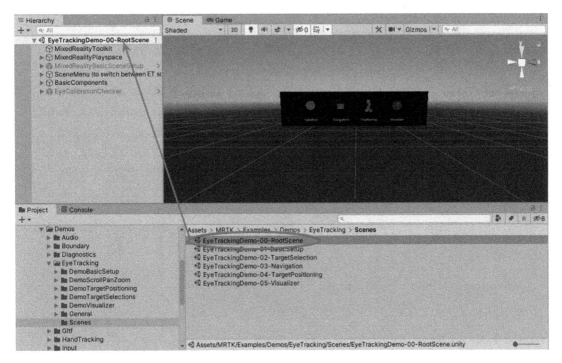

Figure 5-1. *Open the EyeTrackingDemo-00-RootScene from MRTK*

The EyeTrackingDemo-00-RootScene is the foundational scene that needs to be loaded first before trying out different features of eye tracking. The scene contains a graphic menu that owns different eye-tracking samples through which you can switch and enjoy! For the time being, let's focus on the target selection sample and see how it works.

Step 2: Add Scenes to the Build Menu

To try out this feature, you need to add the rest of the scenes to the build menu. Drag and drop the scenes to Build Settings ➤ Scenes In Build menu first, as shown in Figure 5-2.

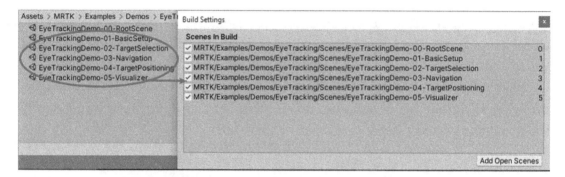

Figure 5-2. *Shows the scenes being added to the Scenes In Build menu*

Navigate to MixedRealityBasicSceneSetup in the Hierarchy window, and ensure that you have checked the check box beside the OnLoadStartScene script, as shown in Figure 5-3. This helps the root scene to understand which demo scene to load first.

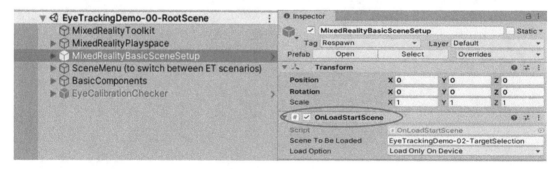

Figure 5-3. *Ensure the OnLoadStartScene script is enabled*

Step 3: Try the Scene!

Within the example scene, you should only see a graphic menu with four options: Selection, Navigation, Positioning, and Visualizer. Go ahead and try the scene by clicking the play button. Feel free to test within the Unity editor or deploy the application to your device.

Let's explore the selection option on the graphic menu; once you select the Selection option on the menu, you will observe several gems appear and the menu at the top, with the demo scene's description. When your gaze hits one of the gems on the scene, it starts rotating, as shown in Figure 5-4. On further looking at the gem, it can be destroyed, as shown in Figure 5-5. On entering the game view on your Unity editor, you must see a small transparent circle that serves as your gaze cursor to stimulate your eye gaze.

Tip   By default, the example scene includes the ability for you to easily navigate your scene using your mouse and keyboard. This is useful if you want to do a quick test without your headset. Hold down the right mouse button and move the mouse to simulate eye movements for gaze. Hold the shift button or spacebar to simulate holding your hand in front of the HoloLens. Left-click to simulate an air-tap gesture (while holding shift or spacebar). Use the keyboard arrow keys to walk around your environment.

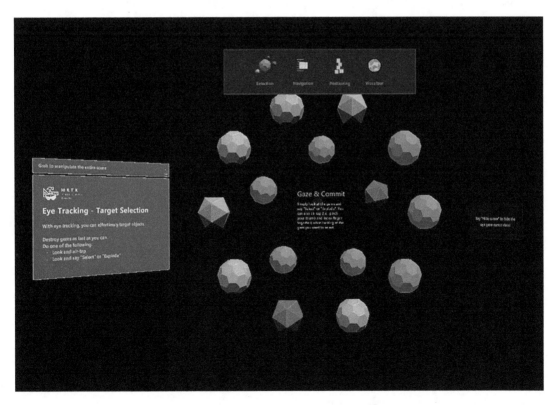

Figure 5-4.   *When playing the scene, your gaze cursor will turn the gems*

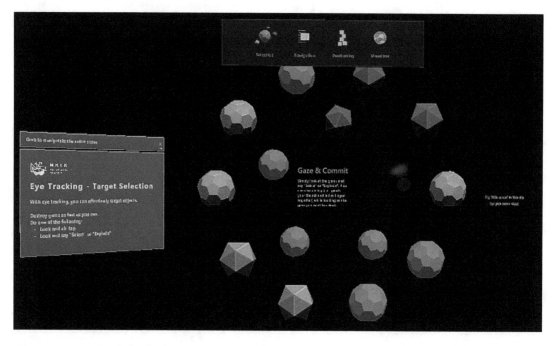

Figure 5-5. *On left-clicking the object under gaze cursor, it is destroyed*

Go ahead and stop the simulation when you are done testing the scene by clicking the play button again.

Step 4: Understanding the Scene

Now that you've experienced the example scene and had some fun, it's time to understand how this scene works and how you can use elements from this scene in your project! Let's start with the Hierarchy and work our way through the elements shown.

To experience smooth and error-free eye tracking, you must do three basic settings. The first one is adding an **Input Data Provider** to your MRTK profile. The Mixed Reality Toolkit input system is an expandable system, which enables input device support. External hardware support can be provided by merely customizing an Input Data Provider. As the name suggests, these Data Providers help in feeding data to a Mixed Reality Toolkit service. To view the Data Providers added to your scene, click the MixedRealityToolkit object on the Hierarchy window. Then in the Inspector window, click the Input tab and expand the Input Data Providers section. Figure 5-6 shows the Input Data Provider named "**Windows Mixed Reality Eye Gaze Provider**" added to your demo scene.

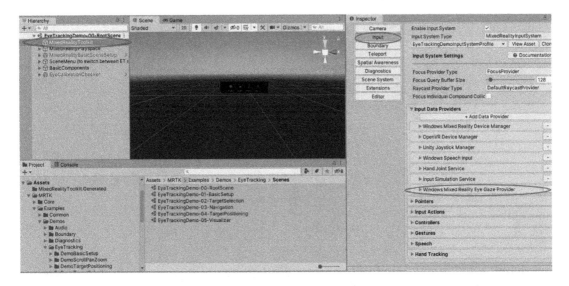

Figure 5-6. *Windows Mixed Reality Eye Gaze Provider added to your demo scene*

Secondly, configuring the **GazeProvider**. A gaze is a form of input that interacts with the surroundings based on where the user is looking. GazeProvider provides this functionality in MRTK. GazeProvider can be configured in the Pointers section of the Input System. Expand the Pointers section in the Input System. Under the Gaze Settings, you can observe that the check box next to the "Is Eye Tracking Enabled" option is ticked. This process ensures that the project uses eye gaze instead of head gaze. Figure 5-7 shows the preceding functionalities.

Since the gaze ray is invisible, we want to use a cursor to represent where the user is gazing and whether the gaze ray is touching a hologram in front of the user. For this, we can see the **EyeGazeCursor prefab**, which is highlighted in Figure 5-7. It represents the end of your gaze ray with a semitransparent circle. See Figures 5-4 and 5-5 for examples of this.

In the demo scene that we saw earlier, when we hover the cursor over the gems, we noticed that the cursor snapped right to the gem's middle. This is a great way to check if all the events are working fine.

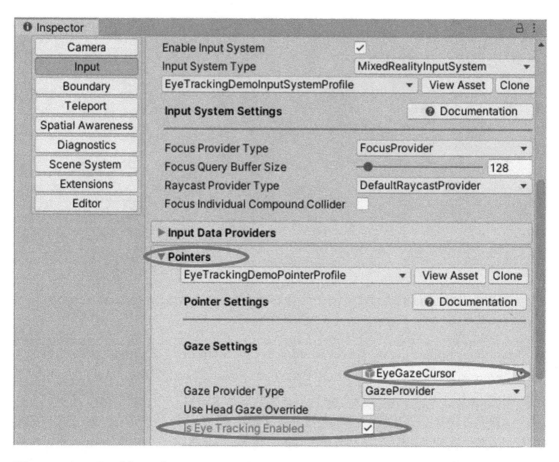

Figure 5-7. *Enabling the Is Eye Tracking Enabled option in the Pointers section of the Input System*

Lastly, to simulate eye-tracking input in your Unity editor, you need to choose the "Default Eye Gaze Simulation Mode" as "Camera Forward Axis." This helps you test your application on an initial stage, that is, before deploying it to your HoloLens 2. The eye gaze signal is simulated by utilizing the camera's location as the eye gaze origin and its vector as eye gaze direction. Open the Input tab, and navigate to Input Data Providers ➤ Input Simulation Service; under Eye Gaze Simulation, you will notice that "Default Eye Gaze Simulation Mode" is set to "Camera Forward Axis." This option is circled in red in Figure 5-8.

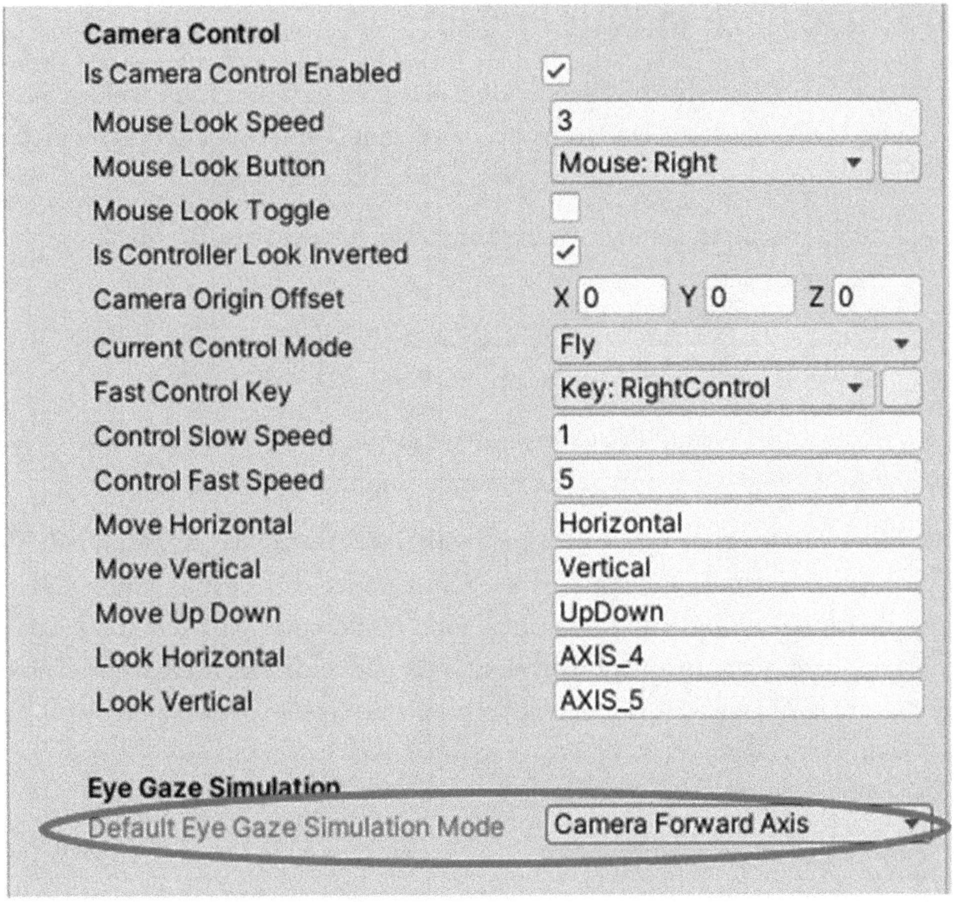

Camera Control

Is Camera Control Enabled	☑
Mouse Look Speed	3
Mouse Look Button	Mouse: Right ▾
Mouse Look Toggle	☐
Is Controller Look Inverted	☑
Camera Origin Offset	X 0 Y 0 Z 0
Current Control Mode	Fly ▾
Fast Control Key	Key: RightControl ▾
Control Slow Speed	1
Control Fast Speed	5
Move Horizontal	Horizontal
Move Vertical	Vertical
Move Up Down	UpDown
Look Horizontal	AXIS_4
Look Vertical	AXIS_5

Eye Gaze Simulation

Default Eye Gaze Simulation Mode	Camera Forward Axis ▾

Figure 5-8. Setting the mode of simulation

Note   Eye Gaze Simulation is a poor substitute for rapid eye movements and unintentional eye movements. Therefore, it is highly recommended to test your application on the HoloLens device rather than compromising on the outcome of the eye gaze simulation option.

Step 5: Use Gaze in Your Project

Now that you have a high-level understanding of the important components of the gaze input method and the cursor, you are aware of the required settings needed to create your own gaze and cursor functionality. Let's review what these are:

- Adding an Input Data Provider to feed data to the Mixed Reality Toolkit service

- Enabling "Is Eye Tracking Enabled" in the Pointers section to enable the eye-tracking feature onto your project

- Setting the "Default Eye Gaze Simulation Mode" to "Camera Forward Axis" to help you simulate the eye gaze feature in Unity editor

Often, it will be far more efficient to start with a preexisting scene that already includes these core items and then use that "template scene" as a foundation for building your application. The EyeTrackingDemo-00-RootScene used in this section does not contain other core functionality and is therefore too limited to be used as an effective template. As we walk through other input methods in this chapter, we will arrive at a full-featured example scene that you can repeatedly use as your template scene each time you start a new project!

Gestures Tutorial

In this section, I'll walk you through using gestures in your application. We'll explore the various classes of gestures and the use cases in which each is appropriate. We'll take a look at the code to see how gestures are implemented.

Step 1. Load Test Scene

For this tutorial, we'll be loading the HandInteractionExamples scene. As you've done with previous test scenes, search or browse for the HandInteractionExamples, and drag it into your hierarchy, as shown in Figure 5-9. Remove any other scenes that you might have opened.

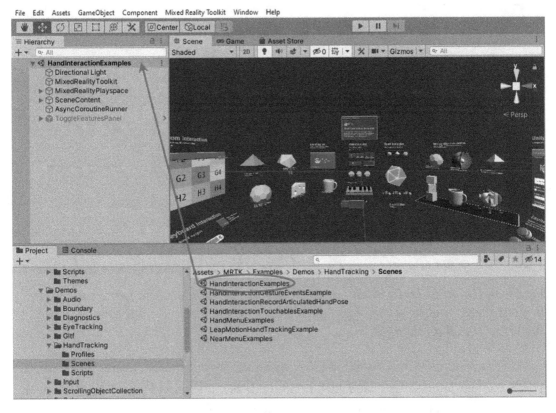

Figure 5-9. *Open the HandInteractionExamples scene. This wonderful test scene is a playground for experimenting with gestures and inputs!*

As shown in Figure 5-9, you'll immediately be greeted with a friendly display reminiscent of an intriguing science fair display.

Step 2. Try It Out!

Go ahead and try this test scene out by clicking the editor's play button, remoting to your device, or deploying to your device. Some features highlighted in this demo include pop-up menus, cursor functionality, the ability to tap objects, drag/move objects, and more!

Are you interested in learning more about something you see in the demo? After you exit the demo (by clicking the play button again), you can select objects of interest within the scene window and view the Inspector to explore which scripts and components are responsible for the object's behavior. In Figure 5-10, I select the coffee cup to view the object's components in the Inspector panel on the right.

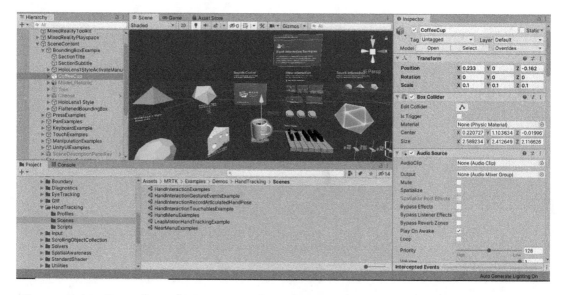

Figure 5-10. *In order to learn more about how each object and feature works in this test scene, highlight the object of interest and explore the components in the Inspector panel on the right*

There are many features of interest in this scene. We've already covered some of the MRTK configuration settings and gaze-related topics in the previous section. We'll walk through some other key features in the next few steps.

Step 3. Bounds Control

Bounds Control allows you to transform objects in mixed reality. You can alter the size and ratios of the objects. It is equivalent to the zoom in and zoom out option but on a 3D scale.

Let us explore this feature by trying it out in the HandInteractionExamples scene. As shown in Figure 5-11, there are five objects under the heading Bounds Control, which will show you how Bounds Control works in both HoloLens 1 and 2.

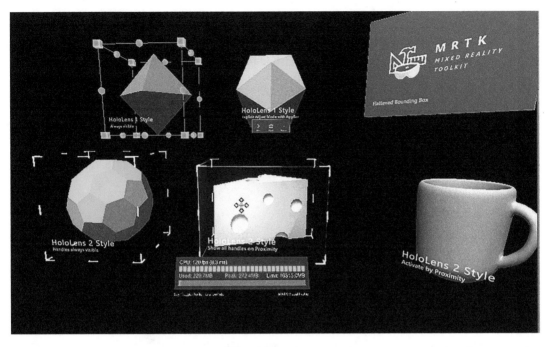

Figure 5-11. *Each of the five objects in the panel responds to the Bounds Control gesture by increasing, decreasing, or rotating*

Handles at the corners help you to scale, rotate, and translate the object. Bounds Control also responds to your input. For example, in HoloLens 2, Bounds Control responds to your finger proximity and provides optical feedback to estimate the object's distance. As shown in Figure 5-12, the script contains several customizable options in the Inspector panel. Let's walk through these:

- **Target Object:** Target Object refers to the object that can be manipulated using the Bounds Control script. If no object is assigned to this, then it will take the owner object as the target object.

- **Behavior:** Behavior settings tell how the Bounds Control should behave when attached to an object. It contains settings to activate Bounds Control, whether the control is flattened at one axis, etc.

- **Smoothing:** It enables you to scale the smoothing behavior while scaling or rotating the object.

- **Visuals:** You can also change the visuals of the Bounds Control by configuring the settings under the Visuals section. They can be either linked or inline scriptable objects.

- **Constraints:** The constraint system helps to control the scaling, rotate, and translate the objects. By configuring these settings, you will be able to restrain movements to a certain extent.

- **Events:** Events help in providing audio feedback once it is activated. There are several events which provide speech or audio feedback like Rotate Started(), Rotate Stopped(), Scale Started(), Scale Stopped(), Translate Started(), and Translate Stopped().

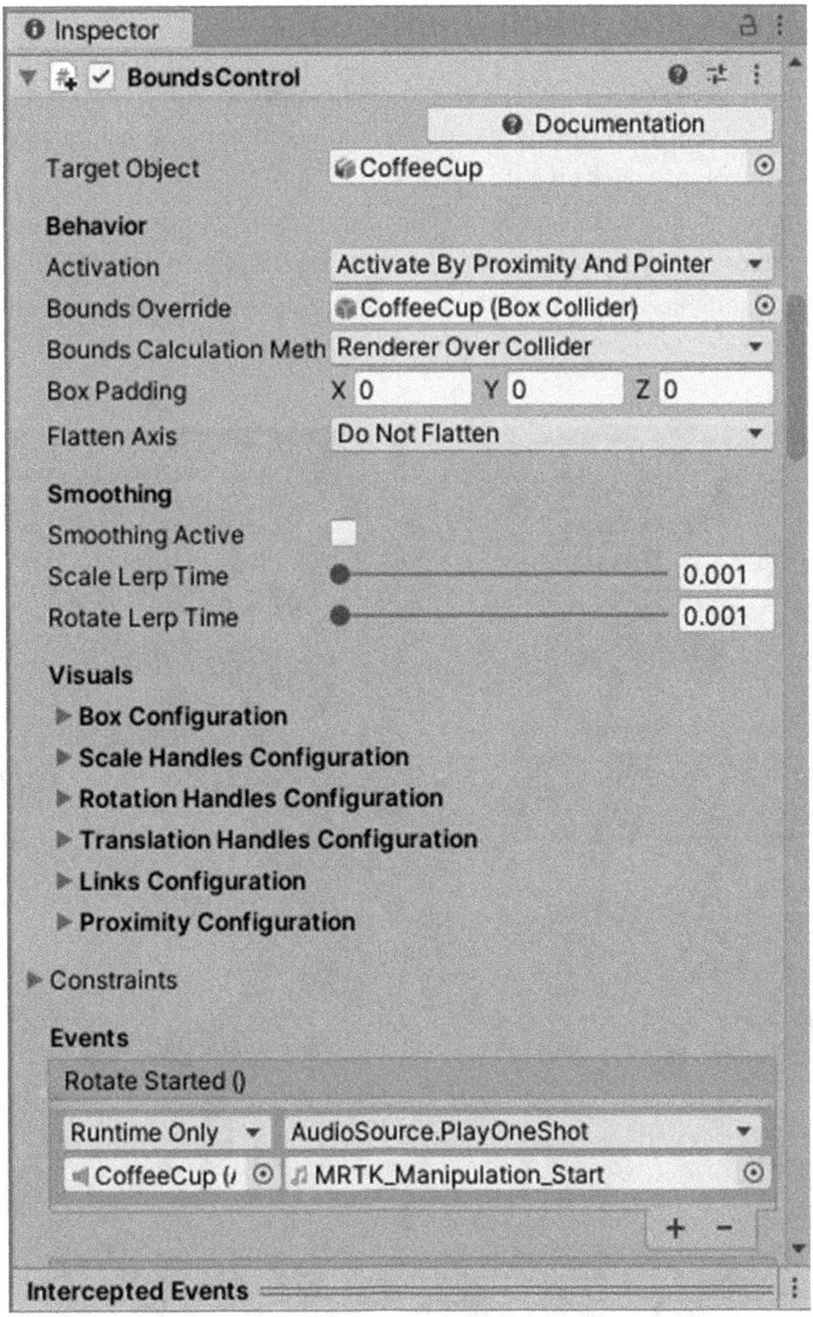

Figure 5-12. *Various customizable elements under the Bounds Control script*

Step 4: Press and Touch Interactions

The most crucial gesture for Windows Mixed Reality devices is the select gesture. For the HoloLens, this is synonymous with the combination of air tap and gazing on object. It is equivalent to the mouse click on a PC.

Let's explore one of the objects in our test scene that responds to the select gesture. As shown in Figure 5-13, there are various buttons and menus in the middle panel. The smaller cube highlighted in Figure 5-13 changes its color to show that the buttons are clicked or selected.

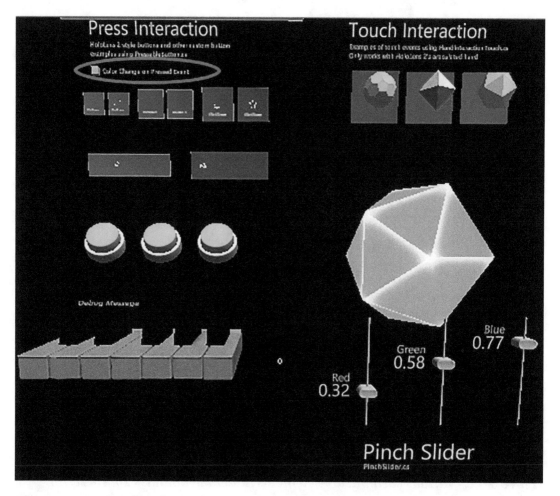

Figure 5-13. *Small cube at the top changes its color every time the buttons are clicked under Press Interaction*

When you select any of the objects, you will notice standard components in the Inspector panel – the PressableButton.cs script, Interactable.cs script, and NearInteractionTouchable.cs as shown in Figure 5-14.

- **PressableButton.cs:** Receives all the input events from the user and reverts it to the PhysicalPressEventRouter, which routes these events to the Interactable.cs. It performs the connected logic of hand pressing the button.

- **Interactable.cs:** The script helps make the objects respond to the user inputs; they can be in any form. You can make the object interactable by adding an Interactable.cs script to your object.

- **NearInteractionTouchable.cs:** The script makes any object touchable and ready to be transformed so that when the PokePointer touches this object, you can perform PointerUp and PointerDown events.

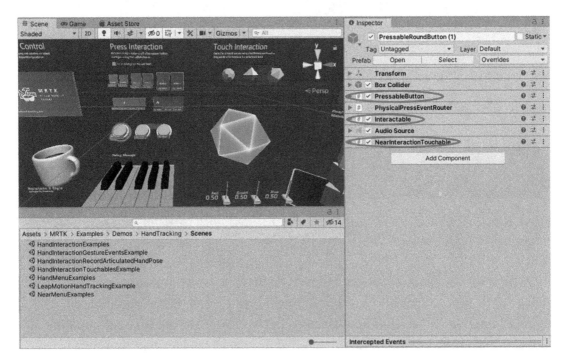

Figure 5-14. *Shows some core components required to perform Press Interaction*

You can attach the preceding scripts to your objects to perform press interactions. To achieve touch interactions, you need to include the HandInteractionTouch.cs and Interactable.cs script components.

Step 5: Object Manipulator

You can move these objects by tapping on a gazed object, holding your finger down, and dragging your hand. Ensure that you are playing the scene in the editor, remoting to your device, or the application is deployed to your device.

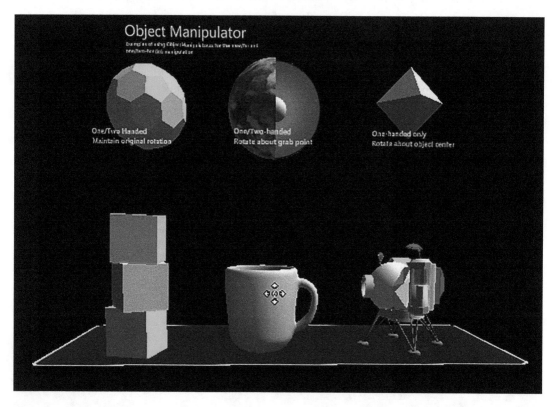

Figure 5-15. *Objects which can be scaled, rotated, and transformed using Object Manipulator component*

Object Manipulator component allows you to scale, rotate, and transform the objects using one or two hands. This feature was previously handled by the Manipulation Handler component, which is now replaced by the Object Manipulator component. You can customize the Object Manipulator component based on various inputs like articulated hand, hand rays, gaze, and gestures.

If you wish to incorporate this feature onto your objects, you need to add the Object Manipulator (script) component to the respective object. Ensure that you also include the collider component in the object. To make your operations more realistic, you can include the RigidBody component in your object; by doing so, your digital objects behave like real ones. They collide with other objects like how natural objects collide; without the RigidBody component, the objects would pass through another object, making it look unrealistic.

Figure 5-16 shows various properties and fields included in the Object Manipulator component. A list of properties and fields is given here:

- **Host Transform:** Includes the object transform, which has to be manipulated.

- **Manipulation Type:** The mode of manipulation can be either one handed or two handed. You can choose both of these settings in this field.

- **Allow Far Manipulation:** Allows you to perform far interaction using pointers.

- **One Handed Manipulation properties:** One-handed manipulation properties look over the operations carried out by a single hand; it might be far or near interaction. Far interactions enable objects to interact through gaze, hand ray, and motion controller's ray. As the name already suggests, users can interact with distant objects. Near interactions are in the form of touches and grabs. Respective touch and grab events are invoked through pointers like PokePointer and SpherePointer.

- **Two Handed Manipulation properties:** One-handed manipulation properties look over the operations carried out by two hands, like move, rotate, and scale.

- **Constraints:** Adding constraints to your objects helps you to restrict the movements of the object. You can select any of the constraint managers that are attached to the object.

- **Physics:** This field is activated only when a RigidBody component is attached to it.

- **Manipulation Events:** A set of events are listed out like OnHoverStarted, OnHoverEnded, OnManipulationStarted, and OnManipulationEnded, which occur in series when an interaction is carried out.

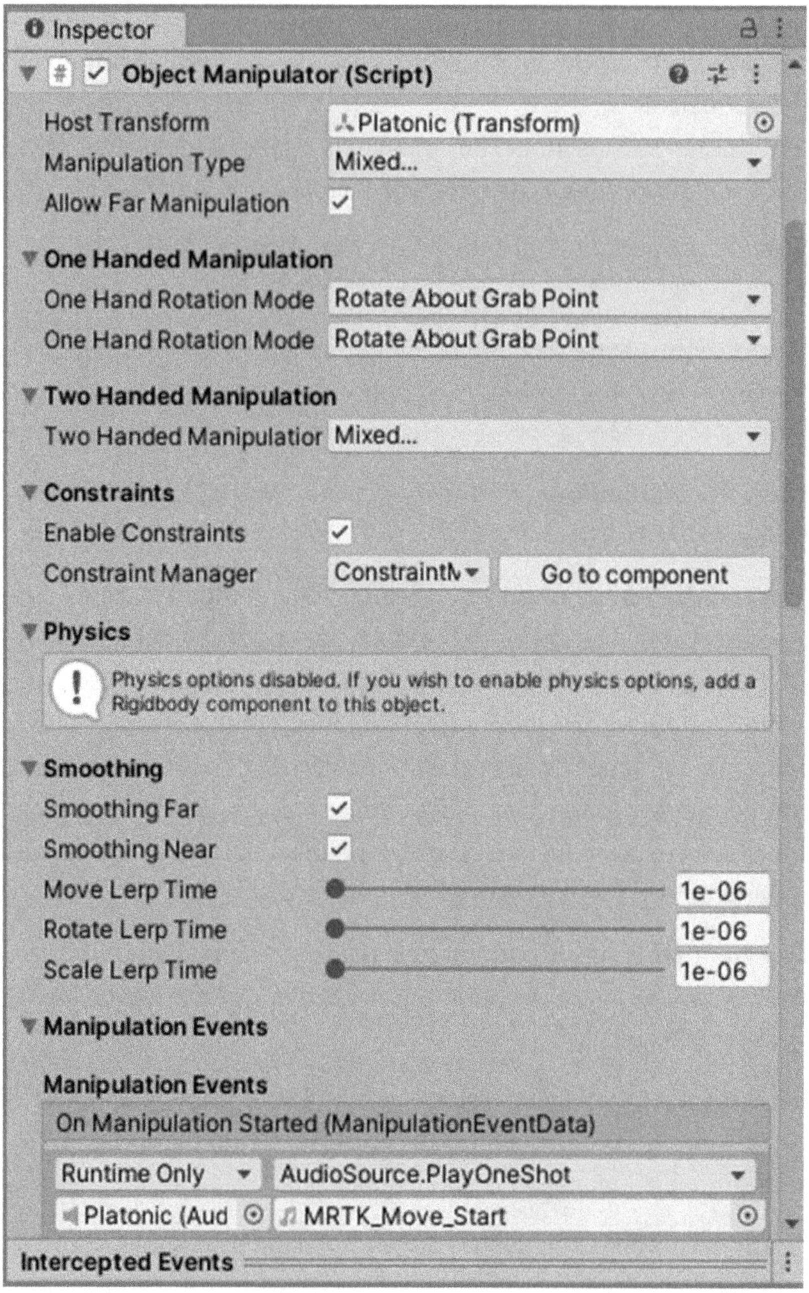

Figure 5-16. *Various properties and fields included under Object Manipulator script*

Step 6: Implementing Gestures in Your Application

Now that you have a high-level understanding of the gesture input methods, you know the required scripts and objects needed to create your gesture functionality. Let's review what these are:

- Bounds Control: Enables you to transform objects in Mixed Reality. You can alter the size and ratios of the objects using handles at the corners of the object.

- Pressable.cs script: Redirects events to PhysicalPressEventRouter and also acts as a connecting logic of hand pressing the button.

- Interactable.cs script: Objects are made interactive by including this component. It enables the objects to respond to user inputs.

- Near Interaction Grabble: Makes the object perceptible and ready to accept inputs.

- Object Manipulator: This allows you to manipulate your object by scaling, rotating, and transforming it. Object Manipulators have various properties and fields for you to customize.

You might want to explore other scripts and objects attached to the example scene to get a more precise insight on how to include gestures in your scene. The HandInteractionExamples scene that we've been exploring in this section is an excellent template scene to use when starting new projects. It contains the essential prefabs listed earlier and several unique examples to modify or expand for your project. As you gain experience, you may also consider building your template scene that contains components you regularly use. If you wish to start with one of the test scenes provided with the Mixed Reality Toolkit, modify it, and save it as your template scene; you may do so by selecting the scene in your Hierarchy and the menu bar selecting File ➤ Save Scene As.

Voice Command Tutorial

In this section, I'll walk you through key elements needed to enable voice commands in your Mixed Reality application. Voice commands are extremely useful when developing Mixed Reality applications because they allow a high level of control and customization without needing a cluttered UI. Users can say a word or series of words to select objects, activate features, and enhance their experience.

Oftentimes, my arms will experience fatigue when using gestures for long periods of time. When this happens, I switch to using voice commands by saying "Select" instead of gestures. This is one example of the power of voice commands. Well thought-out use of voice in your application is key to making a good user experience.

As before, we'll start with a Mixed Reality Toolkit example scene to explore how voice commands work for Windows Mixed Reality.

Step 1: Load the Example Scene

For this tutorial, we'll be loading the "SpeechInputExamples" scene. As you've done with previous test scenes, search or browse for the SpeechInputExamples, and drag it into your hierarchy, as shown in Figure 5-17. Don't forget to unload any other scenes that you might have open.

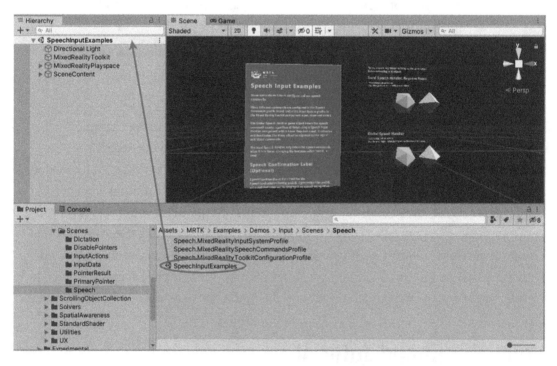

Figure 5-17. *Open the SpeechInputExamples example scene to explore how to use voice commands in your application*

Step 2. Try It Out!

As before, go ahead and try this test scene out by clicking the play button in the editor, remoting to your device, or deploying to your device.

Important   Be sure to add the Microphone capabilities in your app when using voice commands. In Unity, you can check the "Microphone" option at Edit ➤ Project Settings ➤ Player ➤ Settings for Windows Store ➤ Publishing Settings ➤ Capabilities.

Upon starting the example scene, you can see a few game objects with the example scene description and steps that need to be followed. When you gaze at any one of the two game objects at the top and say "Select" out loud, the respective object gets selected. Then say "Change Color" to change the color of the chosen game object as shown in Figure 5-18. The objects need to be selected before you perform the "Change color" operation because it specifically requires focus as the Speech Handler script is locally included.

Saying commands like "Close" and "Open," you can observe that the game objects present at the lower end disappear and appear depending on your speech input. You need not select any objects before providing your command because the Speech Handler script is placed globally. If you are testing via the Unity editor, the voice commands should work if you have a microphone attached to your PC (or if you have a built-in microphone or microphone integrated into your webcam.)

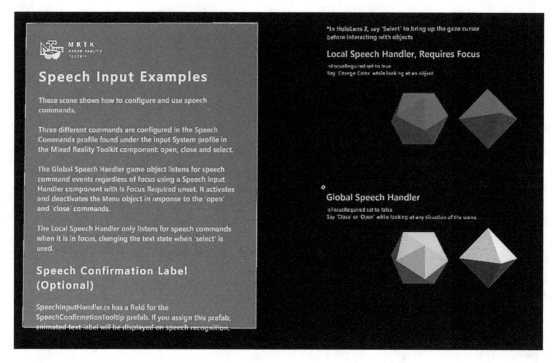

Figure 5-18. *Upon playing the example scene, you will see four objects. Gaze on an object at the top and say "Select" to select it and try saying out loud "Change Color"*

Step 3: Understanding the Scene

Now that you've had some fun trying out voice commands, let's take a deeper look at what makes this experience possible. As shown in Figure 5-19, there are several items included in the Hierarchy of the SpeechInputExamples example scene.

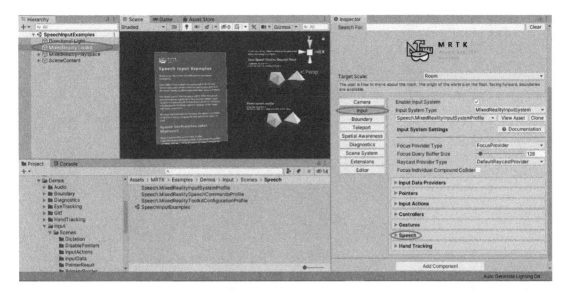

Figure 5-19. *Voice commands are made possible by configuring a few settings in the Speech section of the Input System*

By now, you should be very familiar with some of the objects shown and how to add Input Data Providers to your project. As mentioned earlier, these Data Providers enable you to feed various data or inputs to your Unity project.

Select the Mixed Reality Toolkit object on the Hierarchy window, and navigate the Input Tab ➤ Speech section in the Inspector window, as shown in Figure 5-18. Expand the Speech section to view some of the options. Under the Speech Commands option, you will find input fields to add the keyword to raise speech input events when recognized, as shown in Figure 5-20. Integrating the keywords to your project is the initial step, as your voice commands are identified with these keywords' help.

For each command, you have the option to select Input Action, specify KeyCode, and add a LocalizationKey to be used in UWP apps. These functionalities are displayed in Figure 5-20 which are included in your SpeechInputExamples scene.

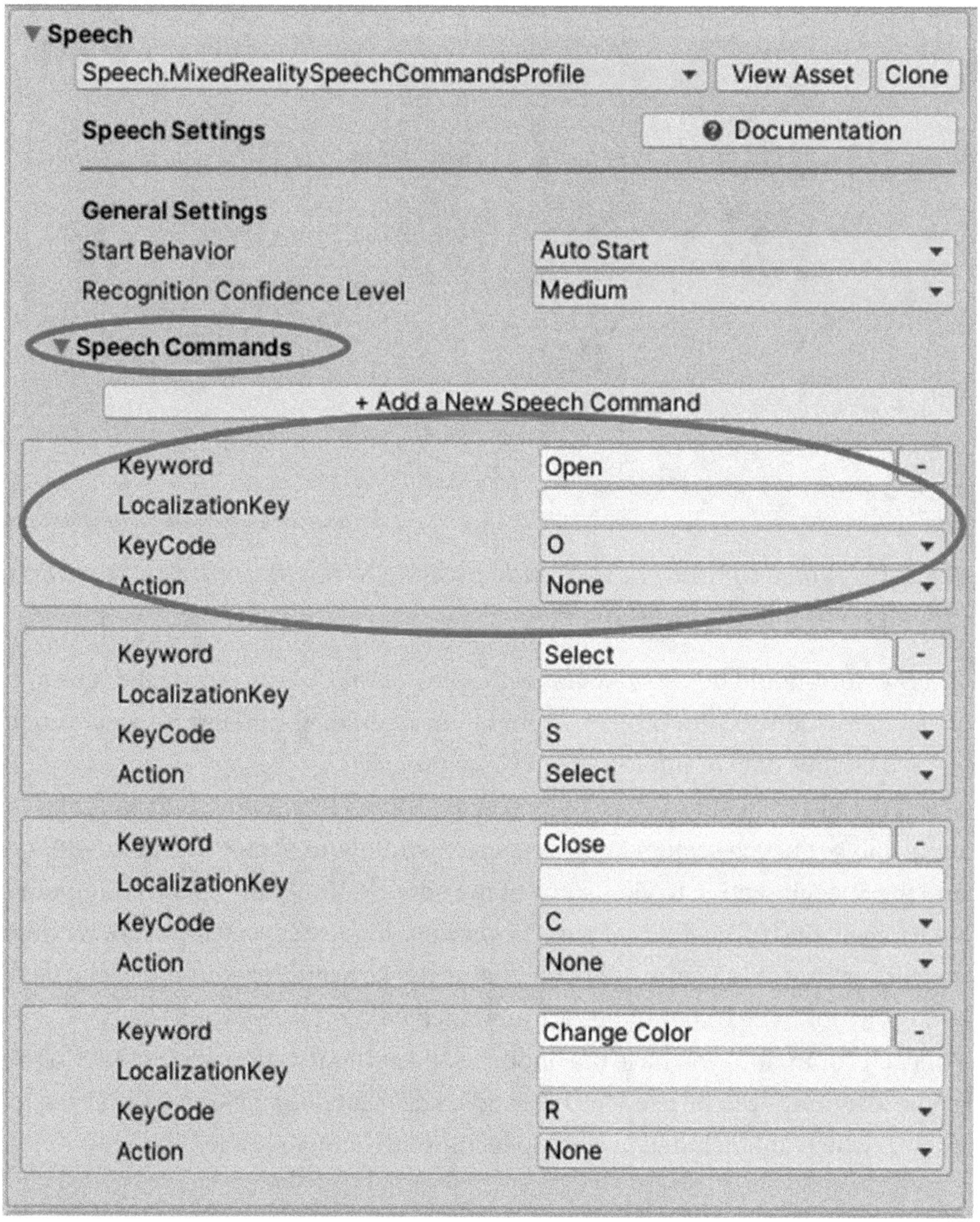

Figure 5-20. Options given for each Speech Commands

After adding the various keywords in your Unity project, we need to attach some functionalities or events to those keywords to perform when recognized. This is taken care of by the Speech Input Handler script. In the Hierarchy window, navigate to SceneContent ➤ LocalSpeechHandlingExample ➤ Platonic2. In the Inspector window, you can see several items included concerning that game object. One of them is the Speech Input Handler script, which helps recognize the keywords and handle the speech input events.

You can also display the recognized text from your voice command by including the SpeechConfirmationTooltip.prefab. This prefab can be assigned to the Speech Confirmation Tooltip prefab field, as shown in Figure 5-21. You can see the Color Changer script, which performs the color-changing operation when the keyword "Change Color" is recognized.

Mesh Filter and Mesh Renderer work hand in hand in delivering the assets onto the scene. The Mesh Filter takes a mesh out of the assets and passes this information to the Mesh Renderer. On the other hand, Mesh Renderer receives the geometry from the Mesh Filter and renders it onto the scene. Box Collider component, which is attached to the object, enables the items to collide with other things on the scene.

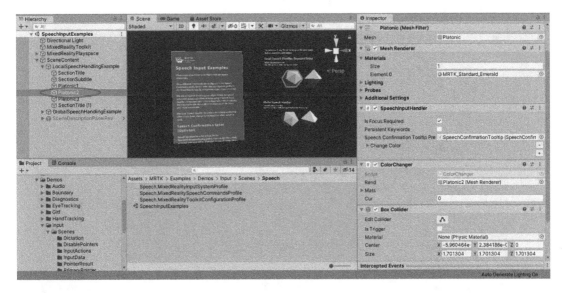

Figure 5-21. *Various items assigned to the object on the scene named "Platonic2"*

Step 4: Add Your Own Voice Command

The best way to learn how something works is to try it yourself! Let's add another voice command to the existing set. The objects currently change color when you say "Change Color," and they disappear and reappear when you say "Close" and "Open." Let's add a voice command for "Move Up" to have the objects move upward.

Select Mixed Reality Toolkit object on the Hierarchy window; in the Inspector window, navigate to Input Tab ➤ Speech sections ➤ Speech Commands. Click the "+Add a New Speech Command" button at the top as shown in Figure 5-22. A new field is added with the same options as the previous speech commands. Fill out the details as shown in Figure 5-21. You have now successfully added a keyword "Move Up" in your Unity project. The keyword is the voice command. Be careful not to put any spaces before the keyword, as it will prevent the code from recognizing your voice command.

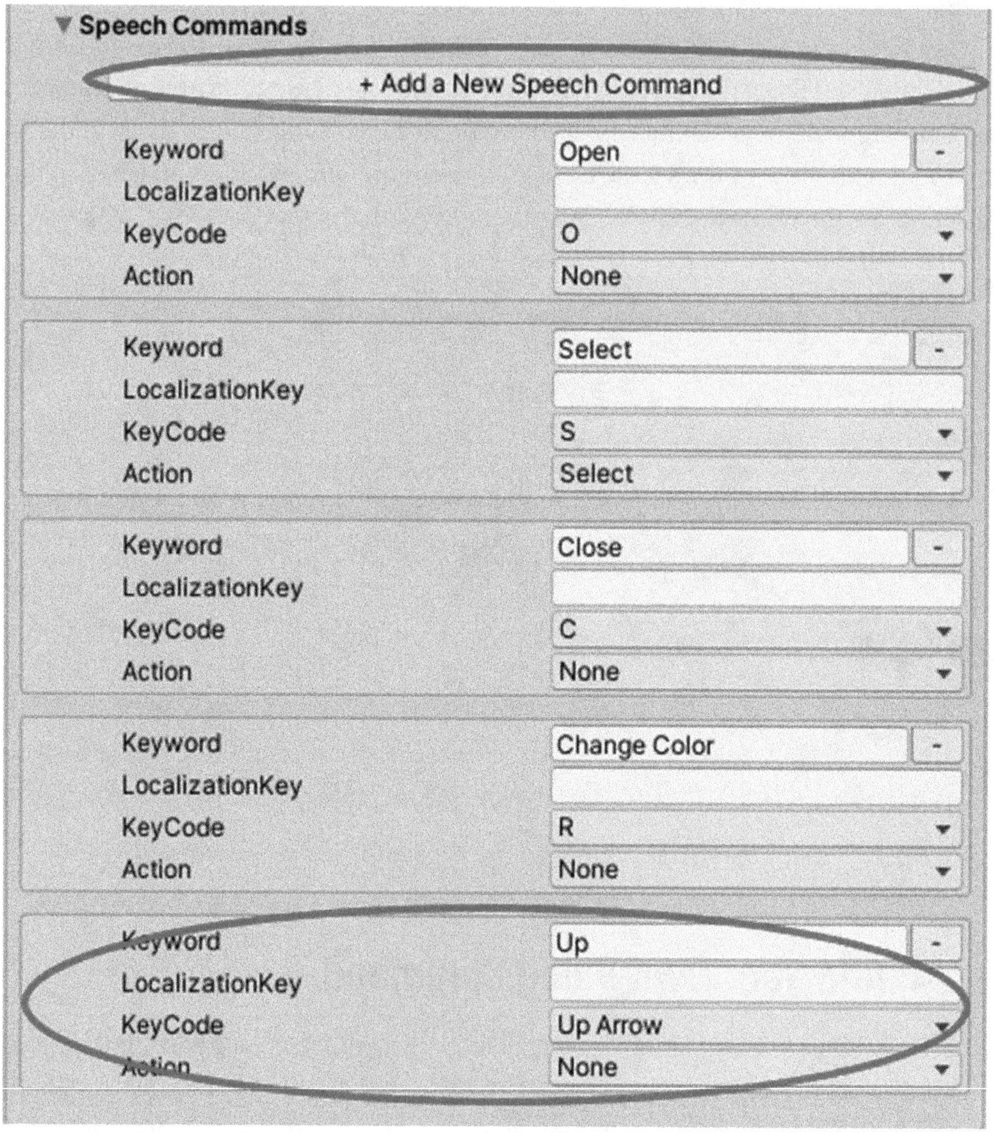

Figure 5-22. *Adding a new speech command*

The next step is to add an event to the keyword through Speech Input Handler Script. For the time being, let's make the "Platonic2" object move up by saying "Move Up." Now, every time you say "Move Up," a message of "OnMoveUp" will be sent to the object you are gazing upon. However, the objects in the scene won't know what to do when they receive the OnMoveUp message. We need to add a method called OnMoveUp() to the script on the game object. Let's take a look at the script attached to the game objects.

You can find the script by searching your Project panel for ColorChanger.cs, or you can find it in the Inspector by going to the "Platonic2" object in your Hierarchy and then double-clicking the "ColorChanger" script that has been attached to the game object in the Inspector panel. Open the script in Visual Studio or any other editor. Go ahead and create the OnMoveUp() method by typing in the following code:

```
public void OnMoveUp()
{
    transform.Translate(0.0f, 0.2f, 0.0f);
}
```

This small addition simply moves the object upward (in the Y direction) by 0.2 units. The previous step is demonstrated in Figure 5-23.

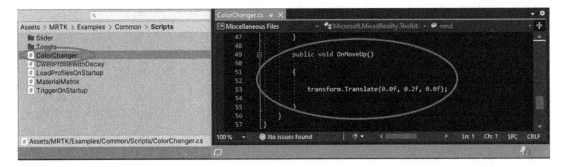

Figure 5-23. *Open the "ColorChanger" code in editor and add the preceding code at the end*

Click the "Platonic2" object on the Hierarchy window; then on the Inspector window, expand the Speech Input Handler script. Click the small "+" mark to add an event to the keyword that you have entered. Fill in the details as shown in Figure 5-24. Make sure that you choose the response event as ColorChanger ➤ OnMoveUp(). This step will help you attach an event to your keyword.

Note   It is important to make sure that the keywords match, or else you'll encounter an error asking for the correct keyword.

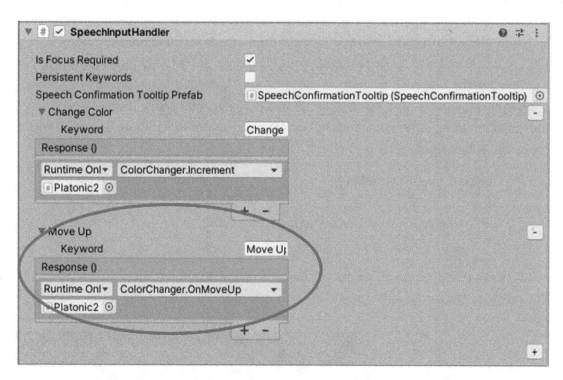

Figure 5-24. *Adding the functionality to the newly added keyword*

Go ahead and try out your shiny new voice command! Gaze on each object and say, "Move Up." You will see the object move up!

Step 5: Using Voice Commands in Your Own Project

Congratulations! You've successfully uncovered how voice commands work with Windows Mixed Reality and how to add your own voice commands to the existing test scene. Adding voice commands to a new scene or a different scene is a simple process. Let's review what you need to do to enable voice commands in your own project:

- Add the required keyword in the Speech section of the Input System in Mixed Reality Toolkit.

- Attach the SpeechInputHandler script to the object on which you have to perform some operations.

- Make sure to select appropriate events for the given keywords.

Implementing voice commands in Windows Mixed Reality is relatively simple but will significantly enhance the user experience of your application. The voice inputs can also be given as complete sentences rather than using single keywords. The next step will discuss some best practices for using voice in your application.

Best Practices for Voice Commands

Voice commands are an excellent way for users to interact with Mixed Reality applications. There are a few HoloLens-specific voice commands which you can try out. Try saying

- "What can I say?"

- "Go to Start" (can be used to open the start menu)

- "Increase Volume"

- "Decrease Volume"

- "How much battery do I have left"

- "Increase Brightness"

- "Decrease Brightness"

- "Start Recording"

- "Stop Recording"

- "Shut down the device"

- "Restart the device"

- "What time is it"

- "Go to sleep"

Here are some best practices to keep in mind for implementing voice in your application:

- Use keywords that have two or more syllables. This helps voice recognition for a wide range of accents.

- Design your app for users accidentally triggering voice commands. Allow users to undo an action, where appropriate (e.g., when deleting an object by accident).

- Make sure all voice commands are distinctive. If two or more commands are similar sounding, the voice recognizer may activate the wrong command.

- Make sure your voice commands are easily recognized across a range of accents, whenever possible.

- Voice commands are a wonderful way to quickly access nested menus or other situations in which multiple gestures may be required.

- Consider providing the user with a list of voice commands, if the UI doesn't already reveal what they are.

- Put a microphone icon next to buttons that can be tapped or activated with a voice command. If possible, make all buttons and UI elements voice enabled.

Other Hardware Input

There are a wide range of hardware options that can be used with Windows Mixed Reality headsets. These include devices such as motion controllers, Bluetooth keyboards and mice, Bluetooth game pads, clickers, and other Bluetooth accessories.

While it is considered a best practice to avoid using traditional PC hardware (keyboards and mice) for Mixed Reality experiences, there may be some applications where these input methods are appropriate.

Game pads are an excellent choice for applications that may involve moving a third-person object, such as a game character, holographic helicopter, or holographic race car.

Summary

Congratulations! In this chapter, we've learned about the primary forms of input for Windows Mixed Reality headsets. We walked through several tutorials on how gaze, gestures, and voice commands work with Mixed Reality. We learned how to enable these features in our own application and how to leverage the Mixed Reality Toolkit to easily implement powerful input features.

As you continue your Mixed Reality development journey, keep in mind that the industry is still in a growing stage. Everyone generally agrees that input methods for Mixed Reality devices are somewhat clunky and awkward at times, lacking precision and elegance. Think about what an ideal input experience would be like, and don't be afraid to try out new ways of interacting with your virtual environment! You never know who will introduce an input method as relevant to Mixed Reality as the mouse was to the PC.

CHAPTER 6

Using Spatial Awareness

In this chapter, we'll learn how to use one of the most defining features of Windows Mixed Reality headsets such as the HoloLens: spatial awareness. We'll learn how to apply spatial awareness in Unity using the Mixed Reality Toolkit and unwrap some neat tricks that you can do with spatial awareness.

What Is Spatial Awareness?

Devices like the HoloLens are constantly tracking their environment and building a 3D model of the area that they are in. This is called *spatial awareness*. Without spatial awareness, holograms would not be able to be set on floors and tables, or be pinned to walls. Objects in other rooms would still be visible, degrading the user's experience.

Spatial awareness is important for several reasons:

- Occlusion: It tells the HoloLens which holograms to hide from view. For example, if you place a hologram in your hallway and then walk into another room, the spatial map of that room's walls will prevent you from seeing the hologram in your hallway. If there was no spatial map, you would see the hologram as if it were visible through your walls, causing an unrealistic experience.

- Placement: It allows users to interact with the spatial map – for example, pin items to your walls, allow characters to sit on your sofa (as seen in Microsoft's "Fragments" app!), or automatically decorate your surroundings.

- Physics: It allows objects to collide with or bounce off your walls, furniture, and floors, resulting in a more realistic experience.

145

© Sean Ong and Varun Kumar Siddaraju 2021
S. Ong and V. K. Siddaraju, *Beginning Windows Mixed Reality Programming*,
https://doi.org/10.1007/978-1-4842-7104-9_6

- Navigation: Use gaze to allow game characters and other holograms to follow along mapped surfaces.

- Persistence: Spatial awareness stores information regarding an object's position in its environment. This is useful in many scenarios. For example, you accidentally close the application after placing your holograms in the desired positions since the positions of the objects are stored. You can find your holograms in the same area on opening your application again.

For more information on spatial awareness and the sensors involved, see Chapter 1.

Spatial Awareness Tutorial

In this section, I'll walk you through setting up some basic spatial awareness capabilities. I'll show which elements from the Mixed Reality Toolkit are needed to enable spatial awareness and provide some tips for a good experience.

Step 1: Set Up Unity Scene

For this tutorial, we will use an example scene from the Mixed Reality Toolkit. If you haven't already, be sure to set up Unity for Mixed Reality development as described in Chapter 4. You may also refer to Chapter 4 for a refresher on how to run Mixed Reality Toolkit example scenes in Unity.

Find the "SpatialAwarenessMeshDemo" example scene (or SpatialAwarenessMeshDemo.unity) in your Project panel by using the search bar, or finding it within the folder structure. Drag the test scene into your Hierarchy, as shown in Figure 6-1. Be sure to unload (disable) all other scenes that you might have open.

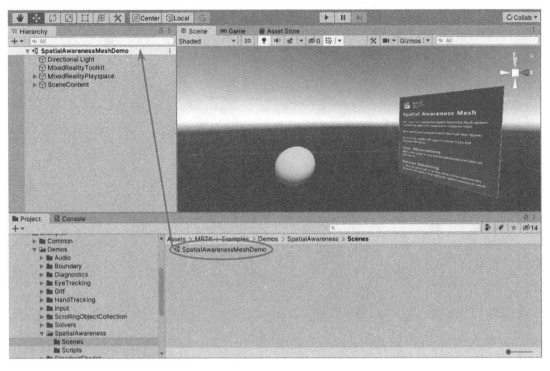

Figure 6-1. *Open the SpatialAwarenessMeshDemo scene from the Mixed Reality Toolkit to explore a basic implementation of spatial awareness*

Step 2. Try It Out!

The next step is to try it out by clicking the play button.

I highly recommend using your HoloLens to experience spatial mesh around you. By using HoloLens, you can observe how the mesh is placed around you and on your objects. If you don't have a device, or prefer not to use it for this test, try on your Unity editor to have a peek on how spatial awareness works.

Note   You need to change the settings as shown in Figure 6-5 in order to test your application on Unity editor. Refer to Step 4 to know how to change the settings.

If wearing the HoloLens, you will see the spatial map well aligned to your physical surroundings, as seen in Figure 6-2.

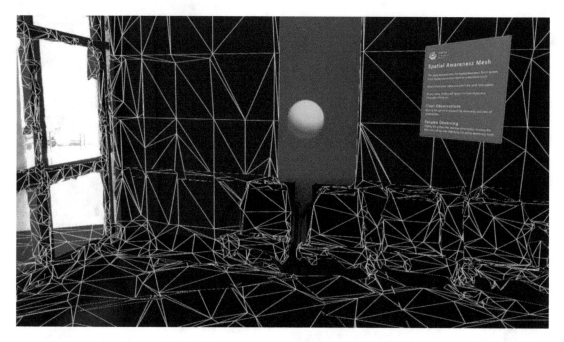

Figure 6-2. *View of the spatial map, as seen through the HoloLens 2*

As you can see, the rendering of the spatial map is a collection of vertices, edges, and faces. Vertices are points where two or more edges meet to form an angle, edges are line segments that are usually straight, and faces are plane surfaces formed from edges meeting at vertices. It looks like a net covering your surroundings (we'll see later how to change the spatial mapping appearance). The 3D object generated by spatial awareness is often called the *spatial object mesh*.

Step 3. Understanding the Scene

Now that you've had the opportunity to experience spatial awareness, let's dig into our scene to learn about the key components that make spatial mapping possible.

Select the Mixed Reality Toolkit object in your Hierarchy window, and observe the Inspector window as shown in Figure 6-3. The Mixed Reality Toolkit object manages the Spatial Awareness System. There are various configuration profiles in the MixedRealityToolkit object, which can be changed and customized based on the application that you are creating. Among configuration profiles, only some have the Spatial Awareness System automatically enabled. One of those profiles is DefaultMixedRealityToolkitConfigurationProfile. The example scene uses this profile as its configuration profile.

Navigate to the Spatial Awareness tab in the Inspector window. You should see a check box named Enable Spatial Awareness System, which is checked. By checking the check box, you are enabling your application to access the Spatial Awareness System.

Note   Settings might not be highlighted as shown in Figure 6-3. This is because you cannot customize standard configuration profiles directly. It would help if you created a clone of that profile to configure the settings. We will discuss more on this step in the upcoming section.

Figure 6-3. *Spatial Awareness settings are all that's needed to enable spatial awareness in your project!*

In the Spatial Awareness System Settings section, you are provided with an option to Add Spatial Observer. By default, the DefaultMixedRealityToolkitConfigurationProfile will have the Spatial Awareness System pre-configured for the Windows Mixed Reality platform, which uses the WindowsMixedRealitySpatialMeshObserver class as shown in Figure 6-4. This setting enables you to visualize spatial mesh when deployed on the device but not on Unity editor.

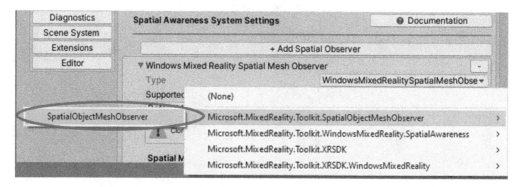

Figure 6-4. *WindowsMixedRealitySpatialMeshObserver class enables you to visualize spatial mesh, when deployed on your device*

For you to test the example scene on your Unity editor, you need to change the "Type" field to "SpatialObjectMeshObserver" class, as shown in Figure 6-5.

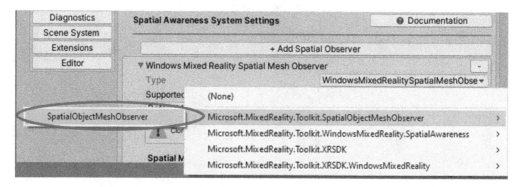

Figure 6-5. *SpatialObjectMeshObserver enables you to visualize spatial mesh when tested on Unity editor*

Click the sphere object in the Hierarchy window. You can observe two scripts attached to the sphere object in the Inspector window. They are *PointHandler.cs* and *ClearSpatialObservations.cs* scripts, which enable you to switch on and off the spatial mesh created by merely tapping on the sphere.

Step 4. Using Spatial Mapping in Your Application

To enable spatial awareness in your future projects, you need to clone the standard Mixed Reality Profiles to begin. Click on the Copy & Customize button highlighted in Figure 6-6 to begin the cloning process. A Clone Profile window pops up where you can provide a new name to the cloned profile and click the "Clone" button as shown in Figure 6-6.

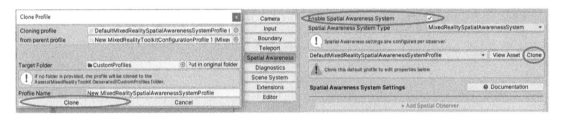

Figure 6-6. *Cloning the DefaultMixedRealityToolkitConfigurationProfile*

The cloned profile is automatically assigned as your configuration profile. You can see a few options getting highlighted after cloning. Now click the Spatial Awareness tab in the Inspector window. Check the Enable Spatial Awareness System check box, as shown in Figure 6-7 to use Spatial Awareness System effectively in your application. To configure Spatial Awareness System Settings, you need to clone the DefaultMixedRealitySpatialAwarenessSystem profile by clicking the Clone button next to it. A Clone Profile window pops up where you can provide your profile name and then click the Clone button shown in Figure 6-7.

Figure 6-7. *Clone the DefaultMixedRealitySpatialAwarenessSystem to access the Spatial Awareness System Settings*

Now you can configure various settings under Spatial Awareness System Settings. Expand the Window Mixed Reality Spatial Mesh Observer section under Spatial Awareness System Settings, and change the "Type" field to the required class based on where you want to test your application. Refer to Figures 6-4 and 6-5 to change the "Type" field.

Occlusion

In this section, I'll walk you through implementing occlusion to your spatial awareness mesh. Occlusion allows parts of objects that are fully or partially behind walls and other surfaces to become invisible – just as they would in the physical world. This increases your holograms' realism and improves your user's experience.

Step 1: Apply Occlusion

To include occlusion in your Unity project, firstly configure the profiles as stated earlier. We have learned how to enable the Spatial Awareness System in our project and clone some standard configuration profiles to customize the settings. Under the Spatial Awareness System Settings, expand the Windows Mixed Reality Spatial Mesh Observer as shown in Figure 6-8. Clone the DefaultMixedRealitySpatialMeshObserverProfile to configure some of its properties. Refer to Figure 6-8.

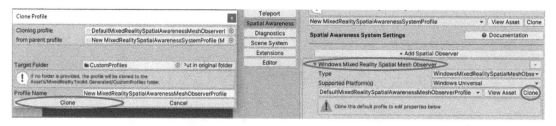

Figure 6-8. *Clone the DefaultMixedRealitySpatialMeshObserverProfile to configure some of the properties*

After cloning, some of the properties and settings get highlighted. Scroll down to the Display setting, and change the Display Option to Occlusion as shown in Figure 6-9. By doing so, you are enabling the Occlusion option to your project. This provides a sense of realism to the application.

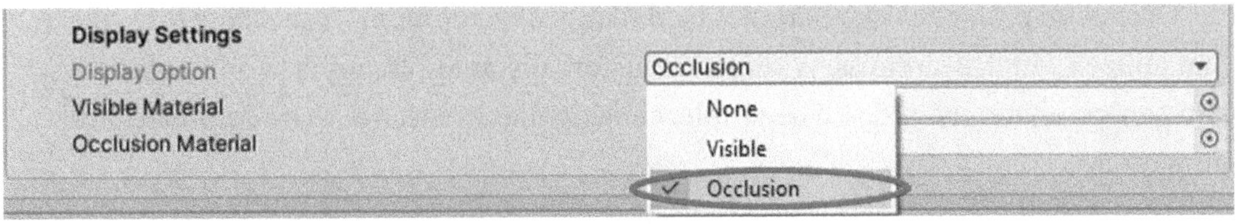

Display Settings

Display Option	Occlusion ▾
Visible Material	None ⊙
Occlusion Material	Visible ⊙
	✓ Occlusion

Figure 6-9. *Change the Display Option to Occlusion*

Step 2: Try It Out!

The occlusion material will be rendered. Since the material is transparent, you will not directly see the spatial mapping mesh, but you will see that part of the object will be occluded by its environment!

As you can see from my tests, the sphere is fully visible when there are no obstructions between me and the sphere, but the sphere is partially visible when obstructions are present (Figure 6-10).

Figure 6-10. *When obstructed (in this case, by door handle), only the unobstructed part of the sphere is visible*

Occlusion is an essential part of mixed reality development – especially for projects that utilize spatial awareness. Without occlusion, distant holograms in other rooms and behind objects would still be visible, causing the experience to be confusing and unnatural.

Scene Understanding

HoloLens has an exceptional understanding of the space around it. It frequently maps the environment present in and builds a 3D mesh that the user can use to analyze. Sometimes the user would prefer a higher level of abstraction with more detailed information about the environment.

Many applications start scanning the scene and placing particular objects on the preferred locations like floor, ceiling, or walls. Having a 3D mesh of the environment proves to be useful for this functionality. However, there are still more processes to be carried out on the mesh to differentiate among various surfaces. This is where Scene Understanding comes in; it allows the user to unlatch more capabilities of the device to reason out scene objects which include walls, ceiling, floor, platform, and so on.

Here are a few things that Scene Understanding allows you to do:

- Place objects on floors, ceilings, and walls.

- Place objects in the air away from you or near you, without touching walls.

- Place objects on the floor away from you or near you.

- Find the largest wall and place objects on it.

- Find sittable surfaces (so you can have characters sit on anyone's chair!).

- Identify chairs and couches.

- Identify large empty surfaces.

- Allows users to "paint" their spatial mesh to limit the scanned area.

- Smooth the spatial mapping mesh.

To have detailed insight on Scene Understanding, refer to `https://docs.microsoft. com/en-us/windows/mixed-reality/develop/platform-capabilities-and-apis/ scene-understanding-sdk#developing-with-scene-understanding`.

Summary

Congratulations! You are now equipped with core knowledge about spatial awareness and can start taking advantage of some cool spatial awareness tools. Let's review what we've learned in this chapter:

- We've learned what spatial awareness is.

- We learned how to enable spatial awareness in your application.

- We learned how to occlude objects using spatial awareness for a more realistic effect.

- We learned how to use Scene Understanding to unleash the power of spatial awareness, identify objects and surfaces in your environment, and place objects on critical surfaces in your environment.

You may not have thought that we had so much to cover on a chapter about spatial awareness! Spatial awareness is essential for Mixed Reality. The headset's understanding of the physical environment warrants the "mixed" in Mixed Reality – allowing our applications to mix the virtual and physical worlds.

We've only touched on the tip of the iceberg concerning spatial awareness. There are so many untapped opportunities waiting to be explored and waiting to be implemented. Here are just a few examples of spatial awareness ideas I've heard mentioned:

- Expanding the spatial mapping mesh to make your room or area appear larger than it is

- Virtually painting your walls and furniture to see what various color options would look like

- Making holes in your walls to give the sensation that you can see through them

As you continue your developer journey, think about creative ways to leverage spatial awareness and all associated tools. Be sure to think outside the box! Keep in mind that your spatial mapping mesh doesn't need to obey physics laws as your real walls and furniture do. The sky's the limit to what you can achieve!

CHAPTER 7

Spatial Sound

In this chapter, I'll walk you through how to make the most of Spatial Sound in your applications! We rely heavily on our ears to precisely locate real objects around us. Our sense of hearing is able to detect extremely small differences in the arrival of sound waves at each of our ears in order to locate the position of the sound source in 3D space.

In the context of Mixed Reality, this is called *Spatial Sound*. Developers can leverage Mixed Reality audio tools that perform complex calculations in order to spatialize sound. These tools determine how sound waves should be modified and adjusted for each ear in order to "trick" our brains into hearing the sound as if it came from a specific point in 3D space and not from the speakers themselves! This vastly increases the feeling of immersion. Users will still be able to hear virtual objects (if the objects are intended to make noise) around them, even if they can't see those objects. This is especially important for devices like the HoloLens, where the field of view is limited and users might not see holograms in their entire peripheral vision.

Here are different ways developers can leverage Spatial Sound:

- Increase immersion. Make the user feel like they are immersed in an experience where the holograms are all around them.

- Call attention to holograms that are outside the field of view. Play audio from a hologram that can't be seen by users in order to prompt the user to look in the direction of that hologram.

- Provide a better interactive experience. When the user interacts with holograms or user interface elements in a Mixed Reality application, having spatial audio cues or effects coming from the point of interaction increases the sense of realism. Think of how satisfying it is to hear the "snap" or a light switch. You can now recreate this satisfaction in your application using Spatial Sound!

© Sean Ong and Varun Kumar Siddaraju 2021
S. Ong and V. K. Siddaraju, *Beginning Windows Mixed Reality Programming*,
https://doi.org/10.1007/978-1-4842-7104-9_7

- Background support. Providing background support to the scene through spatial audio provides the user with a more authentic feel while working with the application.

Note   Spatial Sound only works in Windows 10. If you are developing your Mixed Reality application on a previous version of Windows, Spatial Sound will not work. Spatial Sound can be leveraged by Windows desktop (Win32) apps as well as Universal Windows Platform (UWP) apps on supported platforms

---

Spatial Sound Tutorial

In this section, I'll walk you through a tutorial on how spatial mapping works in a Mixed Reality application.

Step 1: Set Up Unity Scene

For this tutorial, we will use a test scene from the Mixed Reality Toolkit. If you haven't already, be sure to set up Unity for Mixed Reality development as described in Chapter 4. You may also refer to Chapter 4 for a refresher on how to run Mixed Reality Toolkit test scenes in Unity.

Find the "AudioOcclusionExamples" test scene in your Project panel by using the search bar, or finding it within the folder structure. Drag the test scene into your Hierarchy, as shown in Figure 7-1. Be sure to unload (disable) all other scenes that you might have open.

Upon loading the test scene in Unity, you will notice a blue square (the SoundOccluder) with a sphere (the SoundEmitter) behind it. The SoundEmitter is responsible for emitting the sound you will hear when you test this scene. The blue SoundOccluder is responsible for occluding audio. More on that in Step 3!

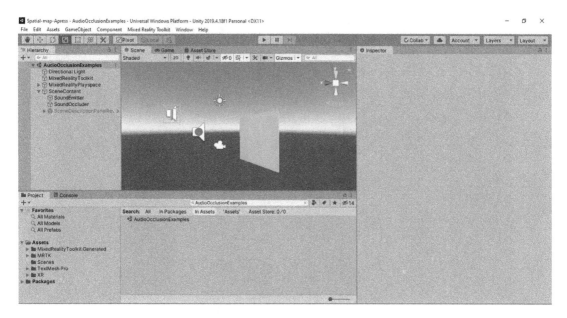

Figure 7-1. *Load the AudioOcclusionTest scene from the Mixed Reality Toolkit by dragging it into your hierarchy*

Step 2: Try It Out!

To experience the Spatial Sound from this test scene, deploy the application to your headset using Visual Studio.

When you are ready, go ahead and click the "play" button to test the application. When you first start the application, you will begin to hear a singing voice that is somewhat muffled.

The sound of the voice is muffled when the blue square is between you and the sphere, as shown in Figure 7-2. When you walk around the square so that it is not between you and the sphere (as shown in Figure 7-3,) you will hear the singing voice loud and clear coming from the sphere.

Figure 7-2. *When you first simulate the test scene, you will see a blue square in front of you and hear a muffled singing voice*

Figure 7-3. *As you walk around the blue square, you will notice that the source of the singing voice is a blue sphere. You will be able to hear the singing voice louder and clearer when the blue square is not obstructing the sound*

Try walking around to various parts of your room or area, and try turning your head in various directions. You will notice that, remarkably, you can hear the singing voices coming from the exact position of the sphere!

Fun Experiment   While the app is running, try closing your eyes, walking around in a few circles, and then putting your fist exactly where you hear the audio source. Now open your eyes. Amazingly, your fist will be at the same exact spot as the sphere! This shows the amazing ability for the brain to spatialize sound, even without visual cues. It also shows the amazing ability for the HoloLens to digitally spatialize sound and sync the audio location to the hologram location.

Step 3: Understanding the Scene

Now that you've had some time to try out Spatial Sound, let's dig a little deeper in the scene to understand all the components that make it work. The only two objects of interest in the Hierarchy are the SoundEmitter object and the SoundOccluder object, as shown in Figure 7-4.

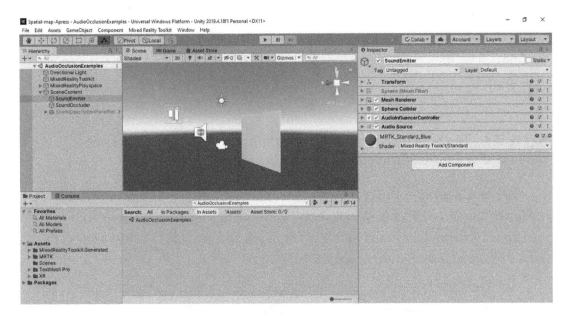

Figure 7-4. *The AudioOcclusionTest scene has two objects that we will focus on in this tutorial, the SoundEmitter and the SoundOccluder*

First, let's look at the SoundOccluder game object. After selecting the SoundOccluder, you will notice a script called AudioOccluder.cs in the inspector panel, as shown in Figure 7-5. The *AudioOccluder.cs* script is a useful script provided in the Mixed Reality Toolkit that allow objects to occlude spatialized audio sources.

Let's see why audio occlusion is a useful feature of Spatial Sound. Think about a band playing music in a room. When you walk out of the room, and close the door, you may still hear the band playing, but the sound you hear will be muffled and a bit quieter. When you open the room's door again, the sound is loud and crisp. The AudioOccluder. cs script allows developers to mimic this behavior in Mixed Reality applications to increase realism for users.

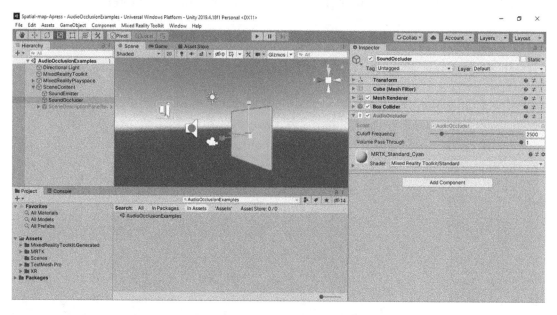

Figure 7-5. *The SoundOccluder object contains the AudioOccluder.cs script, allowing it to "occlude" any sound sources behind it*

When you attach the AudioOccluder.cs script to an object, the object will "muffle" and lower the volume on any spatialized audio sources, if the occlude object is between you (the camera) and the audio sources or emitters. You are able to adjust a few of the script's parameters from the inspector panel:

- The *Cutoff Frequency* parameter allows you to adjust the "muffle" of the occluded sound. This is essentially a low-pass filter.

- The *Volume Pass Through* parameter allows you to adjust how much volume to allow through the occluder.

The second key object in the Hierarchy is the SoundEmitter. The SoundEmitter game object (the blue sphere) is the most important object in this scene, as the audio source is attached to this object and it is where the sound is spatialized. After selecting this object in the Hierarchy, you will notice a somewhat busy inspector panel containing a few important components, as shown previously in Figure 7-4.

The first vital component is the *Audio Source* component. When this component is attached to a game object, it causes it to behave as an audio source. It allows you to select the audio file, spatialize the audio source, adjust the volume, and add effects to your audio. Let's look a few key parameters (as shown in Figure 7-6) of the Audio Source that you can adjust in the inspector panel:

- AudioClip: You may specify the audio file or asset, for example, a .wav or .mp3 file.

- Mute: Check this box to mute the audio. Useful for toggling within your project's scripts.

- Play On Awake: Check this box to play the audio source when the scene loads.

- Loop: Check this box to loop the audio indefinitely.

- Priority: Allows you to set the priority of the audio file. A larger number means a lower priority, while a smaller number means a higher priority. If there are too many audio sources, then sources only with the highest priorities will be heard.

- Volume: Allows you to set the volume of your audio source.

- Pitch: Allows you to speed up or slow down your audio source.

- Spatial Blend: Allows you to set the degree to which your audio source is treated as a 3D spatial audio source. Set the value to 1 for Spatial Sound in the HoloLens.

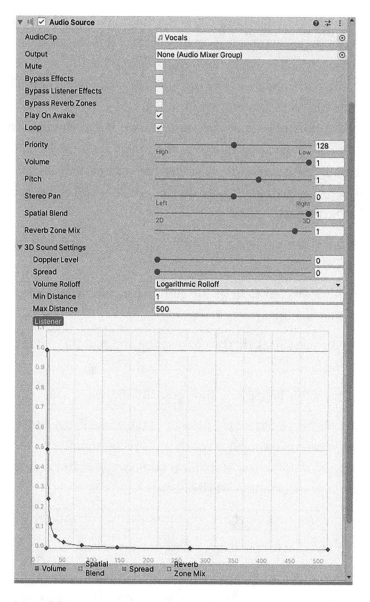

Figure 7-6. *Adjustable parameters of the Audio Source component, as seen in the inspector panel Unity's editor*

The second vital component attached to the SoundEmitter game object is the *AudioInfluencerController.cs* script. This script allows the audio source to be influenced by other game objects in the scene. For example, the SoundOccluder game object (containing the AudioOccluder.cs script) is able to influence this audio source because of the *AudioInfluencerController.cs* script. Let's look at some of the script's parameters (see Figure 7-7) which can be adjusted in the inspector panel:

- Update Interval: The time, in seconds, between audio influence updates. To update each frame, set the value to 0. A longer time period will provide better performance for your application, but also increases the time delay for activating the influencer.

- Max Distance: The maximum distance, in meters, for this object to look when finding the user or influencers.

- Max Objects: The maximum number of objects to consider when looking for influencers.

Figure 7-7. *Adjustable parameters of the AudioInfluencerController.cs script, as seen in the inspector panel Unity's editor*

Step 4: Enabling Spatial Sound in Your Application

Now that you've learned about some of the key elements of Spatial Sound and experienced a working example from the Mixed Reality Toolkit, let's see how to implement Spatial Sound in your own application.

First, you need to enable Spatial Sound in Unity's settings. Go to Edit ➤ Project Settings.

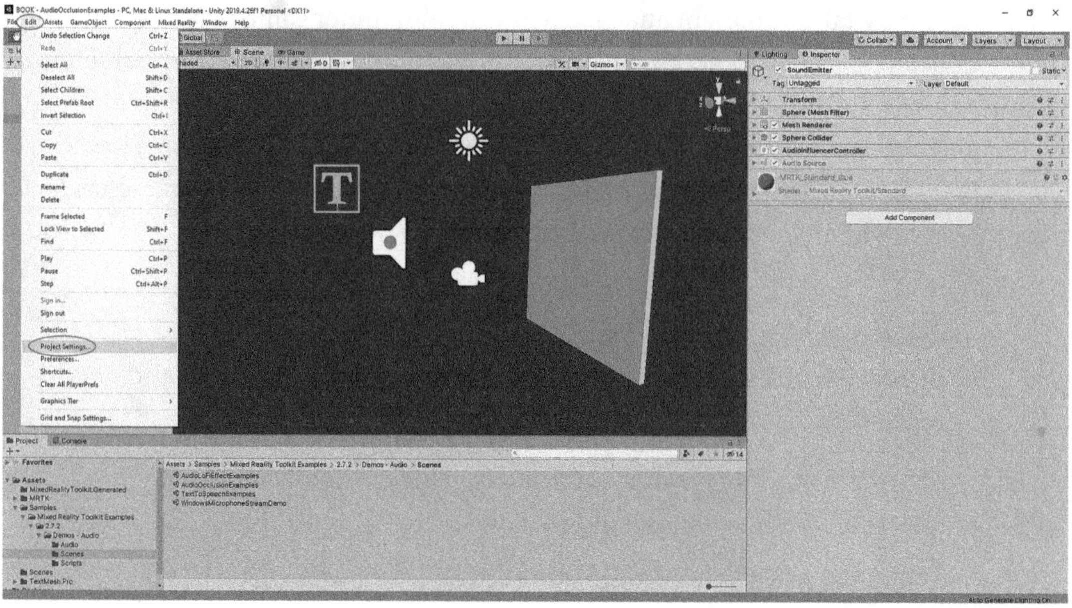

Figure 7-8a. *Selecting Project Settings from edit menu*

Once the Project Settings window opens, select Audio and select the Microsoft HRTF extension in the Spatializer Plugin drop-down, as shown in Figure 7-8a. Set the System Sample Rate to 48000.

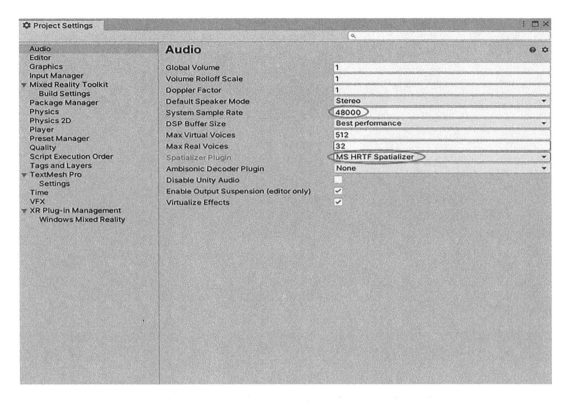

Figure 7-8b. *Enable Spatial Audio in Unity's audio settings. Be sure to select the MS HRTF Spatializer and set the System Sample Rate to 48000*

Second, you need to attach an Audio Source to any game object you wish to behave as an audio source. You can do this by selecting your game object, clicking the "Add Component" button at the bottom of your game object's Inspector panel, and searching for and attaching the Audio Source component, as shown in Figure 7-9. As you can see in Figure 7-9, I created a new cube game object in the AudioOcclusionExamples scene that we've been working with to illustrate creating Spatial Sound on a new game object.

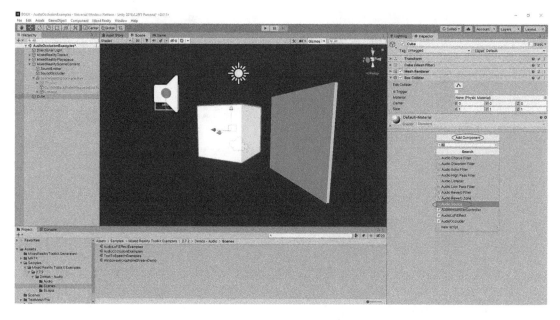

Figure 7-9. *Attach an Audio Source component to the game object you wish to behave as an audio source*

Third, you need to configure the Audio Source for Spatial Sound. There are three parameters in the Audio Source component that you need to set, as shown in Figure 7-10. These are the changes you need to make:

- Enable the *Spatialize* check box.

- Set the *Spatial Blend* to a value of 1.

- Set *Volume Rolloff* to "Custom Rolloff." You may need to expand the "3D Sound Settings" item to see this parameter.

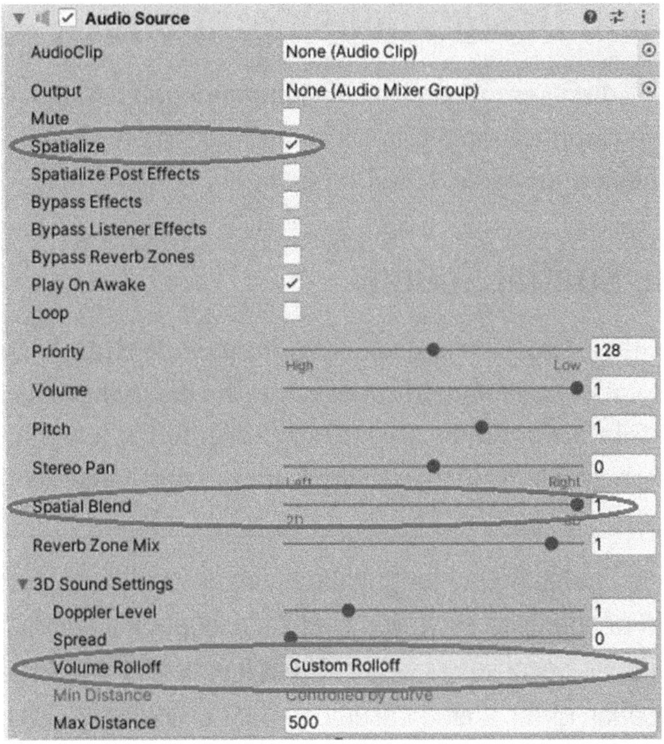

Figure 7-10. *Modify the three parameters shown in the Audio Source component to spatialize your sound*

That's all it takes to enable Spatial Sound in your application! Feel free to drop an audio file from your assets into the AudioClip area, and try it out with your headset.

To turn an object into an audio occluder, simply attach the AudioInfluencerController.cs script to the game object that contains the audio source and attach the AudioOccluder.cs script to the object that you wish to behave as the audio occluder. Be sure that camera has Audio Listener. However, this component is included by default in the HolographicCamera prefab. This determines where the listening point of the audio is and spatializes the sound to produce waveforms at that point.

Note   The "Audio Listener" component is also required to be attached to the camera for audio occlusion and Spatial Sound to work. By default, it is included with the HoloLensCamera prefab in the Mixed Reality Toolkit.

Spatial Sound Design Considerations

In this section, we'll discuss some design considerations and best practices for using Spatial Sound in your application. We'll talk about when to use Spatial Sound and also things to avoid when using Spatial Sound.

When to Use Spatial Sound

Whenever possible, use Spatial Sound to help *guide users*. With such a small field of view, devices like the HoloLens can often frustrate users who are trying to find an object of interest. While a visual arrow can be used to help a user find a hologram to look at, it is much better to leverage our instinctive ability to look in the direction of a sound we hear.

Tip   When using Spatial Sound for guiding users or locating objects, use low- or mid-range audio frequencies. Have you ever tried locating a cricket by its chirp? It's extremely difficult because crickets chirp at a very high frequency. Our brains calculate the location of the sound based on how the sound waves arrive at each ear. Larger sound waves (lower frequencies) are easier to decipher than smaller sound waves (higher frequencies.)

Increase the *realism* and *immersion* of a Mixed Reality experience by attaching *appropriate* spatial sounds whenever possible. I use the world "appropriate" because misuse of Spatial Sound can be annoying and jarring. Avoid loud, obnoxious noises. Add subtle audio effects to objects that collide, to buttons that are clicked, and to holograms that move. Think of Spatial Sound like shadows. We don't really think about shadows on a regular basis. But when shadows are removed from real objects, a scene appears strange and "off." In the same way, the lack of appropriate audio effects in a virtual environment makes it seem inauthentic. The presence of Spatial Sound may go unnoticed, but like shadows, they are necessary to complete the experience. The intention behind Spatial Sound shouldn't be to call attention to the sound itself, but rather to make the user comfortable and immersed in his or her experience.

Whenever possible, you should *spatialize all sound* in your Mixed Reality application. In physical reality, all sound is spatialized – comes from a source or series of sources. Mixed Reality applications should immerse users in a 3D experience – not just visually, but audibly too.

What to Avoid When Using Spatial Sound

Like digital holograms, you are able to do things with Spatial Sound in Unity that defy the laws of physics. Sometimes, these effects can add a special edge to your application. But if not carefully tested and considered, they may create an unnatural or even uncomfortable experience for users.

Invisible audio sources or emitters should rarely be used, if ever. When attaching an audio source to an invisible object, our sense of hearing will be able to precisely locate the source of the audio. However, when the user looks at the location from which the sound is coming from, and does not see any visible objects, it can be an unnerving experience.

Don't mix too many sounds together, and *avoid overpowering spatial sounds with 2D sounds*. As discussed early in this chapter, devices use subtle modifications of sound waves to achieve the Spatial Sound effect. When these are masked or drowned out by ambient noises, such as background music, the Spatial Sound experience can be degraded. When mixing multiple sound sources are needed, be sure the spatial sounds are louder than any ambient sounds.

Try to minimize the use synthesized or artificial sounds. When a sound is unnatural, users may not have a strong intuition on the source of the sound. Instead, use natural sounds like the chirp of a bird, the click of a button, the voice of a person, and other recorded sounds. *Take advantage of human intuition or expectation* when designing your Spatial Sound experience. For example, a human voice is likely to be found at a human height range – so use a voice to guide the user to look at something that is approximately at eye level. Use the sound of rustling tree leaves or birds for objects above the user.

Summary

Congratulations! In this chapter, you learned how Spatial Sound in Mixed Reality development works. We walked through a working Spatial Sound example included in the HoloToolkit, learned how to implement Spatial Sound in your application, and learned some best practices for designing Spatial Sound into your application. You are now equipped with the tools needed to start implementing a great Spatial Audio experience into your application!

When developing an application, it's easy for sound design to be deprioritized or forgotten all together. However, I can't express enough the importance of good sound design when developing for Mixed Reality. I still remember a strong piece of advice I received from a professor during a course I took on video editing:

> *People will forgive bad video if there's good audio. People will not forgive bad audio, even if the video is excellent.*
>
> —*Fred Metzger*

Sound design is extremely important and should be considered as part of your application design from the very beginning, rather than an afterthought.

PART III

Growing As a Holographic Developer

CHAPTER 8

Azure Spatial Anchors

In this chapter, you will learn how to use Azure Spatial Anchors. We'll learn how to anchor the objects in Mixed Reality to experience the real world; you will also explore the various steps required to start and stop an Azure Spatial Anchors session and create, upload, and download Azure Spatial Anchors on a HoloLens 2.

What Is Azure Spatial Anchors?

Azure Spatial Anchors is a cross-platform service that allows developers to create Mixed Reality experiences through objects that endure their positions across various devices over time. This service permits developers to build spatially aware Mixed Reality applications. These applications may support Microsoft HoloLens, iOS-based devices supporting ARKit, and Android-based devices supporting ARCore. Developers can now develop applications that perceive spaces, designate valid points of interest, and recall those points of interest through supported devices. The points of interest are called Spatial Anchors.

Azure Spatial Anchors depends on Mixed/Augmented Reality trackers. These trackers sense the environment around them through cameras and track the device in six degrees of freedom (6DoF) as it passes over space. When a Spatial Anchor is created, the client SDK collects the environment information around the anchor and transmits it to the service. If any other device looks for the anchor in that identical space, similar records transmit to the service. That record is matched toward the surroundings data formerly stored. The position of the anchor relative to the device is then sent back to be used in the application.

© Sean Ong and Varun Kumar Siddaraju 2021
S. Ong and V. K. Siddaraju, *Beginning Windows Mixed Reality Programming*,
https://doi.org/10.1007/978-1-4842-7104-9_8

Azure Spatial Anchors Tutorial

Step 1: Creating new Unity Scene

Start by creating a new Unity project (refer to Chapter 2), name it "Azure Spatial Anchors Tutorial" and save your scene, give it a name that you wish, and be sure to set up Unity for Mixed Reality development as described in Chapter 3.

Step 2: Installing Inbuilt Unity Packages

In this step, you will learn to install the Unity inbuilt package AR Foundation because Azure Spatial Anchors needs it. AR Foundation allows you to work with Augmented Reality platforms in a multi-platform way within Unity.

In the Unity menu, select Window ➤ Package Manager to open the Package Manager window shown in Figure 8-1. Then select AR Foundation and click the Install button to install the package. Refer to Figure 8-2.

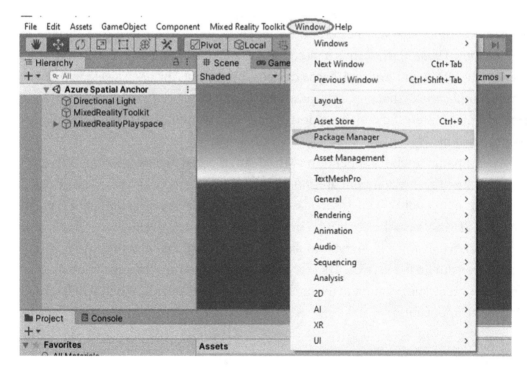

Figure 8-1. *You will notice the package manager once the window button is selected*

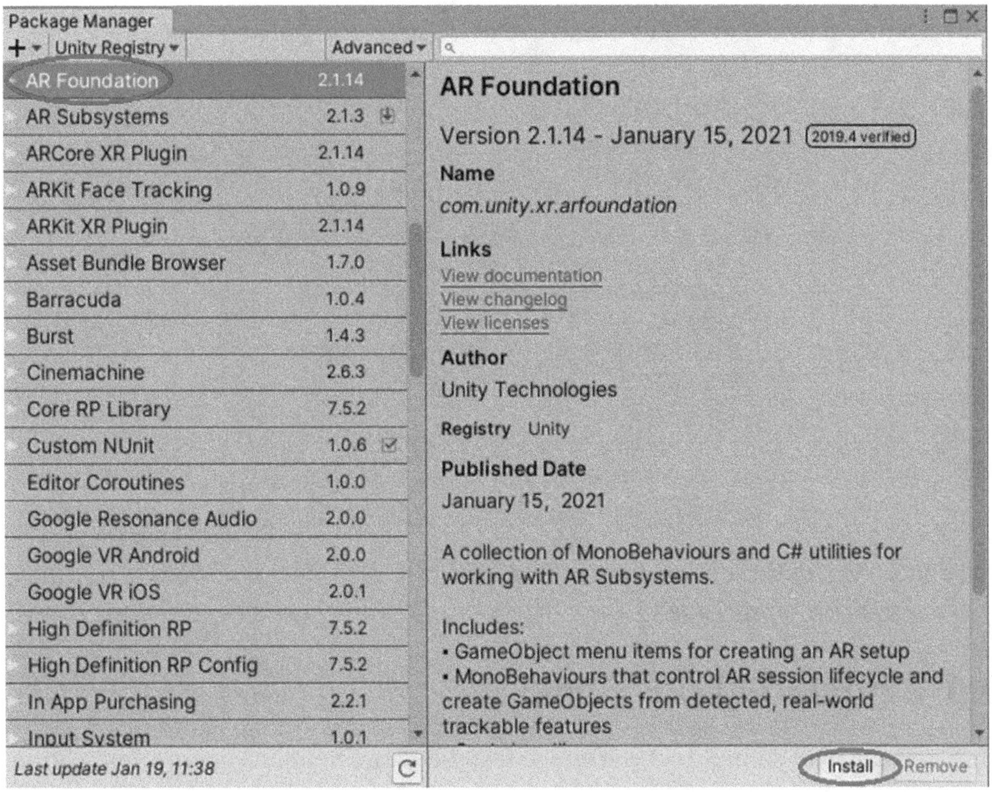

Figure 8-2. *You will find the AR Foundation with a specific version; click the install button to install*

Step 3: Download and Import Tutorial Assets

In this step, you will download and import some of the essential Assets folders used to test the project; you can refer to Chapter 3 to refresh how to import the Unity package.

Download the following asset packages and import them in the order they are listed:

- AzureSpatialAnchors.unitypackage (version 2.2.1)

- MRTK.HoloLens2.Unity.Tutorials.Assets.GettingStarted.2.4.0.unityp ackage

- MRTK.HoloLens2.Unity.Tutorials.Assets.AzureSpatialAnchors.2.4.0.u nitypackage

After you have imported the tutorial assets, your Project window should look similar to that shown in Figure 8-3.

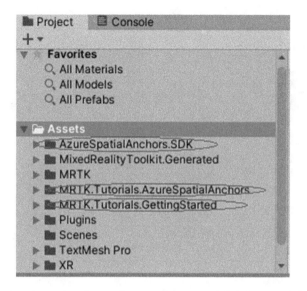

Figure 8-3. *In the Project window, three additional folders will be added after you imported the Unity packages*

Step 4: Preparing the Scene

In this step, you will configure the scene to test the Azure Spatial Anchors application by adding some of the prefabs imported in the previous step.

In the Project window, navigate to the Assets ➤ MRTK.Tutorials. AzureSpatialAnchors ➤ Prefabs folder, and then click and drag the following prefabs into the Hierarchy window to add them to your scene:

- ButtonParent prefabs

- DebugWindow prefabs

- Instructions prefabs

- ParentAnchor prefabs

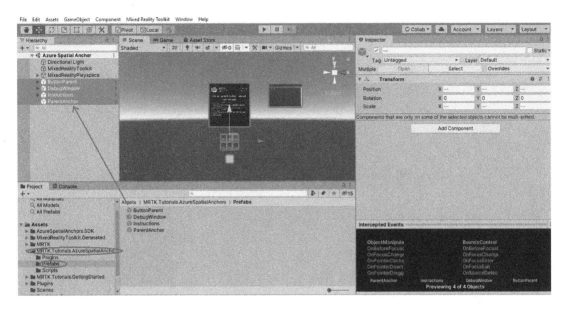

Figure 8-4. *Select all the four prefabs by holding the shift button and drag and drop to the Hierarchy*

Step 5: Configuring the Buttons to Operate the Scene

In this step, you will configure the buttons by adding scripts to demonstrate the fundamentals of how both local anchors and Azure Spatial Anchors behave in an app.

For you to layout the holograms and objects persistently on the screen, the device must be capable of understanding your surroundings and then let you place objects in the environment. When you start an Azure Session, it scans your environment and obtains the mapping. By doing so, you can determine where the anchors are located. Mobile Platforms (iOS and Android) need to remind their camera to scan the environment, whereas HoloLens is continuously monitoring the environment. To start an Azure Session, follow the succeeding instructions.

In the Hierarchy window, expand the ButtonParent object, and select the first child object named StartAzureSession. Then navigate to the Button Config Helper (Script) in the Inspector window. Configure the OnClick() event attached to the script as shown in Figure 8-5.

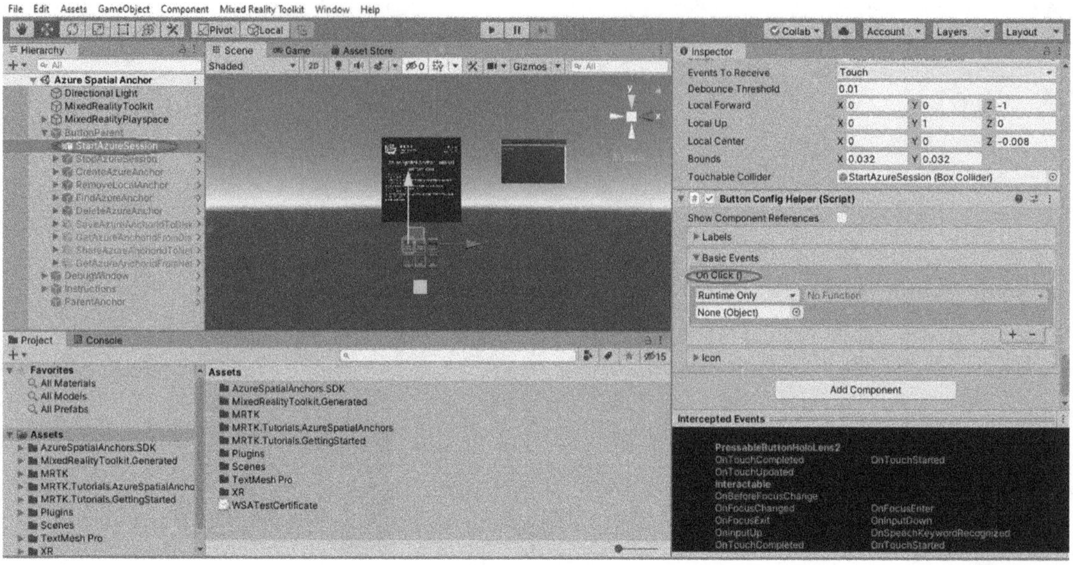

Figure 8-5. *In the Inspector window, we can find the On Click() event under Basic Events*

Now we have to configure the On Click event of StartAzureSession buttons.

Select the ParentAnchor object, and drag and drop to the None (Object) field in On Click event. Refer to Figure 8-6.

From the No Function drop-down, select AnchorModuleScript ➤ StartAzureSession () to set this function as the action to be executed when the event is triggered. Refer to Figure 8-7.

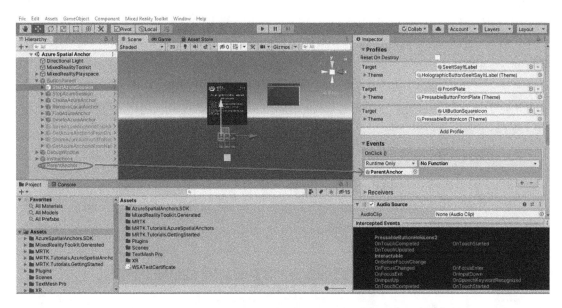

Figure 8-6. *Drag and drop the ParentAnchor to the None (Object) field in On Click event under Basic Events*

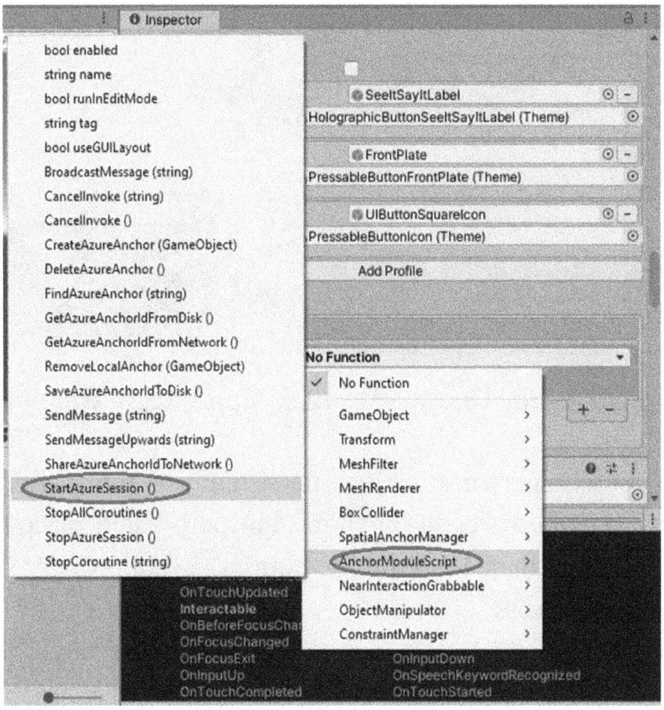

Figure 8-7. *In the drop-down list, select AnchorModuleScript ➤ StartAzureSession () function*

To stop the Azure Session, you can click the StopAzureSession, which will stop the environment processing and any watchers. To configure the StopAzureSession button, follow the given instructions.

In the Hierarchy window, select the next button named StopAzureSession; then in the Inspector window, configure the Button Config Helper (Script) component's OnClick() event as follows:

- Assign the ParentAnchor object to the None (Object) field.

- From the No Function drop-down, select AnchorModuleScript ➤ StopAzureSession () to set this function as the action to be executed when the event is triggered.

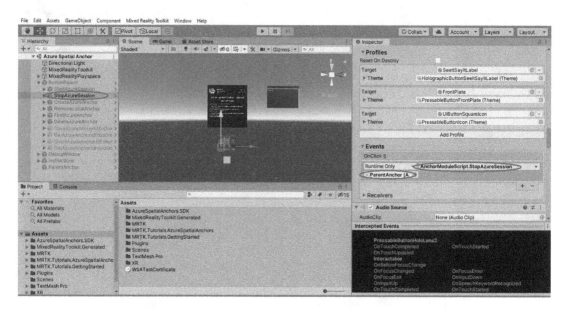

Figure 8-8. *Configuring the On Click event of StopAzureSession button*

If you wish to place holograms or objects persistently on the environment across different platforms, you need to create anchors to be perpetually placed. You can create an anchor by clicking the CreateAzureAnchor button. The following instructions will guide you through this process.

In the Hierarchy window, select the button named CreateAzureAnchor; then in the Inspector window, configure the Button Config Helper (Script) component's OnClick() event as follows:

- Assign the ParentAnchor object to the None (Object) field.

- From the No Function drop-down, select AnchorModuleScript ➤ CreateAzureAnchor() to set this function as the action to be executed when the event is triggered.

- Assign the ParentAnchor object to the empty None (Game Object) field to make it the argument for the CreateAzureAnchor () function.

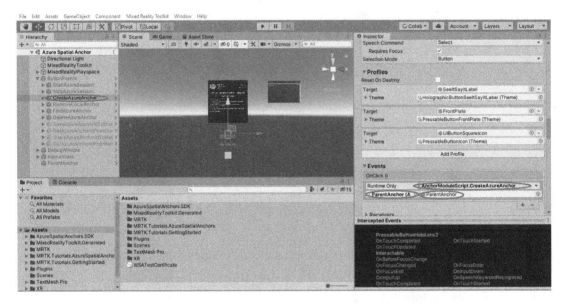

Figure 8-9. *Configuring the On Click() event of CreateAzureAnchor button*

If you are not satisfied with the already created anchor, you can easily reset it by first removing it and creating it again. To remove your local anchors, you can click the RemoveLocalAnchor button. The following steps will guide you on how to configure the RemoveLocalAnchor button.

Similarly, in the Hierarchy window, select the next button named RemoveLocalAnchor; then in the Inspector window, configure the Button Config Helper (Script) component's OnClick() event as follows:

- Assign the ParentAnchor object to the None (Object) field.

- From the No Function drop-down, select AnchorModuleScript ➤ RemoveLocalAnchor () to set this function as the action to be executed when the event is triggered.

- Assign the ParentAnchor object to the empty None (Game Object) field to make it the argument for the RemoveLocalAnchor () function.

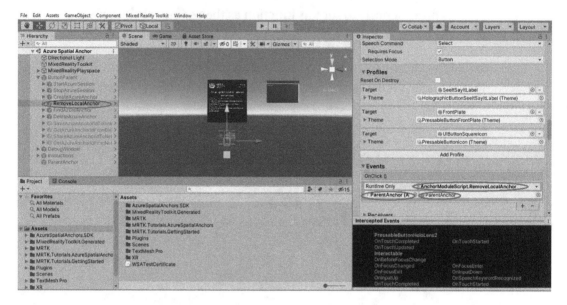

Figure 8-10. *Configuring the On Click event of RemoveLocalAnchor button*

Being able to locate the previously saved anchors is one of the reasons for using Azure Spatial Anchors. Azure Spatial Anchors uses the information collected during the session to locate the formerly saved anchors in the environment. You can perform this function using the FindAzureAnchor button. Follow the succeeding steps to configure the FindAzureAnchor button.

In the Hierarchy window, select the button named FindAzureAnchor; then in the Inspector window, configure the Button Config Helper (Script) component's OnClick() event as follows:

- Assign the ParentAnchor object to the None (Object) field.

- From the No Function drop-down, select AnchorModuleScript ➤ FindAzureAnchor () to set this function as the action to be executed when the event is triggered.

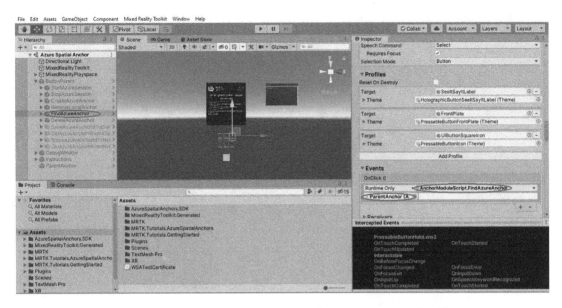

Figure 8-11. *Configuring the On Click event of FindAzureAnchor button*

If the created anchors are not in use, it is a good practice in the development process to delete those anchors as it will help you to keep the resources clean and avoid confusion in the future. To delete your anchors, you can click the DeleteAzureAnchor button. The following steps will guide you on how to configure the DeleteAzureAnchor button.

Similarly, in the Hierarchy window, select the next button named DeleteAzureAnchor; then in the Inspector window, configure the Button Config Helper (Script) component's OnClick() event as follows:

- Assign the ParentAnchor object to the None (Object) field.

- From the No Function drop-down, select AnchorModuleScript ➤ DeleteAzureAnchor () to set this function as the action to be executed when the event is triggered.

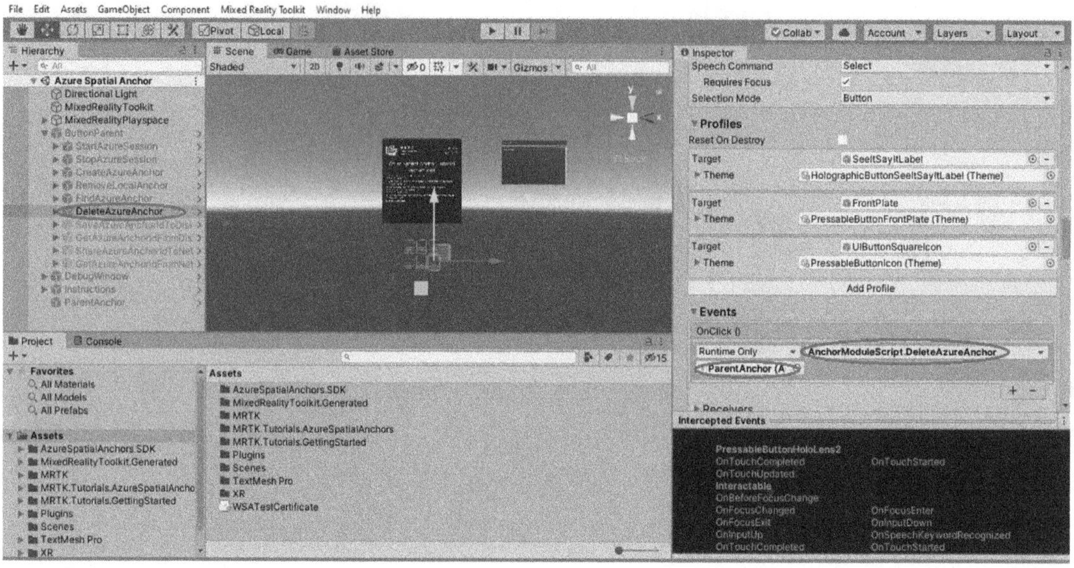

Figure 8-12. *Configuring the On Click event of DeleteAzureAnchor button*

Step 6: Connecting the Scene to the Azure Resource

In this step, we are going to connect our created scene to the Spatial Anchor (Azure resource) created in Azure portal. Once you have created the Azure resource, you will get the access key and account ID.

Note   Refer to the following link to create a Spatial Anchor resource from which the access key and account ID can be retrieved. Link: `https://docs.microsoft.com/en-us/azure/spatial-anchors/quickstarts/get-started-unity-hololens?tabs=azure-portal#create-a-spatial-anchors-resource`

In the Hierarchy window, select the ParentAnchor object; then in the Inspector window, locate the Spatial Anchor Manager (Script) component. Here, you can find two empty fields, Spatial Anchors Account Id and Spatial Anchors Account Key field.

- In the Spatial Anchors Account Id field, paste the account ID from your Azure Spatial Anchors account.

- In the Spatial Anchors Account Key field, paste the primary or secondary access key from your Azure Spatial Anchors account.

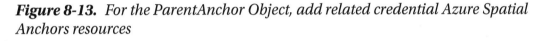

Figure 8-13. *For the ParentAnchor Object, add related credential Azure Spatial Anchors resources*

Step 7: Test the Application in Device

You cannot run the Azure Spatial Anchors in Unity editor, so to test the Azure Spatial Anchors functionality, you need to build the project and deploy the app to your device.

When the application loads in the device, please follow these instructions:

- Move the cube to a different location.

- Start Azure Session.

- Create Azure Anchor (creates an anchor at the location of the cube).

- Stop Azure Session.

- Remove Local Anchor (allows the user to move the cube).

- Move the cube somewhere else.

- Start Azure Session.

- Find Azure Anchor (positions the cube at the location from Step 3).

- Delete Azure Anchor.

- Stop Azure session.

You can also find this instruction in the Instruction panel present in the Unity scene.

Note   Azure Spatial Anchors uses the Internet to save and load the anchor data, so make sure your device is connected to the Internet.

Summary

Congratulations! In this chapter, you learned how to perform various operations on anchors. We walked through creating, removing, finding, and deleting the Spatial Anchors on the scene. You are now equipped with the tools needed to start implementing Spatial Anchors in your application.

CHAPTER 9

Shared Experiences

In this chapter, we'll learn the fundamentals of building a multiuser experience using Photon Unity Networking (PUN). PUN is one of several networking options available to Mixed Reality developers to create shared experiences.

What Are Shared Experiences?

A shared experience is exactly what it sounds like: seeing, hearing, or doing the same thing as someone else. Here, you will be sharing each other's interactions using the Photon platform.

Shared experiences create moments, no matter how small, of belonging, as well as offering opportunities to take our relationships to even greater levels of trust and intimacy.

Multiuser Capabilities Tutorial

In this section, I'll walk you through a tutorial on how multiuser capabilities tutorial works in a Mixed Reality application.

Setting Up Photon Unity Networking

In this section, you will prepare for creating a shared experience using Photon Unity Networking (PUN). You will learn how to create a PUN app, import PUN assets into your Unity project, and connect your Unity project to the PUN app.

189

© Sean Ong and Varun Kumar Siddaraju 2021
S. Ong and V. K. Siddaraju, *Beginning Windows Mixed Reality Programming*,
https://doi.org/10.1007/978-1-4842-7104-9_9

Step 1: Creating New Unity Scene

We will create a new Unity project (refer to Chapter 2), name it "MultiUserCapabilities" and save your scene, give it a name that you wish, and be sure to set up Unity for Mixed Reality development as described in Chapter 3.

Step 2: Enabling Additional Capabilities

In this step, you will learn to enable Internet Client Server capability and Private Network Client Server capability, which are required for sharing each other's interactions. In the Unity menu, select Edit ➤ Project Settings to open the Player Settings window, and then locate the Player ➤ Publishing Settings section (Figure 9-1).

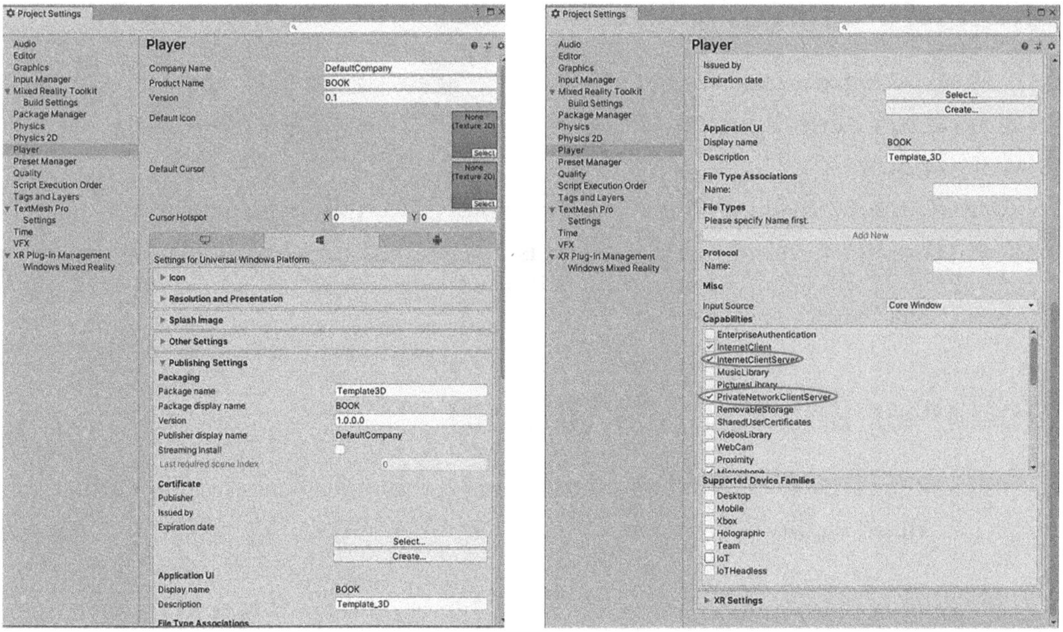

Figure 9-1. *Enable Internet Client Server and Private Network Client Server capabilities*

In the Publishing Settings, scroll down to the Capabilities section and double-check that the InternetClient, Microphone, SpatialPerception, and GazeInput capabilities enabled during configuring the Unity project step earlier are enabled.

Then enable the following additional capabilities:

- InternetClientServer capability

- PrivateNetworkClientServer capability

Step 3: Installing Inbuilt Unity Packages

In this step, you will learn to install the Unity built-in package AR Foundation. AR Foundation allows you to work with Augmented Reality platforms in a multi-platform way within Unity. In the Unity menu, select Window ➤ Package Manager to open the Package Manager window, and then select AR Foundation, and click the Install button to install the package (Figure 9-2).

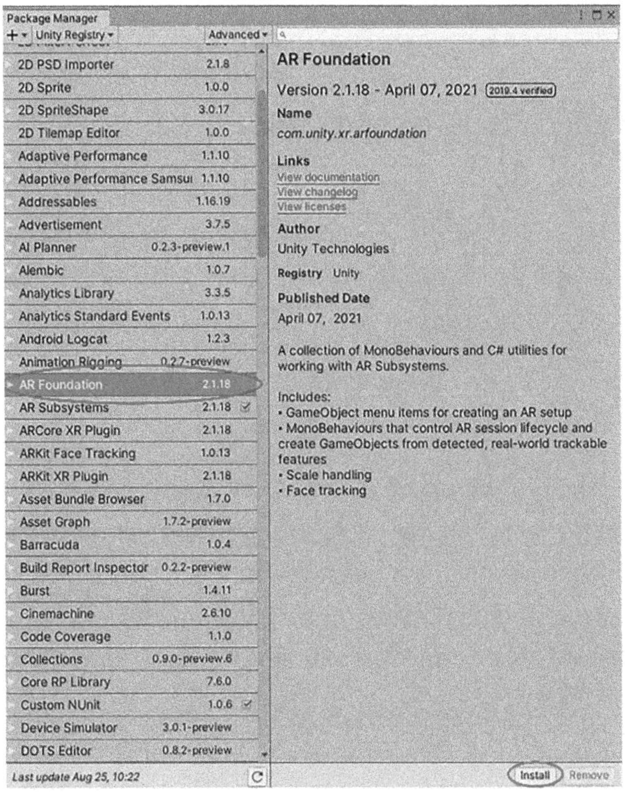

Figure 9-2. *You will find AR Foundation with a specific version; click Install button to install*

Step 4: Importing the Tutorial Assets

Add AzureSpatialAnchors SDK V2.7.1 into your Unity project (you need to see Chapter 3 – the Unity Package Manager uses a manifest file [manifest.json]). At the same level as the Dependencies section, at the top of the file, add Listing 9-1 to include the Azure Spatial Anchors registry to your project. The scopedRegistries entry tells Unity where to look for the Azure Spatial Anchors SDK packages.

Listing 9-1. Code to include Azure Spatial Anchors registry to your project

```
{
  "scopedRegistries": [
    {
      "name": "Azure Mixed Reality Services",
      "url": "https://api.bintray.com/npm/microsoft/AzureMixedReality-NPM",
      "scopes": [
        "com.microsoft.azure.spatial-anchors-sdk"
      ]
    }
  ],
  "dependencies": {
"com.microsoft.azure.spatial-anchors-sdk.android": "2.7.1",
    "com.microsoft.azure.spatial-anchors-sdk.ios": "2.7.1",
    "com.microsoft.azure.spatial-anchors-sdk.windows": "2.7.1",
```

(After importing the MultiUserCapabilities tutorial asset package, you will see several **CS0246** errors in the Console window stating that the type or namespace is missing. This is expected and will be resolved in the next section when you import the PUN assets.)

To add the packages, download and import the following Unity custom packages in the order they are listed (see Chapter 4, if you need a reminder on how to do this):

- MRTK.HoloLens2.Unity.Tutorials.Assets.GettingStarted.2.5.0.1.unity package

- MRTK.HoloLens2.Unity.Tutorials.Assets.MultiUserCapabilities.2.4.0. unitypackage

After you have imported the tutorial assets, your Project window should look similar to that shown in Figure 9-3.

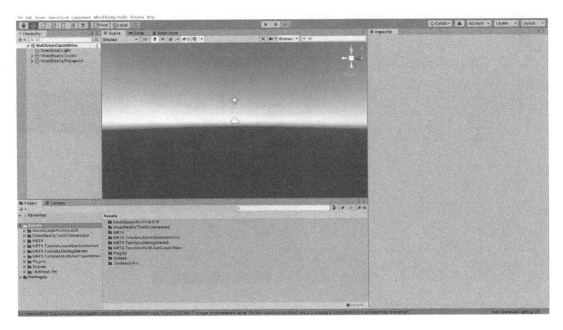

Figure 9-3. *After importing tutorial assets, your project window should look similar to this*

Step 5: Importing the PUN Assets

PUN enables you to add multiuser to your network and launch them globally quickly. In the Unity menu, select Window ➤ Asset Store to open the Asset Store window, search for and select PUN 2 - FREE from Exit Games, and click the Download button to download the asset package to your Unity account. When the download is complete, click the Import button to open the Import Unity Package window (Figure 9-4).

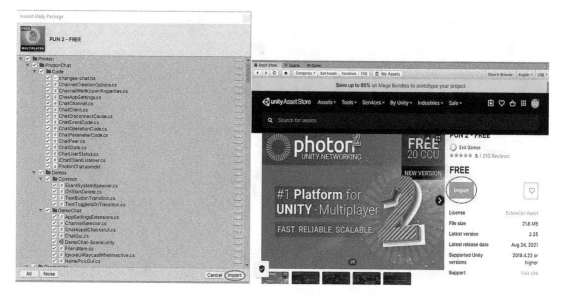

Figure 9-4. *Importing PUN asset to your project*

In the Import Unity Package window, click the All button to ensure all the assets are selected, and then click the Import button to import the assets. Once Unity has completed the import process, the Pun Wizard window will appear with the PUN Setup menu loaded; you can ignore or close this window for now (Figure 9-5).

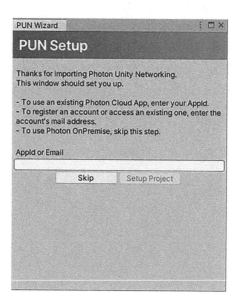

Figure 9-5. *PUN Wizard window*

Step 6: Creating the PUN Application

In this section, you will create a Photon account, if you don't already have one, and create a new PUN app. Navigate to the Photon dashboard (`https://cutt.ly/4nUQsgb`) and sign in if you already have an account you want to use; otherwise, click the "Create one" link, and follow the instructions to register a new account (Figure 9-6).

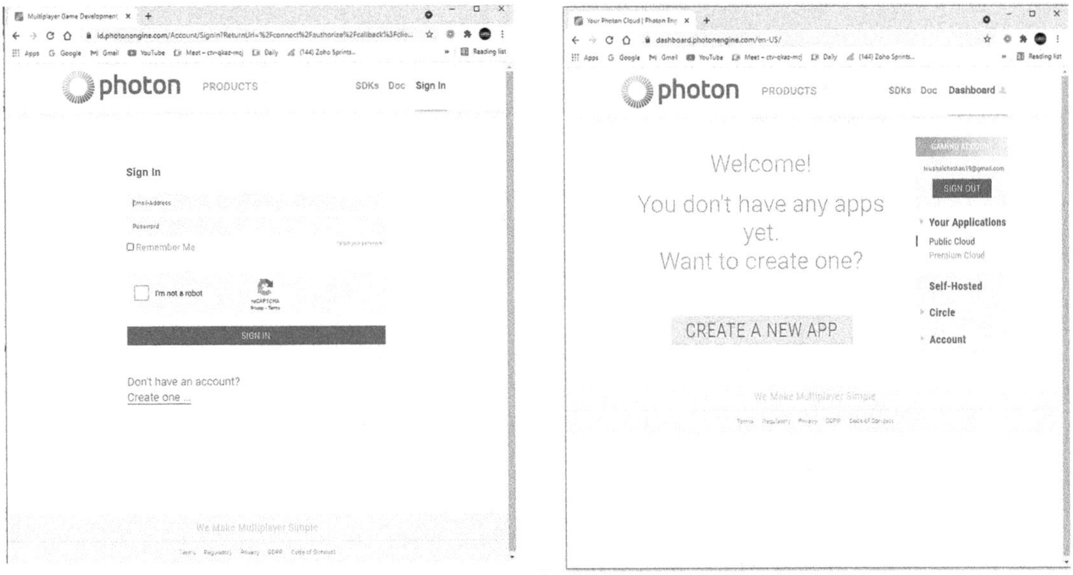

Figure 9-6. *Sign in to PUN application*

Once signed in, click the Create a New App button. On the Create a New Application page, enter the following values as shown in Figure 9-7:

- For Photon Type, select Photon PUN.

- For Name, enter a suitable name, for example, MRTK Tutorials.

- For Description, optionally enter a suitable description.

- For Url, leave the field empty.

Then click the Create button to create the new app.

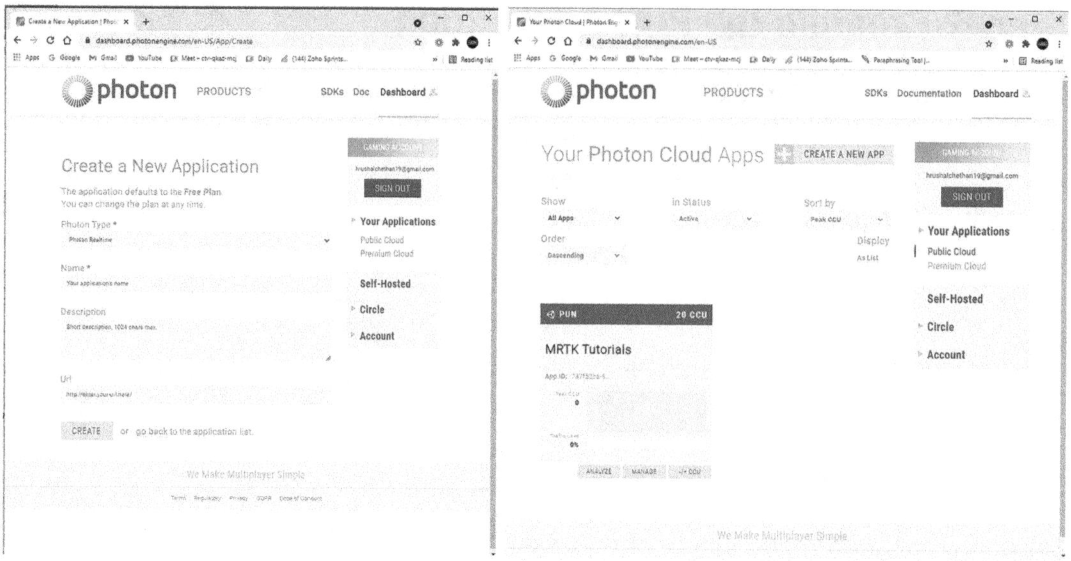

Figure 9-7.   *Creating the PUN application*

Once Photon has finished the creation process, the new PUN app will appear on your dashboard.

Step 7: Connecting the Unity Project to the PUN Application

In this section, you will connect your Unity project to the PUN app you created in the previous section. On the Photon dashboard, click the App ID field to reveal the app ID, and then copy it to your clipboard (Figure 9-8).

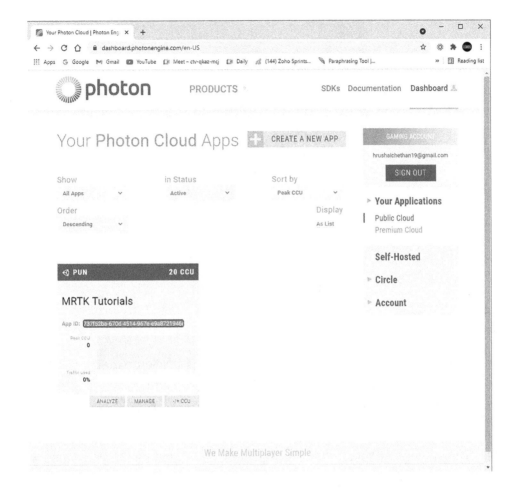

Figure 9-8. *PUN application ID*

In the Unity menu, select Window ➤ Photon Unity Networking ➤ PUN Wizard to open the Pun Wizard window, and click the Setup Project button to open the PUN Setup menu. In the AppId or Email field, paste the PUN app ID you copied in the previous step. Then click the Setup Project button to apply the app ID (Figure 9-9).

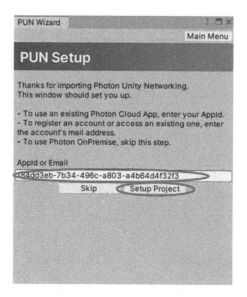

Figure 9-9. *Paste PUN application ID to Connecting the Unity project to the PUN application*

Once Unity has finished the PUN setup process, the PUN Setup menu will display the message Done! and automatically select the PhotonServerSettings asset in the Project window, so its properties are displayed in the Inspector window (Figure 9-10).

Note   The settings might already be displayed, but to update the properties, you need to close it and open it again.

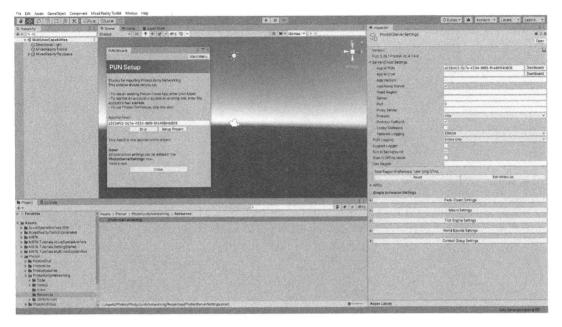

Figure 9-10. *Confirmation message of connecting the Unity project with the PUN application*

Connecting Multiple Users

In this section, you will learn how to connect multiple users as part of a live shared experience. By the end of this section, you will be able to run the app on multiple devices and have each user see the avatar of other users move in real time.

Step 1: Preparing the Scene

In the Project window, navigate to the Assets ➤ MRTK.Tutorials.MultiUserCapabilities ➤ Prefabs folder, and then click and drag the following prefabs into the Hierarchy window to add them to your scene:

- NetworkLobby prefab
- SharedPlayground prefab

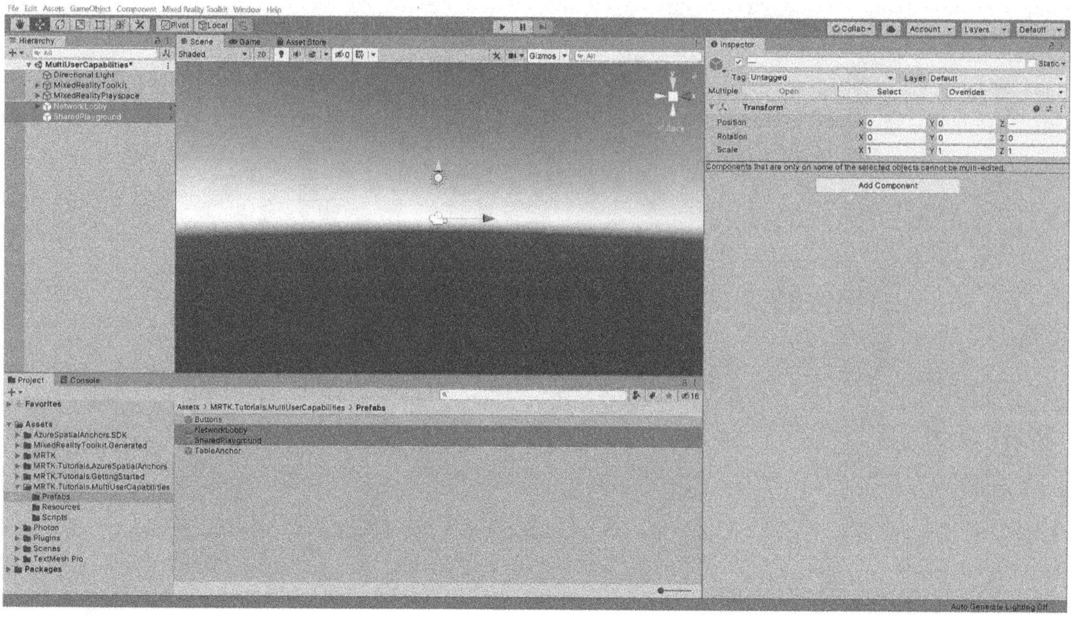

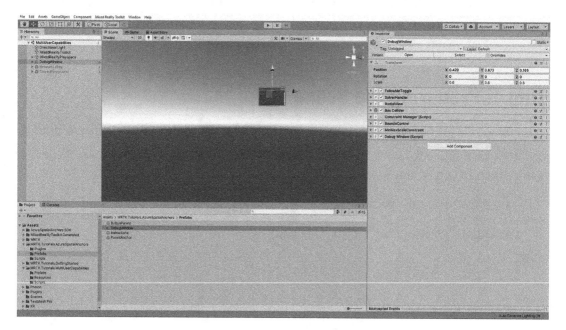

Figure 9-11. *Adding NetworkLobby and SharedPlayground prefabs to scene*

In the Project window, navigate to the Assets ➤ MRTK.Tutorials.
AzureSpatialAnchors ➤ Prefabs folder, and then click and drag the DebugWindow
prefab into the Hierarchy window to add it to your scene (Figure 9-12).

Figure 9-12. *Adding DebugWindow prefabs to the scene*

Step 2: Create and Configure the User

- In the Hierarchy window, right-click an empty area, and select Create Empty to add an empty object to your scene, name the object PhotonUser, and configure it as follows:

  Ensure the Transform Position is set to X = 0, Y = 0, Z = 0.

- In the Hierarchy window, select the PhotonUser object; then in the Inspector window, use the Add Component button to add the Photon User (Script) component to the PhotonUser object (Figure 9-13).

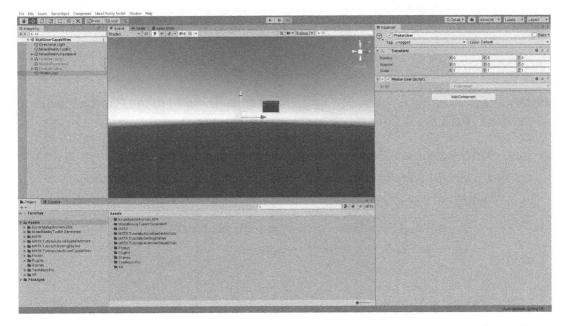

Figure 9-13. *Create PhotonUser component, and add the Photon User (Script) to it*

- In the Inspector window, use the Add Component button to add the Generic Net Sync (Script) component to the PhotonUser object, and configure it as follows:

  - Check the Is User check box.

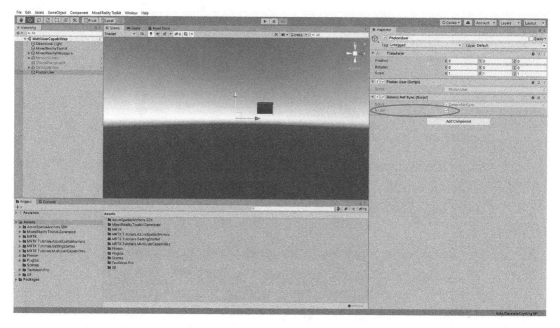

Figure 9-14. *Add the Generic Net Sync (Script) component to the PhotonUser object, and check the Is User check box*

- In the Inspector window, use the Add Component button to add the Photon View (Script) component to the PhotonUser object, and configure it as follows:

  - Ensure that the Observed Components field is assigned with the Generic Net Sync (Script) component.

Figure 9-15. *Add the Photon View (Script) component to the PhotonUser object, and ensure the Observed Components field is assigned with the Generic Net Sync (Script) component*

Step 3: Create the Avatar

In the Project window, navigate to the Assets ➤ MRTK ➤ StandardAssets ➤ Materials folder to locate the MRTK materials. Then, in the Hierarchy window, right-click the PhotonUser object and select 3D Object ➤ Sphere to create a sphere object as a child of the PhotonUser object, and configure it as follows:

- Ensure the Transform Position is set to X = 0, Y = 0, Z = 0.

- Change the Transform Scale to a suitable size, for example, X = 0.15, Y = 0.15, Z = 0.15.

- To the MeshRenderer ➤ Materials ➤ Element 0 field, assign the MRTK_Standard_White material.

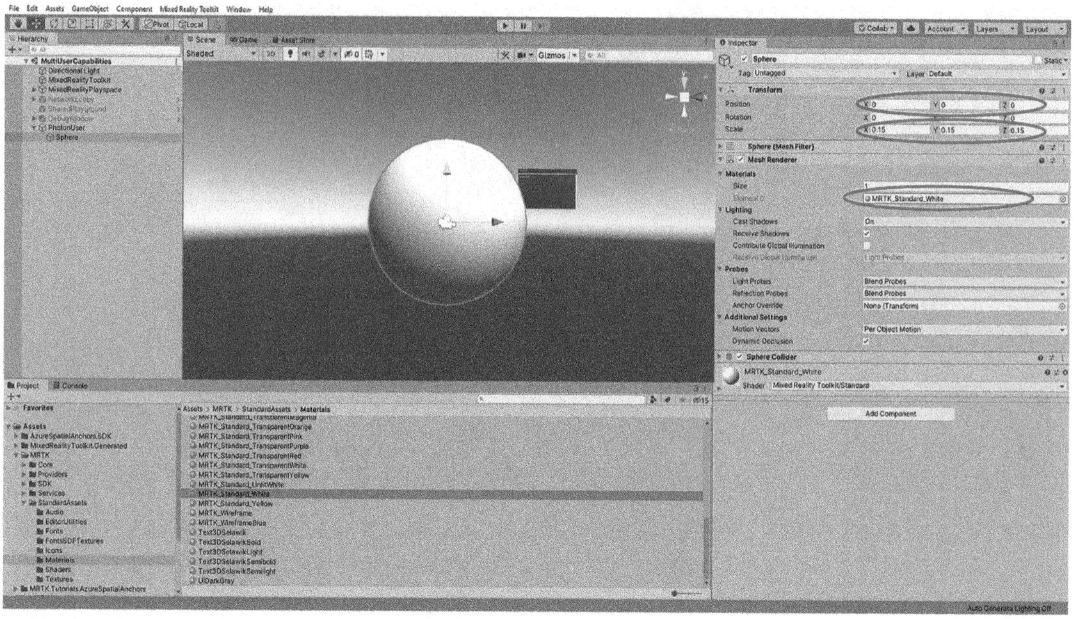

Figure 9-16. Add the 3D sphere and assign a standard material to it

Step 4: Create the Prefab

In the Project window, navigate to the Assets ➤ MRTK.Tutorials.MultiUserCapabilities ➤ Resources folder. With the Resources folder still selected, click and drag the PhotonUser object from the Hierarchy window into the Resources folder to make the PhotonUser object a prefab.

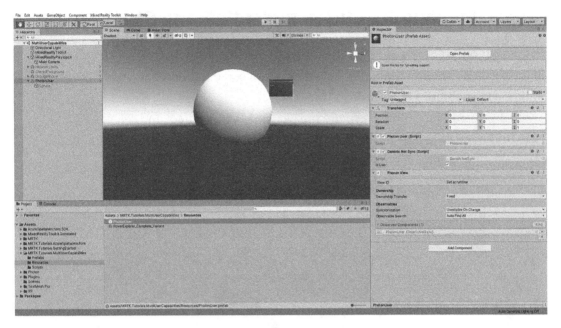

Figure 9-17. *Create PhotonUser prefab*

In the Hierarchy window, right-click the PhotonUser object, and select Delete to remove it from the scene (Figure 9-18).

Figure 9-18. *Delete PhotonUser game object from Hierarchy window*

Step 5: Configuring PUN to Instantiate the User Prefab

In this section, you will configure the project to use the PhotonUser prefab you created in the previous section. In the Project window, navigate to the Assets ➤ MRTK.Tutorials. MultiUserCapabilities ➤ Resources folder.

In the Hierarchy window, expand the NetworkLobby object and select the NetworkRoom child object; then, in the Inspector window, locate the Photon Room (Script) component and configure it as follows:

- To the Photon User Prefab field, assign the PhotonUser prefab from the Resources folder.

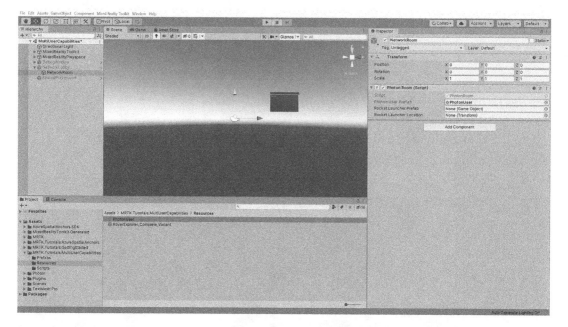

Figure 9-19. *Assign Photon User Prefab field with Photon User Prefab from the Resources folder*

If you now build and deploy the Unity project to your HoloLens and then, back in Unity, enter Game mode while the app is running on your HoloLens, you will see the HoloLens user avatar move when you move your head (HoloLens) around.

Sharing Object Movements with Multiple Users

In this section, you will learn how to share the movements of objects so that all participants of a shared experience can collaborate and view each other's interactions.

Step 1: Preparing the Scene

In the Project window, navigate to the Assets ➤ MRTK.Tutorials.MultiUserCapabilities ➤ Prefabs folder, and drag the TableAnchor prefab onto the SharedPlayground object in the Hierarchy window to add it to your scene as a child of the SharedPlayground object.

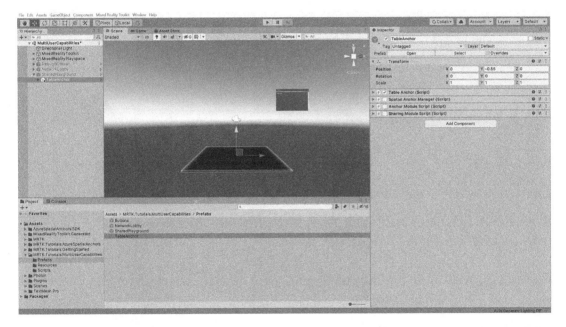

Figure 9-20. *Make TableAnchor prefab as child of SharedPlayground object in the Hierarchy*

Step 2: Configuring PUN to Instantiate the Objects

In this step, you will configure the project to use the Rover Explorer experience. In the Project window, navigate to the Assets ➤ MRTK.Tutorials.MultiUserCapabilities ➤ Resources folder. In the Hierarchy window, expand the NetworkLobby object, and select the NetworkRoom child object; then, in the Inspector window, locate the Photon Room (Script) component and configure it as follows:

- To the Rover Explorer Prefab field, assign the RoverExplorer_ Complete_Variant prefab from the Resources folder.

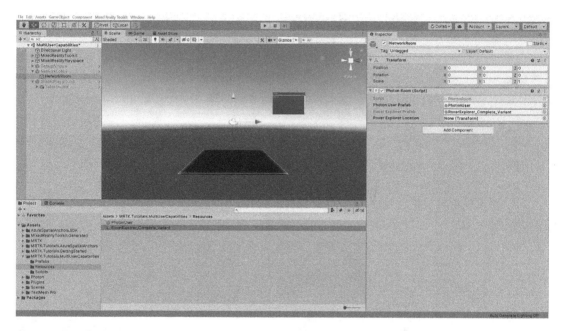

Figure 9-21. *Assign Rover Explorer Prefab field with RoverExplorer_Complete_ Variant prefab from the Resources folder*

With the NetworkRoom child object still selected, in the Hierarchy window, expand the TableAnchor object; then in the Inspector window, locate the Photon Room (Script) component and configure it as follows:

- To the Rover Explorer Location field, assign the TableAnchor ➤ Table child object from the Hierarchy window.

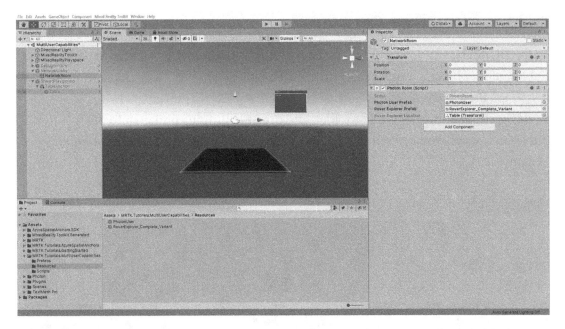

Figure 9-22. *Assign Rover Explorer Location field with TableAnchor child object "Table" from the Hierarchy window*

If you now build and deploy the Unity project to your HoloLens and then, back in Unity, click the play button to enter Game mode while the app is running on your HoloLens, you will see the object move in Unity when you move the object in HoloLens.

Integrating Azure Spatial Anchors into a Shared Experience

In this section, you will learn how to integrate Azure Spatial Anchors (ASA) into the shared experience. ASA allows multiple devices to have a common reference to the physical world so that the users see each other in their actual physical location and see the shared experience in the same place. Refer to Chapter 8 for more information on Azure Spatial Anchors.

Step 1: Preparing the Scene

In the Hierarchy window, expand the SharedPlayground object, and then expand the TableAnchor object to expose its child objects.

In the Project window, navigate to the Assets ➤ MRTK.Tutorials. MultiUserCapabilities ➤ Prefabs folder, and drag the Buttons prefab onto the TableAnchor child object to add it to your scene as a child of the TableAnchor object (Figure 9-23).

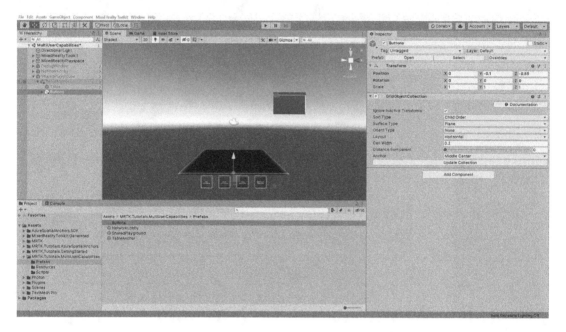

Figure 9-23. *Make Buttons prefab as child of TableAnchor object in the Hierarchy*

Step 2: Configuring the Buttons to Operate the Scene

- In this step, you will configure a series of button events demonstrating the fundamentals of how Azure Spatial Anchors can be used to achieve spatial alignment in a shared experience.

- In the Hierarchy window, expand the Button object and select the first child button object named StartAzureSession.

- In the Inspector window, locate the Interactable (Script) component and configure the OnClick () event as follows:

  - To the None (Object) field, assign the TableAnchor object.

  - From the No Function drop-down, select the AnchorModuleScript ➤ StartAzureSession () function.

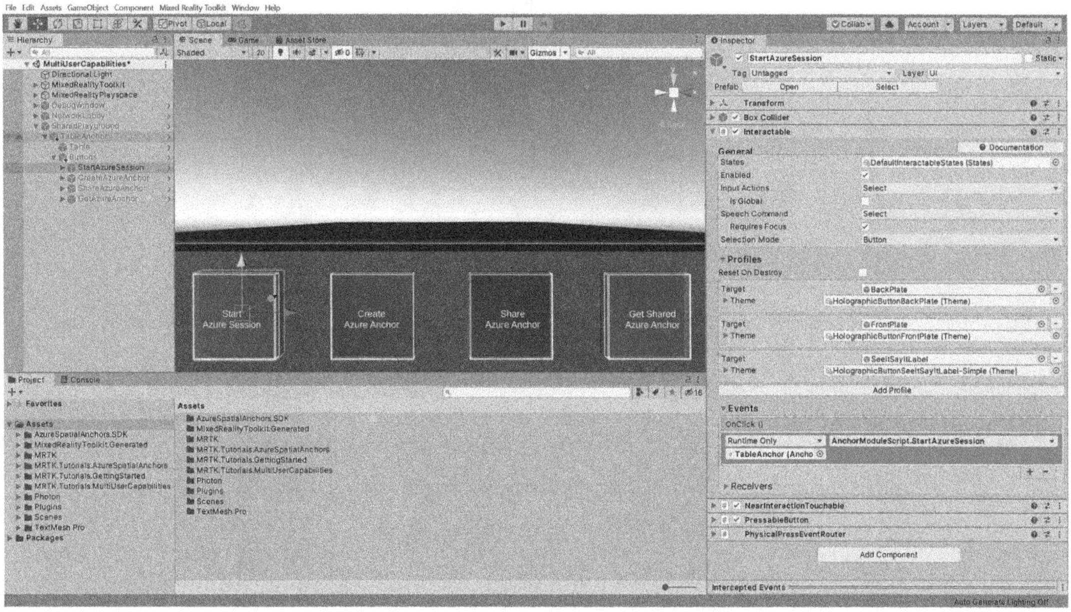

Figure 9-24. *Configure the StartAzureSession Button OnClick() event*

- In the Hierarchy window, select the second child button object named CreateAzureAnchor; then in the Inspector window, locate the Interactable (Script) component and configure the OnClick () event as follows:

  - To the None (Object) field, assign the TableAnchor object.

  - From the No Function drop-down, select the AnchorModuleScript ➤ CreateAzureAnchor () function.

  - To the new None (Game Object) field that appears, assign the TableAnchor object.

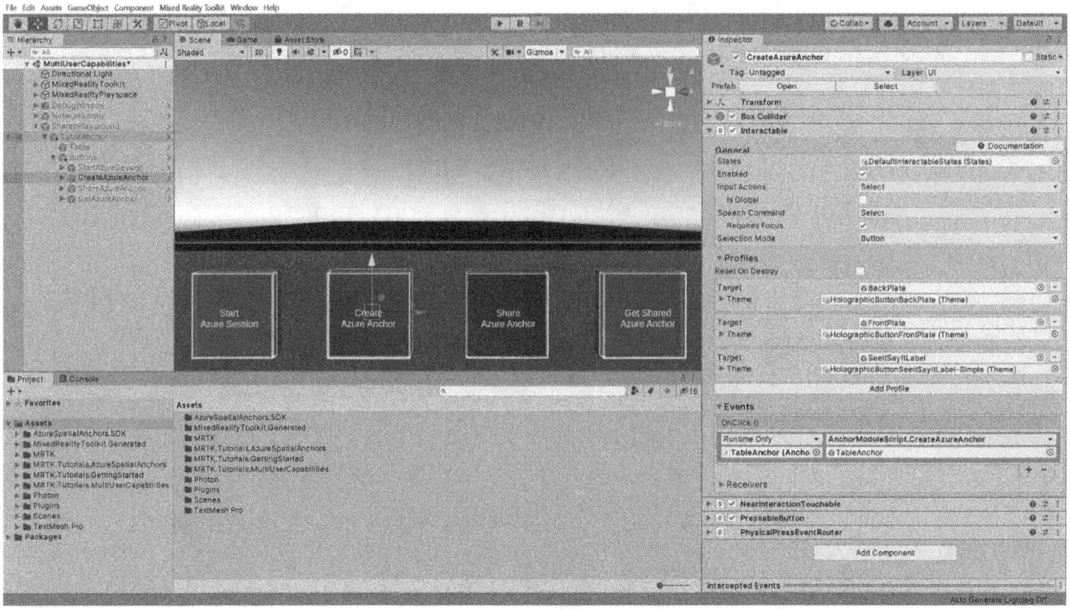

Figure 9-25. *Configure the CreateAzureAnchor Button OnClick() event*

In the Hierarchy window, select the third child button object named ShareAzureAnchor; then in the Inspector window, locate the Interactable (Script) component and configure the OnClick () event as follows:

- To the None (Object) field, assign the TableAnchor object.

- From the No Function drop-down, select the SharingModuleScript ➤ ShareAzureAnchor () function.

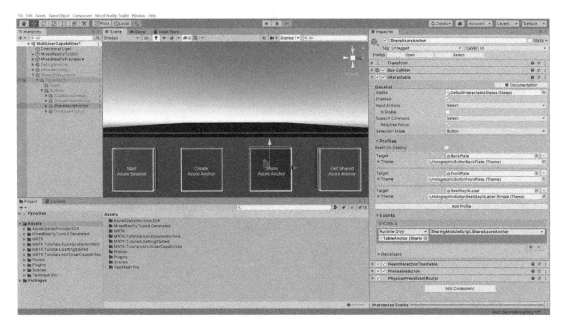

Figure 9-26. *Configure the ShareAzureAnchor Button OnClick() event*

In the Hierarchy window, select the fourth child button object named GetAzureAnchor; then in the Inspector window, locate the Interactable (Script) component and configure the OnClick () event as follows:

- To the None (Object) field, assign the TableAnchor object.

- From the No Function drop-down, select the SharingModuleScript ➤ GetAzureAnchor () function.

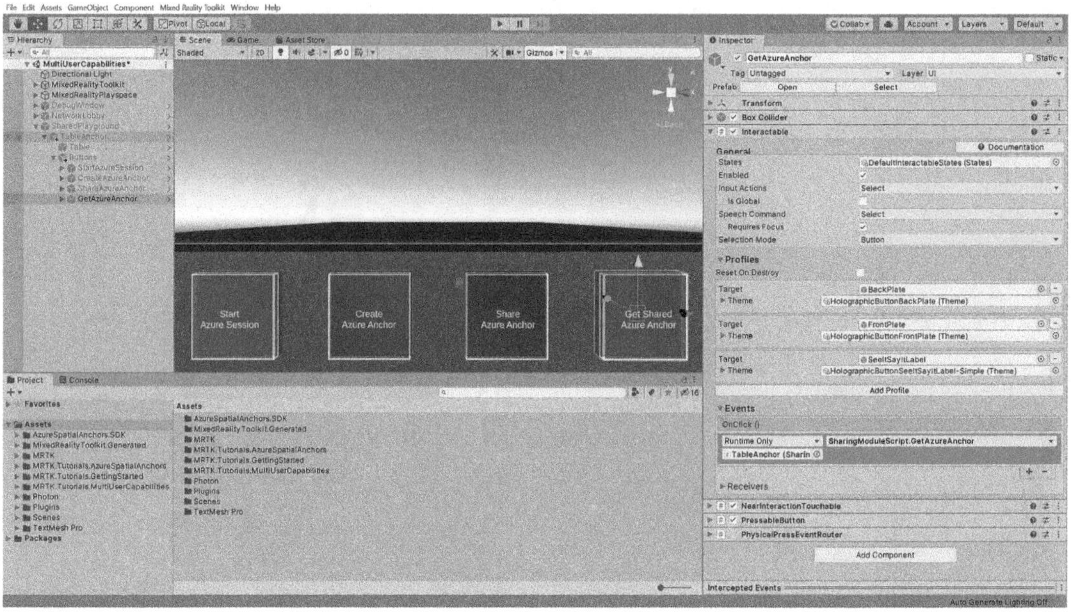

Figure 9-27. *Configure the GetAzureAnchor Button OnClick() event*

Step 3: Connecting the Scene to the Azure Resource

In the Hierarchy window, expand the SharedPlayground object and select the TableAnchor object. In the Inspector window, locate the Spatial Anchor Manager (Script) component, and configure the Credentials section with the credentials from the Azure Spatial Anchors account created as part of the prerequisites for this tutorial series:

- In the Spatial Anchors Account ID field, paste the account ID from your Azure Spatial Anchors account.

- In the Spatial Anchors Account Key field, paste the primary or secondary access key from your Azure Spatial Anchors account.

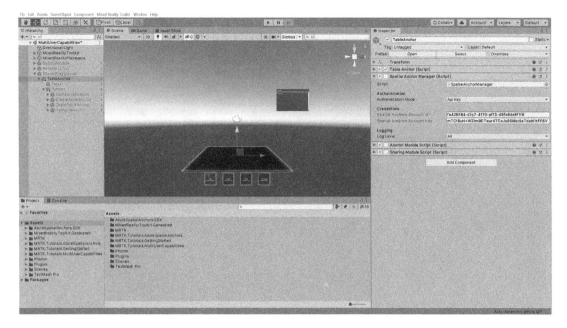

Figure 9-28. *Enter the Spatial Anchors Account ID and Spatial Anchors Account Key*

In the Hierarchy window, select the TableAnchor object; then in the Inspector window, locate the Anchor Module (Script) component and configure it as follows:

- In the Public Sharing Pin field, change a few digits, so the pin becomes unique to your project.

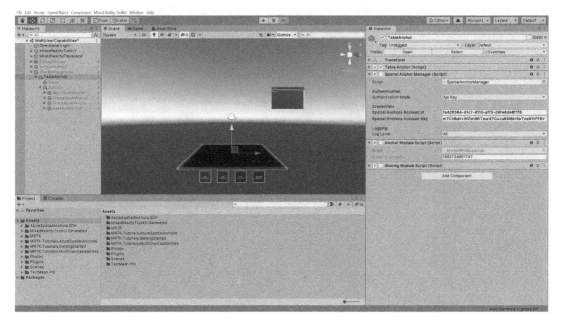

Figure 9-29. *Enter the unique Public Sharing Pin to your project*

With the TableAnchor object still selected, in the Inspector window, make sure all the script components are enabled:

- Check the check box next to the Spatial Anchor Manager (Script) components to enable it.

- Check the check box next to the Anchor Module Script (Script) components to enable it.

- Check the check box next to the Sharing Module Script (Script) components to enable it.

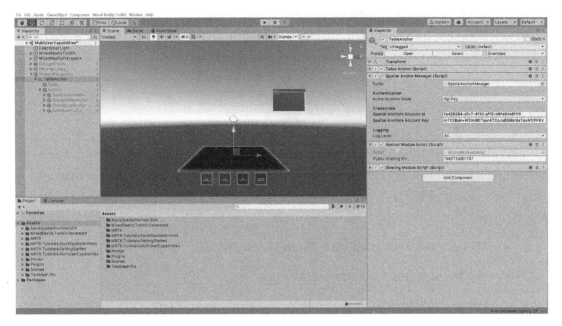

Figure 9-30. *Enable all the script components attached to TableAnchor object*

Trying the Experience with Spatial Alignment

If you now build and deploy the Unity project to two devices, you can achieve spatial alignment between the devices by sharing the Azure Anchor ID. To test it out, you can follow these steps:

On device 1: Start the app (the Rover Explorer is instantiated and placed on the table).

On device 2: Start the app (both users see the table with the Rover Explorer, but the table does not appear in the same place, and the user avatars do not appear where the users are).

On device 1: Click the Start Azure Session button.

On device 1: Click the Create Azure Anchor button (creates an anchor at the location of the TableAnchor object and stores the anchor information in the Azure resource).

On device 1: Click the Share Azure Anchor button (shares the anchor ID with other users in real time).

On device 2: Click the Start Azure Session button.

On device 2: Click the Get Azure Anchor button (connects to the Azure resource to retrieve the anchor information for the shared anchor ID, then moves the TableAnchor object to the location where the anchor was created with device 1).

Summary

Congratulations! Having created your shared experiences, you are well on your way to becoming a Mixed Reality developer. Building a multiuser experience using Photon Unity Networking (PUN) is a very satisfying experience! Let's recap what we've learned in this chapter:

- You learned how to set up a Photon account.

- You learned how to create a PUN app.

- You learned how to integrate PUN into the Unity project.

- You learned how to configure user avatars and shared objects.

- You learned how to align multiple participants using Azure Spatial Anchors.

You have now developed one of the exciting projects for Mixed Reality development. In the next chapter, we will also develop a few more exciting projects for Mixed Reality development.

CHAPTER 10

Awe-Inspiring Experiences

In this chapter, I'll walk you through some tips and tricks on making awe-inspiring Mixed Reality experiences! By now, you've learned all the basics you need to make compelling applications. There are dozens of books that can be written on advanced Mixed Reality development and techniques – and even more, Mixed Reality techniques that are yet to be discovered! I'll give you a taste of some things you can do to enhance your applications and experiences by introducing you to some design concepts, HoloLens project samples, and some third-party tools that you can use.

What Makes an App Awe Inspiring?

There's a certain feeling of awe and magic when you experience a well-made application. The Microsoft-published experiences do a great job showcasing what's possible with the HoloLens. Applications like Fragments, RoboRaid, HoloStudio, Vivo, Actiongram, and Galaxy Explorer provide an unforgettable experience for users. Apps like these run smoothly, take full advantage of spatial sound and spatial mapping, and make excellent use of shaders and colors.

Here are some key features of an awe-inspiring experience:

- An awe-inspiring app allows the user to forget about the headset and feel immersed in the experience. It fully takes advantage of spatial sound and spatial mapping so that holograms feel like they are really in the user's environment.

- It provides stunning visuals, as opposed to boring or plain visuals. It uses transparency, light, colors, and motion appropriately.

© Sean Ong and Varun Kumar Siddaraju 2021
S. Ong and V. K. Siddaraju, *Beginning Windows Mixed Reality Programming*,
https://doi.org/10.1007/978-1-4842-7104-9_10

- It runs smoothly and maximizes the frame rate. A choppy frame rate causes user to be disoriented and the experience to feel artificial. A smooth frame rate (60 frames per second) makes the application feel real and responsive.

- It provides an element of magic, or the ability to do something the user didn't think was possible. A few examples of this are using image recognition to identify objects in the user's scene, using spatial understanding to allow digital characters to sit on real sofas and chairs, and being able to use voice commands in unexpected ways.

While Microsoft and a handful of Mixed Reality studios have published what I would consider awe-inspiring experiences, I want to reiterate one of the big assumptions of this book, which is that we're all still very early in determining best practices for Mixed Reality. There are a few resources available for current best practices. For example, Microsoft has released documentation that highlights best practices for designing Mixed Reality experiences, which can be found at `https://docs.microsoft.com/en-us/windows/mixed-reality/design/design`.

However, there's still so much left to discover. The few tips and tricks I highlight in this chapter shouldn't be considered the best achievable, but rather the minimum starting point from which to improve.

Many Mixed Reality developers (myself included) obtain inspiration from movies with a lot of special effects, such as science fiction movies. When watching these movies, you'll find many great ideas for what makes a hologram look amazing. You'll see colors and textures that elicit awe, excellent examples of fluid animations and transitions, and sound effects that work well.

Optimization and Performance

In this section, I'll walk you through best practices for optimizing your Mixed Reality application. The key metric in optimization is frame rate, or frames per second (FPS.) Other crucial factors include CPU usage and impact on battery life. However, the frame rate of your application directly impacts how the user experiences your application and can make the difference between a choppy, frustrating experience and a smooth, wonderful experience.

Optimizing for performance is one of those necessary, but annoying aspects of development. When asked about my experiences developing for the HoloLens, I often tell people this:

I can make just about anything I want in Mixed Reality. That's the easy part. What's hard is optimizing for the best performance.

I've talked to countless HoloLens and Mixed Reality developers – and all developers, both experienced and beginners, suffer from the pain of optimization. The reason is that all devices – whether it's a HoloLens, immersive headset, or powerful gaming PC – have limits to the amount of content it can render before running into hardware and performance limitations. As developers, it's easy to want to include high-detail 3D models, extravagant colors, extremely realistic lighting effects, and complex animations. However, all these additions take processing power to render. When you have too much content in your experience, your device responds by a drop-in frame rate.

In essence, optimization of your application is a form of art. You need to learn the perfect balance between content and performance. Maximizing the look and feel of your content while maintaining 60 FPS is the ultimate goal of performance optimization in any Mixed Reality experience.

While you should always strive to achieve 60 FPS, you may notice that lower frame rates (30–60 FPS) might be acceptable, depending on the use case. When you are out of optimization options, you may need to make a difficult decision to include certain features or objects at the expense of frame rate.

Note   Since the HoloLens is a self-contained holographic computer (not tethered to a more powerful PC), it has more performance constraints than tethered Mixed Reality headsets. Because of this, the performance optimization conversation in this section will be focused on the HoloLens. Performance will be less of an issue when using tethered headsets connected to a powerful gaming PC. That said, all performance suggestions given can help when optimizing any experience, both small and large. Also, when developing for tethered headsets, it's important to consider individuals who may be running your application on a less powerful PC. I recommend testing on a minimum-specification PC for performance monitoring when developing for tethered Mixed Reality headsets.

How to Monitor for Performance

Before we dive into best practices, you should first know how to measure the performance of your applications. The best place to see all performance metrics of the HoloLens is through the *Windows Device Portal*. To access the Windows Device Portal, make sure your headset is turned on and either connected to the same Wi-Fi network as your PC or connected via USB cable.

Ensure that you have already set up developer mode on your device (as discussed in Chapter 3) and that the "Device Portal" option is enabled. You can find the "Device Portal" setting in your HoloLens at Settings ➤ Update and Security ➤ For Developers ➤ Device Portal.

If your device is connected to your PC via the included USB cable, you may type in this address into your web browser: 127.0.0.1:10080

Note   If you're having issues with USB connectivity, double-check that the USB Device Connectivity optional component is installed as part of your Visual Studio tool package.

If you are using Wi-Fi, you may type in the IP address of your headset. If you don't know your IP address, you can access it on your HoloLens by going to Settings ➤ Network & Internet ➤ Advanced Options. See Figure 10-1 for guidance on where to find the IP address in your HoloLens' Settings app.

Figure 10-1. *Illustration of where to find your HoloLens IP address in the Settings app*

Once you log into the Windows Device Portal, navigate to "System Performance" on the left menu bar. You will see real-time performance tracking and metrics, as shown in Figure 10-2.

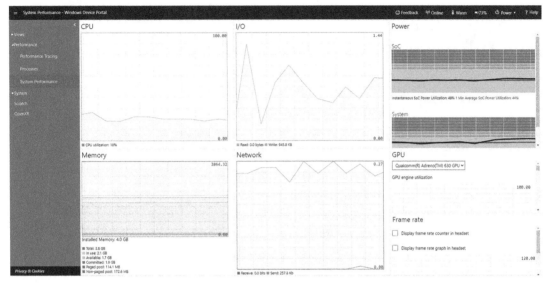

Figure 10-2. *Real-time performance metrics for the HoloLens can be tracked via the Windows Device Portal*

When within the Device Portal, you'll see several metrics. The following outline describes each of these metrics:

- *System power* is the total power consumption of the HoloLens. Monitor this to ensure power consumption is kept within the green and orange areas, to avoid the generation of heat. Be sure to measure system power when the device isn't charging, as it will not measure while charging.

- *SoC power* is the combined power consumption of only the CPU, GPU, and memory unit. As with system power, be sure SoC power is kept within the green and orange areas to avoid overheating of the device.

- *Frame rate* is the rendered frames per second of your 3D application. If you are developing a 2D application that will run within the Windows shell, then the frame rate will be the frame rate of the shell, and not your 2D application.

223

- *CPU* shows the load of your central processing unit.

- *GPU* shows the load of your graphics processing unit. It shows the percentage of time that the GPU is active with tasks. Note: The GPU is primarily responsible for rendering while the HPU controls Augmented Reality processing, which combines real world and data. The HPU handles all of the data integration and user input.

- *I/O* shows the disk usage for all processes.

- *Network* shows the network/Wi-Fi usage for all processes.

- *Memory* shows the total memory committed by all processes on your device. To see memory usage for an individual process, see the Processes tab in the Windows Device Portal.

While maintaining a high FPS is key, it is also important to consider the preceding metrics when optimizing your application. If you maintain 60 FPS, but your application is very demanding on these other metrics, your device may overheat which can eventually lead to shutdown of the device, which will cause your application to be terminated or even shut down the device to protect itself. The following is a summary of essential performance targets for the HoloLens:

- Maintain frame rate at 60 FPS.

- Keep power consumption within orange and green areas.

- Keep memory usage of your application under 900 MB.

Another excellent tool for monitoring performance of your application during development is the *VisualProfiler* included in the Mixed Reality Toolkit. *VisualProfiler* provides you information regarding frame rate, frame time, frame graph, and memory utilization. (The Diagnostics System Settings in the MRTK Profiles Inspector can be used to set up the Visual Profiler.)

Best Practices for Performance

As mentioned earlier in this section, performance optimization is a big challenge, even for experienced developers. The guidelines provided here will help when optimizing, but you should be prepared to spend a good chunk of time on optimizing and troubleshooting performance issues.

Start Monitoring and Optimizing Early

As a rule of thumb, you should consider performance and optimization *very early* in your development cycle. If you start too late, you may have a difficult time identifying objects in your scene that are causing performance issues. If you start out with a smooth application at the beginning, then you'll be able to easily identify when additions to your project start to impact performance. You'll only be able to accurately test performance when deployed to your device. Playing your device in the Unity editor will not give you many insights regarding the actual frame rate and hardware usage when your application is deployed to your headset. This might feel like you're spending more time deploying and testing upfront, but it will save you time troubleshooting performance issues later in your development cycle.

Optimize Polygons and Textures

All 3D objects rendered by the HoloLens are made up of triangles or polygons, including the spatial mapping mesh. While polygon count isn't the only factor affecting performance on the HoloLens, it is one of the easiest ways to begin optimizing your experience.

Models with many polygons are typically referred to as *high poly*, while models with fewer polygons are referred to as *low poly*. There's no strict definition for the number of polygons that constitute high- or low-poly models, as it depends on the size and complexity of the model. In general, high-poly models appear smooth and curved, while low-poly models appear somewhat blocky. Refer to Figure 10-3.

High-poly 3D models are sure to slow down your frame rate. Low-poly models, when combined with other best practices, will allow your experience to perform well. In general, the HoloLens can render up to about 80,000 triangles while maintaining 60 FPS, if optimal shaders are used. Frame rate drops to about 30 FPS with 200,000 triangles. In most cases, you'll want to stay safe in the 20,000–60,000-triangle range to give yourself some room to work with.

Figure 10-3 shows a few different views of a 3D model of an apple. The apple on the left is high poly, while the apple on the right is low poly. You can see that the high-poly apple looks much smoother and more realistic than the low-poly model. In the middle row of Figure 10-3, I turned on the wireframe so you can visualize the individual triangles that comprise each 3D model. In the top row, the high-poly apple uses the standard shader, allowing it to look shiny, but also impacting performance negatively. The low-poly apple in the top row uses the legacy diffuse shader, making it look dull but allowing for much better performance. In the bottom row, I swap the shaders between the two apples, to illustrate that shaders can make low-poly models look better and vice versa.

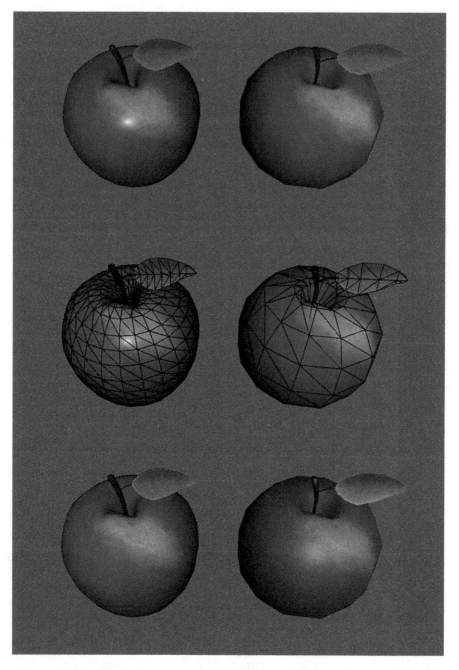

Figure 10-3. *Illustration of how polygon count and shader can impact the visual appearance of 3D models*

As you can see, optimizing your HoloLens application sometimes means making difficult trade-offs between visually appealing models and fast performance. There are tricks to making low-poly models look stunning, even with high-performing shaders. 3D artists can color model textures to give them an illusion of appearing shiny or extremely detailed. For example, in Figure 10-4, the sofa appears to have a high level of detail, with folds in the cushion and light reflections at the edges. However, the sofa model is actually a low-poly model, as shown in the lower image. The cushion folds and reflections came from the texture image applied to the 3D model. I was able to achieve both high performance and a stunning visual of a sofa in the HoloLens because I was able to minimize my polygon count and use a fast shader.

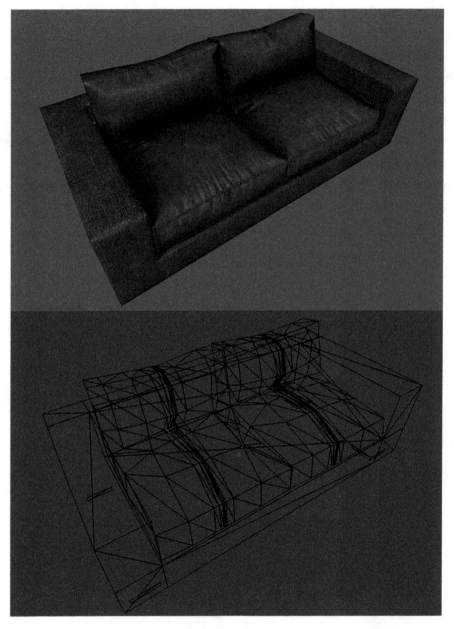

Figure 10-4. Low-poly models can be given the appearance of looking detailed with some creativity in the texture image applied

As much as possible, you should strive to use one texture per model, as opposed to a model comprised of many texture files. You should also minimize shader switching. Try to use the same type of shader for all objects in view.

Level of Detail Rendering

Level of detail (LOD) rendering is a performance technique whereby you reduce the polygon count and appearance of objects that are further away from view. It's a waste of computing power to render a high-quality model that's far from the user, since the model will appear small when far away, and the user will not be able to appreciate the model's detail. Unity provides a component called *LOD Group*, which allows you to change how an object is rendered at various distances. Figure 10-5 shows what this component looks like in Unity. You may add various levels of details by right-clicking the colored bars, drag each bar to specify distance from the camera, and add models of varying polygon counts and shaders for each LOD. For additional information, see `https://docs.unity3d.com/Manual/class-LODGroup.html`.

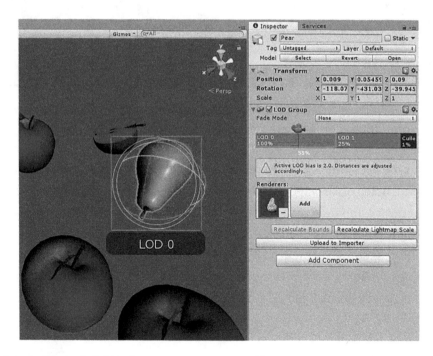

Figure 10-5. *Unity's LOD Group component allows you to specify how your model will be rendered based on distance from the camera. You will be able to render a lower-quality model when the camera is far from the object*

Culling

Another effective performance strategy is called *culling*, which means to not render models that will not be seen. By default, Unity uses *frustum culling*, which means that anything outside of the user's view or frustum is not rendered. Figure 10-6 illustrates the camera's frustum, shown with the white lines. Avoiding rendering objects outside of the camera's view limits what needs to be drawn and increases performance.

Figure 10-6. *Frustum culling ensures that anything outside of the camera's frustum (shown in green here) is not rendered*

Another type of culling is called *occlusion culling*, which allows you to not render objects that are being obstructed by other objects in your scene, thereby reducing the load on your device and increasing performance. To enable occlusion culling, go to Window ➤ Rendering ➤ Occlusion Culling, and click the "Bake" button in the Occlusion Culling window, as shown in Figure 10-7. You will also need to ensure that the Occlusion Culling setting is enabled in your camera. For more information on occlusion culling, see https://docs.unity3d.com/Manual/OcclusionCulling.html.

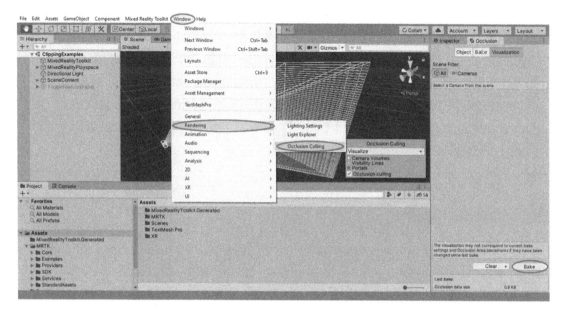

Figure 10-7. *You may enable Occlusion Culling by going to Window ➤ Rendering ➤ Occlusion Culling. Occlusion Culling increases performance by preventing obstructed objects from being rendered*

Enable Single-Pass Instanced Rendering

Hidden in your Player settings (Edit ➤ Project Settings ➤ XR Plugin Management ➤ Oculus), you'll find an option to change your stereo rendering method between Multi Pass and Single Pass Instanced. This option significantly reduces CPU processing time by rendering both eyes at the same time, instead of one eye at a time. Figure 10-8 illustrates where you can find the stereo render setting. For more information on single-pass instanced rendering, see `https://docs.unity3d.com/Manual/SinglePassStereoRendering.html`.

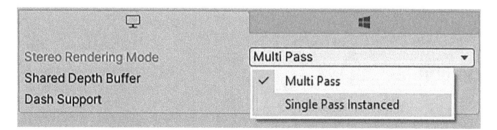

Figure 10-8. *You can switch between stereo rendering modes in your player settings*

> **Warning**   Not all shaders are compatible with single-pass instanced rendering. If you are using shaders outside of those included with the Mixed Reality Toolkit, keep an eye out for differing views between your left and right eyes. If this happens, you may need to revert to multi-pass rendering or update your shaders as described here: `https://docs.unity3d.com/Manual/SinglePassStereoRendering.html`.

Optimize Shaders

Shaders are scripts or programs that perform calculations responsible for producing light levels, darkness, color, reflectivity, and special effects for objects. Shaders are an extremely important factor for how your object appears, but they can significantly contribute to performance issues in your application, arguably more so than your object's polygon count.

Typically, any special object visualization you would like to achieve in your experience will require a shader that decreases performance. Examples of special object visualizations include highly reflective metals or mirrored surfaces, glass-like or transparent objects, and glowing or neon-like effects on objects.

The topic of shaders and shader optimization is a large part of the 3D modeling and graphics industries. Many books have been written on the topic, and advanced developers will inevitably need to write custom shaders to perform specific visualizations while maintaining good performance. I won't go into the details of writing your own shaders in this book. For beginners, I recommend leveraging shaders offered in the Mixed Reality Toolkit. For advanced tips and guidelines when working with or writing your own shaders, Microsoft's Mixed Reality documentation provides many good shader suggestions here: `https://developer.microsoft.com/en-us/windows/mixed-reality/performance_recommendations_for_hololens_apps`.

Simplygon

What if you have a 3D model you would like to use, but find that it has too many polygons and contains large texture files? *Simplygon* is a tool (acquired by Microsoft in 2016) that allows users to reduce the number of polygons and reduce the complexity of textures of a 3D model without noticeably impacting the visual appearance of the model!

Figure 10-9 shows an example of the Simplygon user interface. Simplygon also provides a plug-in for Unity, which allows you to optimize models from within Unity. To sign up for an account and download Simplygon for free, visit this URL: `www.simplygon.com/Downloads`.

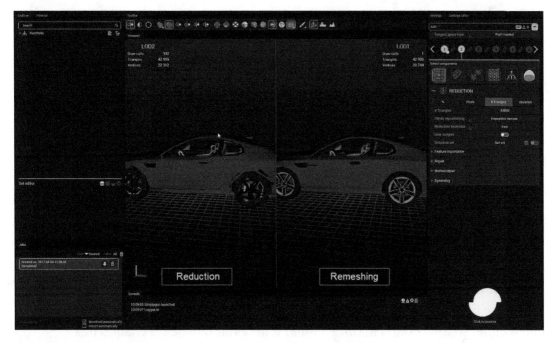

Figure 10-9. *Simplygon allows you to convert large, complex 3D models into beautiful, low-poly models that perform well in the HoloLens*

Stabilization Plane

The HoloLens performs special hardware-assisted stabilization to keep holograms appearing stable in your environment. Since the HoloLens can't stabilize all holograms in your scene, an invisible plane in your scene, called the *stabilization plane*, is used to select objects that receive the maximum amount of stabilization. Figure 10-10 shows the script (*stabilizationplanemodifier.cs*) that manages this plane in the Inspector panel. By default, the stabilization plane will attempt to find appropriate holograms without requiring an additional setup. However, for best results, you can help the plane find appropriate objects to stabilize within your script and also within the stabilizationplanemodifier.cs script.

▼ # ✓ **StabilizationPlaneModifier**		❓ ⇄ ⋮
Script	StabilizationPlaneModifier	⊙
Mode	Fixed	▼
Use Unscaled Time	✓	
Lerp Power Closer	4	
Lerp Power Farther	7	
Target Override	None (Transform)	⊙
Track Velocity	✓	
Default Plane Distance	2	
Draw Gizmos	✓	
▶ Override Plane		

Figure 10-10. *The stabilization plane helps the HoloLens prioritize which objects receive the greatest amount of stabilization for a better experience*

The stabilizationplanemodifier.cs script is useful for adjusting the behavior of the stabilization plane. (StabilizationPlaneModifier controls the stabilization plane in a variety of settings. It accomplishes this by taking care of the platform call to HolographicPlatformSettings. SetFocusPointForFrame is a method for setting the focus point for a frame. StabilizationPlaneModifier will take precedence over DepthLSR. The depth buffer sharing option in Unity's Build settings automatically enables this. Consolidation PlaneModifier is recommended for HoloLens 1; however, it can also be used for HoloLens 2, and it has no effect on WMR.) Here is a brief description of each setting in the script:

- *Mode* allows the stabilization plane to be created and placed automatically, based on your gaze, a fixed distance, or a target that you provide.

- *Use unscaled time* modifies the way the plane moves by making it independent of frame rate, pausing, or other time manipulations.

- *Lerp power closer* is the speed at which the plane moves toward the camera.

- *Lerp power farther* is the speed at which the plane moves away from the camera.

234

- *Target override* allows you to override the location of the stabilization plane. Use this when you want to stabilize specific holograms in your scene.

- *Track velocity* keeps track of the velocity of your target object, so that the plane can accurately follow and anticipate the target object's movement rather than reacting to it.

- *Default plane distance* is the distance from the camera that the plan will float, if no target object is specified or identified.

- *Draw gizmos* allows you to visualize the stabilization plane when testing or running your application.

To manually set the stabilization plane on a target object via scripting, you can use the SetFocusPointForFrame() function. See the following for an example of this:

```
public GameObject objectToFocusOn;
void Update ()
{
    var normal = -Camera.main.transform.forward;
    var position = focusedObject.transform.position;
    UnityEngine.VR.WSA.HolographicSettings.SetFocusPointForFrame(position,
    normal);
}
```

In the preceding code, you provide a normal and a point to define the plane. The point (position) is the position of your target object (objectToFocusOn). Feeding these variables into the SetFocusPointForFrame() function allows the stabilization plane to be placed at your desired location.

The following are some general tips to get the most out of your stabilization plane:

- Try to use the plane to cover as much of your content as possible. For example, if your content is a plane (2D image, text, UI plane, or other flat surface), then align the stabilization plane to your 2D surface.

- Do your best to have your plane cut through all relevant holograms in your scene, to stabilize as many objects as possible.

- Place the stabilization plane on objects that are further away from the camera, as those tend to be more unstable.

- Never place the plane outside of your camera's view. There's no point wasting precious stabilization resources on objects that you can't see. Stabilize objects that the user will be looking at.

- Don't let the stabilization plane touch or cut through the user.

For more information and best practices for the stabilization plane, feel free to review the following resources:

```
https://microsoft.github.io/MixedRealityToolkit-Unity/
Documentation/hologram-stabilization.html?q=hologram%20
stability
```

```
https://developer.microsoft.com/en-us/windows/mixed-
reality/focus_point_in_unity
```

```
https://developer.microsoft.com/en-us/windows/mixed-
reality/case_study_-_using_the_stabilization_plane_to_
reduce_holographic_turbulence
```

Design and Magic

In this section, I'll focus on design elements, tools, and best practices that will help your application to stand out visually and provide a good user experience. There are many ways that developers can add 3D objects and holograms to a scene. However, when visuals feel dull or cheesy, it's a lost opportunity for a truly awe-inspiring experience. Incorporating good design and magical experiences into your application takes more thought and effort. In the long run, however, you'll have a Mixed Reality experience that you can feel proud about and perhaps provide users with an excuse to keep coming back to your app.

To get us started, I'll first provide you with some best practices for Mixed Reality design, followed by some design-related tools and resources you can use. I'll also provide a brief tutorial on using Vuforia and talk about ways to incorporate some magic into your experiences.

Best Practices for Design

In the short period of time that the HoloLens and other Mixed Reality devices have been around, a few key best practices for design have emerged. While there's still so much more to be learned by developers (that's you!), these best practices will help your design process in the short term.

Spatial Mapping

As much as possible, try to consider the use of spatial mapping in your application. It's easy to forego spatial mapping. You might think that it's not worth the effort or adds little value to your project. I am also guilty of wondering why I should add spatial mapping when it would only limit where my holograms can go. However, a big benefit of devices like the HoloLens is its powerful ability to interact with the physical world. Take advantage of that by allowing your objects to be able to rest on floors and surfaces, be pinned to walls and ceilings, and be occluded by real objects in your scene. It's an easy way to add magic to your experience without trying to invent something new.

The Mixed Reality Toolkit provides different options for visualizing your spatial mapping mesh. Spatial mesh can vary in different colors and textures based on your requirements. It can vary from Figure 10-11 to Figure 10-12.

Figure 10-11. *The default shader for visualizing the spatial mapping mesh is functional, but not very pretty*

Figure 10-12. *Smoothing out the mesh and tinting the lines green, as is done with the spatial understanding mesh, improves the experience*

However, scanning your environment using spatial mapping is a technologically magical feat. As such, visualization of the mesh should be equally impressive. Microsoft-published applications like Fragments or Young Conker use vibrant colors and lighting effects to really breathe life into the spatial mapping mesh. The specific shader used in Fragments and Young Conker is not available to developers as of this writing; there are similar shaders that can be downloaded for use in your application. One of my favorite examples can be found at this URL, Pulse Shader, which provides an optical pulse illusion on surface reconstruction: `https://microsoft.github.io/ MixedRealityToolkit-Unity/Assets/MRTK/SDK/Experimental/PulseShader/README. html`.

Figure 10-13. *Adding regularity, color, texture, and animations to the spatial mapping mesh significantly boosts design (Source: Microsoft)*

Distance from User

Microsoft recommends that optimal placement of holograms is between 1.25m and 5m, with 2m being the best place. Holograms placed too close to users may result in discomfort or a jarring experience. By default, the HoloLens camera prefab in the Mixed Reality Toolkit culls any holograms that are closer than 0.85m (using frustum culling). This is why you often cannot view details when you approach a hologram too closely.

In my experience, reducing frustum culling from 0.85m to 0.20m is acceptable, depending on the use case of your application. This allows users to view intricate details close-up, without the model frustratingly disappearing. This value can be set by adjusting the "Near" Clipping plane in the camera GameObject.

Shadows

Our brain heavily relies on shadows as a cue for where objects are in the world around us. Shadows are also an important part of 3D design. As such, the use of shadows can help increase realism and provide a greater sense that digital holograms are anchored in the real world.

While Unity can easily create shadows in your scene, devices like the HoloLens are unable to display shadows because it can only add light to the display and cannot darken an area (displays that work in this manner are referred to as *additive displays*). The trick to overcoming this limitation is to use a technique called *negative shadowing*. Negative shadowing adds a small amount of light or glow around your object and then removes the light where the shadow would normally appear. The user will not be able to perceive the light glow, but will be able to perceive the shadow.

Voice

Whenever possible, add voice commands to your application. This is especially true for UI elements. If your application has a button that says "start," be sure to add a voice command for "start." A best practice is to add a small microphone icon on or near your button to cue users that the button is voice enabled. For bonus design points, you can have the icon of the microphone appear after the user has gazed at the object for a certain period of time (0.5–1 second should be sufficient).

Sharp Text

As of this writing, it's very common to see blurry text in many HoloLens applications, especially those in the Windows Store. Using Unity's default fonts causes fonts to appear blurry in the HoloLens due to scaling. Figure 10-14 illustrates Unity's default text (the upper "Testing") and text written using the Mixed Reality Toolkit's UITextSelwik prefab (the lower "Testing").

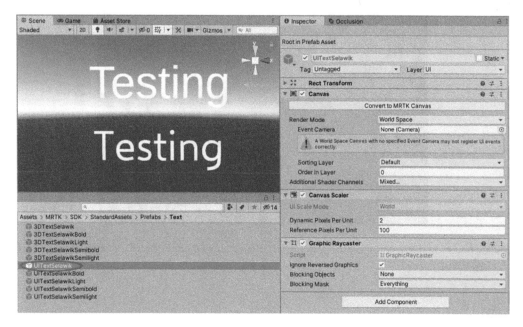

Figure 10-14. *Use typography resources included with the MixedRealityToolkit, such as the UITextSelawik, to achieve sharp-looking text in the HoloLens. Default Unity text resources appear blurry and unappealing*

As a rule of thumb, text also looks best in the HoloLens when the font is white against a colored or darker (but not black) backdrop. Avoid outlining your text.

Bounds Controls

When users have the option of manipulating (moving, rotating, scaling) a hologram, be sure to add a Bounds Control with "handles" that users can use for manipulation. The Bounds Controls should appear invisible when the hologram is not selected, but appear when the hologram is selected.

Figure 10-15. *Example of Bounds Control around a selected hologram to assist with manipulation*

Toolbars

I also recommend using toolbars and app bars in Mixed Reality applications. Toolbars with minimalistic buttons evoke a feeling of cleanliness and make your experience feel modern. Figure 10-16 illustrates what a well-designed toolbar looks like. Each button should respond to being gazed at, such as the heightened button shown in Figure 10-16.

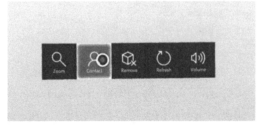

Figure 10-16. *Use clean and modern toolbars for your menu items*

Colors

While you may be tempted to make your application or experience shine vividly with all the colors that the HoloLens can render, a great design strategy is to use only one color on any object that you want to appear as a traditional hologram. From sci-fi movies, we've come to expect holograms to have a certain monochromatic glow. Rendering an object with a single blue or green color evokes a special feeling and makes the hologram appear real.

Use only one or two colors as a theme for your application. You can see by the previous menu item in Figure 10-16 that the simple color choices result in a UI that appears modern.

Design Experiences to Avoid

Never headlock content. While heads-up display (HUD) UI may sound fun, it doesn't feel good in devices like the HoloLens. If an information panel or object needs to follow the user's gaze, be sure to give it a slight delay, so it appears to chase and catch up to your gaze. The RadialView.cs script included with the HoloLens already provides the delayed follow functionality.

Avoid using loud sound effects, especially when they are triggered by gaze. This may result in an annoying experience for users.

Avoid making the user type information unless absolutely necessary. Text input on devices like the HoloLens is difficult and cumbersome.

Additional Resources

The HoloLens design team has provided a valuable resource for implementing many design best practices into your project. Separate from the Mixed Reality Toolkit, you'll find another repository on GitHub called the Mixed Reality Design Labs. This is an excellent resource for finding prefabs and scripts for bounding boxes, app bars, progress bars, and more!

You can find the repository at `https://github.com/Microsoft/MRDesignLabs_Unity`.

Adding Magic: Vuforia

Devices like the HoloLens are already a feat of modern engineering and magical in and of itself. However, there are many ways that developers can add more magic to their applications. It's difficult to define magic in this context, but I tend to define it as any experience that amazes the user due to it being pleasantly unexpected or seemingly impossible.

The most powerful way to invoke the feeling of magic is to couple your Mixed Reality application with artificial intelligence or "cognitive services." Services like IMB Watson, Microsoft Azure, and more allow applications to perform amazing tasks, such as image recognition, custom speech/chat capabilities, real-time translation, and more!

You may review Azure's list of cognitive services to get a feel for the type of resources available: https://azure.microsoft.com/en-us/services/cognitive-services/.

One of my favorite examples of adding magic to your application is the use of a powerful tool called Vuforia. Vuforia allows your headset to recognize 2D images and 3D objects in your real world and place a hologram at or near the recognized image/object in real time! In the following, I provide a brief tutorial on how to download and set up an experience that's powered by Vuforia.

Step 1: Install the Vuforia Sample

Open a new Unity project, and go to asset store and search for Vuforia engine asset. Click Download. See Figure 10-17.

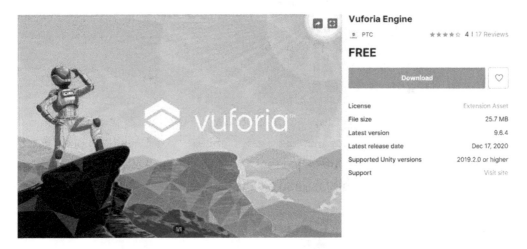

Figure 10-17.   *Click the Download button to download your asset*

After downloading, click Import.

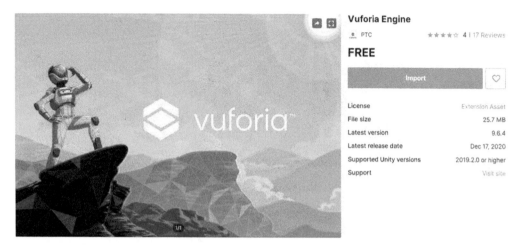

Figure 10-18. *Click Import button to import all the packages*

After importing the asset, search for the scene with name "0-Main" in project window, and open the 0-Main scene. See Figure 10-19.

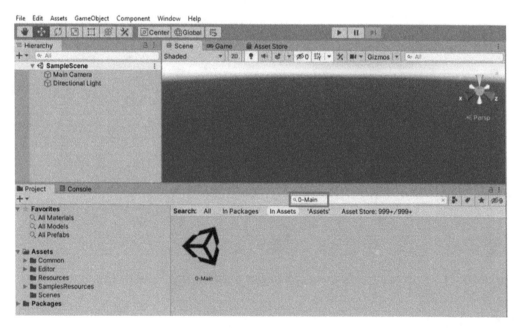

Figure 10-19. *Search for "0-Main" scene*

Select ARCamera in the Hierarchy window, and click Open Vuforia Engine configuration in the Inspector window.

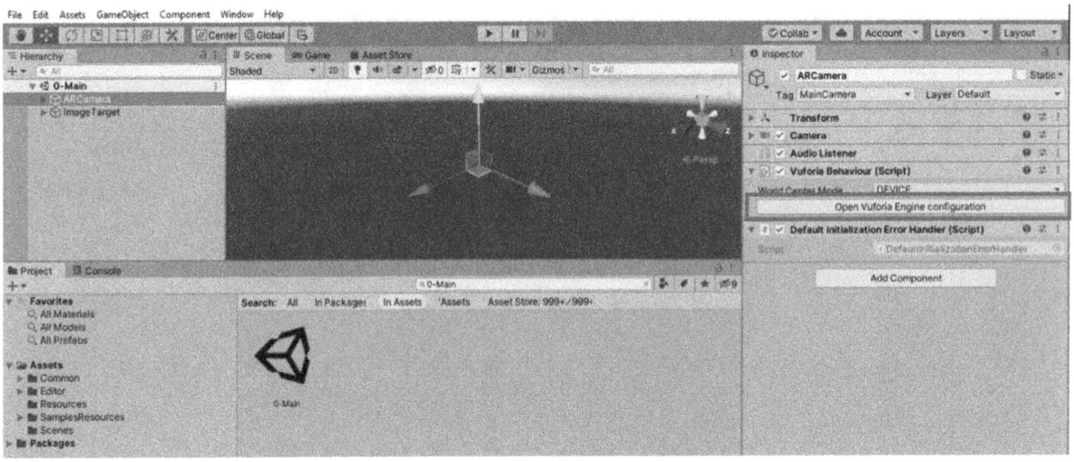

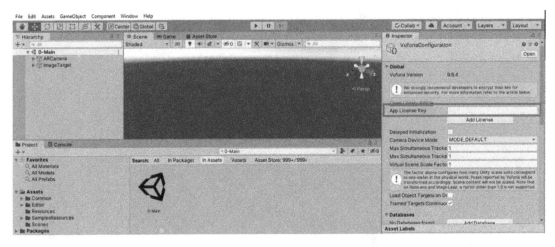

Figure 10-20. *Open Vuforia Engine configuration in the Inspector Window*

Now enter the Vuforia license key on the App License Key text box.

Here is the link to create and use the Vuforia license key: `https://library.vuforia.com/articles/Training/Vuforia-License-Manager.html`.

Figure 10-21. *Provide the license key in the field highlighted in the figure*

Step 2: Try It Out!

To experience the application in action, you will need to print out Vuforia's target image. You can download the image from this URL: `https://library.vuforia.com/sites/default/files/vuforia-library/docs/target_samples/unity/mars_target_images.pdf` (consider only the first target image out of six target images). No additional settings are required with the app package you imported into Unity. You may test out the application using holographic remoting or by deploying it to your device. I recommend deploying the application to your HoloLens for the smoothest experience.

When you launch the Vuforia application, you will notice a 3D astronaut appearing above the image of the astronaut that you printed out! Figure 10-22 illustrates what this looks like. Try to move the paper around on your desk, hold it up, and rotate it. You will notice that the teapot is perfectly attached to the image of the rocks. A truly magical experience!

Figure 10-22. *Like magic! A holographic image appears on the image of a card with Vuforia's HoloLens sample*

Be sure to sign up for a Vuforia account to gain access to the ability to add your own custom image targets and to learn more about the platform. For more information, visit `https://developer.vuforia.com/`.

Summary

Creating awe-inspiring applications for Mixed Reality is ultimately about providing a great experience for users. In this chapter, I provided you with a few guidelines and resources that will help you on your journey toward creating your own awe-inspiring experiences. I talked about the importance of optimizing the performance of your application, provided you with some insights to speed up your application, walked you through several best practices for good design, and provided you with an example of how to add a little magic to your application.

There's really no limit to how creative you can get when designing for Mixed Reality. There's not much art you can do on a 1D line. But vast possibilities are unlocked when painting and developing on a 2D canvas. Bigger yet is the jump to the 3D stage of Mixed Reality, where there are infinite possibilities waiting to be discovered and created.

I encourage you to build upon the best practices and tools provided in this Chapter. Try new design experiences – test what works and what doesn't. The best way to gauge whether or not your application is awe inspiring is to closely observe the reactions of others when they try your experience. You will quickly perceive if your app invokes a sense of wonder and amazement. Finally, don't forget to share your lessons learned with the broader Mixed Reality development community (more on this in Chapter 12!).

CHAPTER 11

Turning Holograms into Money

In this chapter, I'll introduce you to several ways that independent developers can monetize Mixed Reality development activities. From the app model to offering your services as a freelancer, there are many ways that independent developers can earn money from Mixed Reality today! Developing for Mixed Reality is fun and rewarding, but there are also plenty of business opportunities that arise from such a revolutionary new medium. Note that as of this writing, the vast majority of monetization opportunities (if not all) are for the enterprise and business sector rather than the consumer sector. We will discuss this in more detail later in this chapter.

When I bought my first HoloLens unit in the spring of 2016, I started developing for the platform as a hobby and for side projects. I worked on a few applications, both for myself and also others (at no cost). As the year progressed, I started observing that there was a fairly active market for HoloLens developers. I responded to several project bid requests and quickly transitioned to becoming a full-time HoloLens developer.

The biggest financial opportunities for Mixed Reality, however, will come from the sheer fact that these devices will replace the way we do computing today. There's an immense amount of financial potential, and we don't need to wait for a mythical forthcoming device or form factor to start dipping into that potential. In the next few sections, I'll provide you with plenty of resources and discussions for turning holograms into money today!

© Sean Ong and Varun Kumar Siddaraju 2021
S. Ong and V. K. Siddaraju, *Beginning Windows Mixed Reality Programming*,
https://doi.org/10.1007/978-1-4842-7104-9_11

Publishing Your App to the Microsoft Store

In this section, I'll provide a discussion on publishing and monetizing your applications through the Microsoft Store. Perhaps the most direct way to monetize your Mixed Reality experiences is to publish them to the Microsoft Store. The *Microsoft Store* is Microsoft's online shop for apps, media, and other products. Figure 11-1 illustrates just a few of the many HoloLens applications on the Microsoft Store.

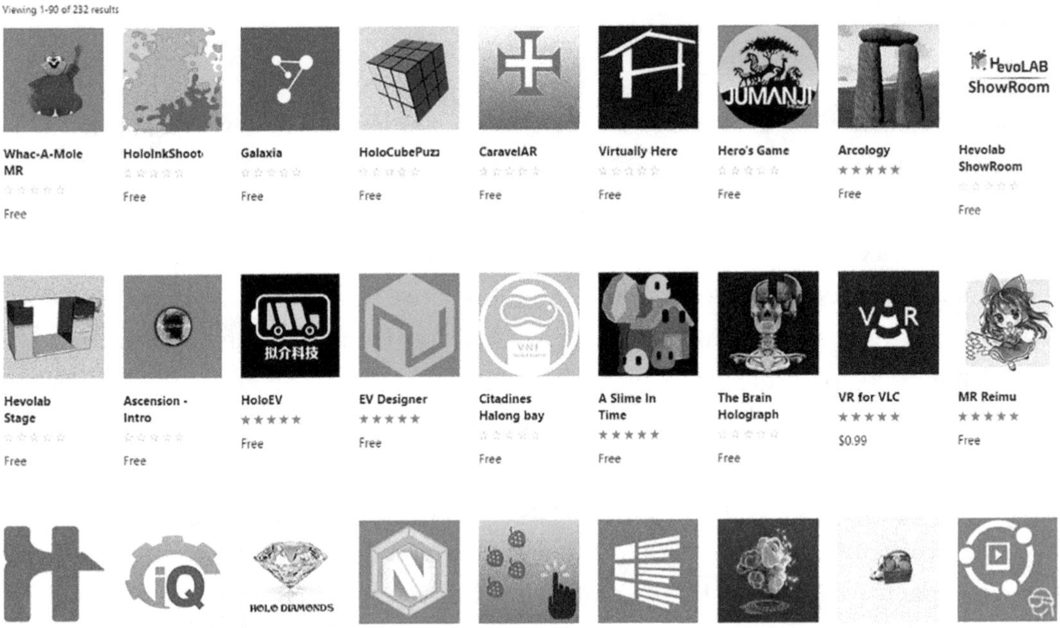

Figure 11-1. *The Microsoft Store contains hundreds of apps, with more being added each month*

When you publish to the Windows Store, you have several options for monetization:

- *Free* apps are applications that users can download at no cost. You won't receive any direct revenue from this approach, but it's a fantastic way to build your portfolio and reputation and may lead to other financial opportunities. Developers may also have a portfolio of many applications, where free applications may lead users to download other paid applications from the same developer.

- *Free with ads* are applications that users can download at no cost but include in-app advertising. Revenue comes from ad clicks and impressions. This is a fairly popular approach among mobile applications; however, it is still unproven in Mixed Reality as of this writing.

- *Freemium* apps are apps that users can download for free, but may opt to pay a premium for additional features, in-app resources, or to remove advertising.

- *Paid* apps are apps that users pay for before downloading. Developers have the option of offering a limited trial period, before requiring users to pay.

I've not found any statistics from Microsoft regarding Mixed Reality app downloads, user engagement, and revenue. However, the general consensus among developers is that monetization opportunities on the Windows Store are still fairly low.

Freelancing and Contracts

In this section, I'll talk about being an independent Mixed Reality developer and share best practices for successfully finding and securing opportunities. I'll share a little bit of my story to illustrate how you can be fully supported by Mixed Reality contracts.

I started developing for the HoloLens shortly after I received one of the first HoloLens (first-generation) units in the spring of 2016. However, I primarily created experimental applications with no firm monetization strategies in mind. What I didn't realize, however, is that the creation of these experimental Mixed Reality applications served to build my portfolio, which would later prove essential to securing my first set of Mixed Reality contracts.

In late 2016, I took note of several requests for bids on Microsoft's Mixed Reality forums that I visited regularly. Companies from Shanghai and Dubai were looking for HoloLens developers to create business-related experiences, including architecture visualization apps and higher education apps. I took a plunge into the brave new world of professional Mixed Reality development by submitting proposals for these projects. I was granted these contracts in part due to my portfolio. Looking back, I wouldn't necessarily consider my portfolio particularly impressive; however, it was rare to find any developer with a HoloLens-related portfolio in those early months after the release of the first-generation HoloLens.

The contracts I secured were relatively small in scope and did not provide enough revenue for full-time work. As such, I still needed to continue working other jobs to meet a livable wage. However, securing and fulfilling those contracts signaled the beginnings of my Mixed Reality journey.

A key turning point in my career was in January of 2017, which marked the point at which I started developing full time for the HoloLens and was fully supported financially by Mixed Reality freelancing opportunities. Thereafter, the number and size of HoloLens and Mixed Reality contract opportunities continued to expand year over year. To meet growing demand, I eventually needed to expand beyond freelancing and started a Mixed Reality development agency. This agency has since spun off several subsidiaries and helped support the growth of partner Mixed Reality agencies. As of this writing, these opportunities have directly resulted in many new companies being incorporated or expanded, supporting dozens of developers, contractors, and employees in the United States, India, and around the world.

Earning a living using Mixed Reality is rewarding and exciting. It also enables you to have a grounded perspective on how Mixed Reality applications are used in business.

Where to Find Mixed Reality Freelance Opportunities

I was first made aware of opportunities by monitoring requests through forums and online communities, which are discussed in detail in Chapter 12. I typically see about three to five freelance and job opportunities per week in the Virtual Reality and Mixed Reality communities I follow online.

The benefit of finding opportunities through these online communities is that you are able to interact directly with the individuals who need help, and a hiring decision can be made swiftly. If you are active in these communities and frequently help others, showcase your work, and contribute to the community, then you will have a much higher chance of being recognized, sought out, and securing new opportunities.

In addition to online communities, job boards and freelance websites are also an excellent source of contracts that you can bid on. It's harder to stand out on freelance sites, and you often don't have the opportunity to connect directly with the manager. However, there is usually a much larger pool of projects to bid to, with new projects being added daily. One website I monitor closely is upwork.com, which has been my most consistent source of Mixed Reality contracts. While contracts on Upwork typically start with a relatively small scope, some opportunities eventually evolve into lasting client relationships.

Increasing Your Chances of Winning a Contract

In winning and losing many HoloLens opportunities, I've observed a few patterns that will help increase your chances of landing a Mixed Reality job:

- Managers are interested in seeing your portfolio of apps. Try to have at least two to three good applications that you can refer prospective clients to. Have at least one stunning application that you can point to first. There are many software developments firms that claim to have Mixed Reality development capabilities, but without any real qualifications or prior experience. Managers have a very difficult time trying to filter out true Mixed Reality developers from those with no experience. A portfolio of applications quickly lets managers know that you have hands-on experience with the technology.

- Submit a proposal. Sometimes, it's easy to think that a casual conversation or email bid will suffice. When I take the time to develop a thought-out proposal, I have a much higher chance of winning the contract. I recommend developing a proposal template that you can use to quickly put together for projects you bid to.

- Keep in touch! My most successful projects have come out of lost-bid opportunities. Regardless of whether you lost a bid, or weren't called back after an initial phone call, keep a record of your various opportunities and follow up from time to time. It keeps you fresh on your client's minds and lets them know you're a dedicated Mixed Reality developer.

You'll always have plenty of competition, regardless of what industry you freelance or consult in. It's no different with Mixed Reality. However, because Mixed Reality is an emerging platform, there are many ways that you can stand out as a developer. Making unique contributions to the community, creating a great application, and making a splash on social media with something cool you did are all ways that you can stand out and start freelancing in Mixed Reality.

Future Opportunities Today

By now, I hope that I've instilled in you a sense of where Mixed Reality is headed. A world in which everyone interacts with holograms instead of 2D screens means that a lot of industries will be disrupted, many new businesses will be created, and there will be many financial opportunities.

The truth is that this future is not a far-off science fiction prediction. It is something that is here today. We have the technology and the resources to start building out this future, and there's no reason we shouldn't. Yes, technology will continuously improve (when does it ever stop?), and yes, devices will get smaller, lighter, and less expensive. The HoloLens, however, is a revolutionary device that's fully capable of ushering in our Mixed Reality future.

Imagine taking a PC back in time, several decades before computers were widely used in businesses. Do you think you could walk into just about any business and show them how valuable a computer would be for their company? From document and spreadsheet editing, digital art, record keeping, audio recording, and much more. I suspect you'd be able to sell them on buying a computer without much persuasion. In the same way, Mixed Reality is here to usher in the next computing paradigm and start disrupting the status quo. Whenever you visit or drive by any office or business, start thinking about how that business could leverage Mixed Reality technology. Start thinking about the types of applications and experiences you could build that would add value to those companies.

There's nothing stopping you from scheduling a free demo to several companies local to you and pitch them on transitioning to the holographic age. If you're equipped with a compelling solution that will add value, I doubt many will turn down the offer for a fun Mixed Reality demo! In this way, you could create new and larger opportunities for yourself (and the industry).

Summary

In this chapter, I provided several insights into ways you can earn money as a Mixed Reality developer. I discussed various monetization models for the Microsoft Store, provided several insights for successfully securing freelance and contract opportunities, and provided some inspiration for creating new opportunities all around you.

Ultimately, a technology platform will be widely accepted and embraced if it adds real value. So far, Mixed Reality is living up to its promise by demonstrating that it does indeed add value across a wide range of sectors. As you and other developers continue to build new experiences, discover new ways to interact with holograms, and find new ways this platform can add value to businesses, the financial opportunities of Mixed Reality will grow exponentially.

CHAPTER 12

Community Resources

In this chapter, I'll introduce you to some valuable online and community resources that will help you on your journey as a Mixed Reality developer. Examples of these resources include relevant community forums, online groups, notable events, and other information that will help during the development process.

I cannot underscore the importance of leveraging community resources during application development of any kind. This is especially true for Mixed Reality development, where the platform is still new, and developers everywhere are exchanging valuable lessons learned. As you've heard me echo throughout this book, the world has yet to unlock a good user experience when it comes to immersive computing. I anticipate dozens of "Eureka!" moments over the next few years as we (Mixed Reality developers) come to grips with this revolutionary technology. As such, it would be extremely advantageous to be plugged into the community to exchange ideas, help one another, and build upon others' successes.

HoloDevelopers Slack Team

The HoloDevelopers Slack Team is my personal favorite HoloLens and Mixed Reality community online and by far what I consider the most helpful for new developers. In this section, I'll introduce the HoloDevelopers Slack Team, including information on how to join the group and the best way to participate in this community.

What Is Slack?

For those not familiar with Slack (`https://slack.com/`), it is a fantastic collaboration and communication tool for groups. It can be thought of as a big chat room platform, where a community can discuss ideas and share content across multiple chat rooms. The power of Slack is its cross-platform compatibility (Web, iOS, Android, Mac,

© Sean Ong and Varun Kumar Siddaraju 2021
S. Ong and V. K. Siddaraju, *Beginning Windows Mixed Reality Programming*,
https://doi.org/10.1007/978-1-4842-7104-9_12

Windows, Windows Phone, HoloLens, and more) as well as the ability to chat with and interact with large groups of people across multiple chat rooms (called "channels"), where each channel is dedicated to specific topics of discussion. Anyone can create a Slack team, and thousands of Slack teams exist for a wide range of topics. Slack is also popular among businesses, being utilized as an employee communication tool.

What Is the HoloDevelopers Slack Team

The HoloDevelopers Slack team is the "semi-official" developer Slack team for all things HoloLens and Windows Mixed Reality. It's a place where developers can share experiences, ask questions, and talk about Windows Mixed Reality. I say "semi-official" because this Slack team was not founded by Microsoft, yet it has become so foundational that Microsoft now recognizes this resource on their website (*https://developer.microsoft.com/en-us/mixed-reality/*) and there are dozens of Microsoft employees from the HoloLens team that regularly contribute and participate in the HoloDevelopers Slack.

The HoloDevelopers Slack team was founded by Jesse McCulloch after being frustrated by some of the shortcomings of Microsoft's official Windows Mixed Reality developer forums. The Slack team was intended to provide Mixed Reality developers with a greater sense of community and quicker, more interactive feedback when asking questions.

The HoloDevelopers Slack team contains an evolving list of many relevant discussion channels, each active with lively conversations. Figure 12-1 illustrates a snapshot of one conversation on this Slack team. As of this writing, the HoloDevelopers Slack contains nearly *10,000* members and growing at a rate of about 25 to 30 new members per week. You can find the Slack team at this URL: *https://holodevelopers.slack.com/*.

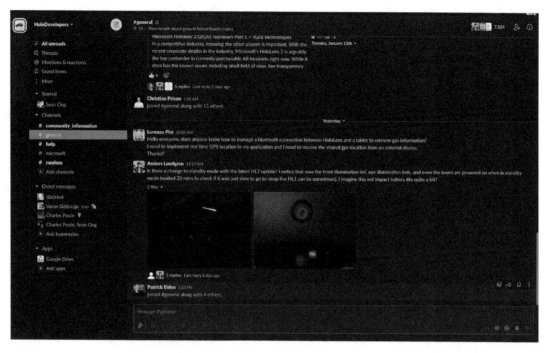

Figure 12-1. *The HoloDevelopers Slack Team is a lively group of HoloLens and Windows Mixed Reality developers*

How to Join the HoloDevelopers Slack Team

Joining the HoloDevelopers Slack team is easy. Enter your email address at this link: `https://holodevelopersslack.azurewebsites.net/`, as shown in Figure 12-2. You'll instantly receive an invitation to join the Slack team, at which point you can sign up for your account.

Figure 12-2. *Use the sign-up link to get an instant invite to join the HoloDevelopers Slack Team*

Participating in the HoloDevelopers Slack Team

Once you are a member of the HoloDevelopers Slack team, introducing yourself to the community is a great way to kick off a conversation.

I recommend using the *#help* channel for any project-related questions you may have. Use the *#general* channel for general Windows Mixed Reality discussions, and use the *#random* channel for anything unrelated to Mixed Reality or whenever you're unsure if your content fits within the *#general* discussion.

Here are some general tips to make the most of being part of this Slack community:

- Microsoft has HoloLens employees actively participating in this community. Be sure to reach out to them whenever appropriate!

- Don't be afraid to ask tough questions. This Slack team boasts some amazing talent, and there's always someone happy to help. If your question goes unanswered, be persistent in asking the community!

- Make some money! Check the #job-opportunities channel regularly for fun employment and contract opportunities.

- Be sure to install the Slack app on your phone and PC to get notifications and easily follow discussions you're interested in.

- Use the direct messaging feature to have one-on-one conversations with individuals.

- Share your work! Everyone in the Mixed Reality community loves to see each other's progress and accomplishments. Share your work and share lessons learned.

Overall, if there's only one Windows Mixed Reality community to be part of, I would definitely choose the HoloDevelopers Slack team. The community, level of engagement, and quality of developers in this group make it second to none. I highly recommend joining and checking in regularly on this community.

Other Online Communities and Resources

In this section, I'll introduce other online HoloLens and Windows Mixed Reality communities and groups that you can participate in.

HoloLens Developers Facebook Group

As expected with the Internet, there are hundreds (and possibly thousands) of online groups, forums, and communities that you can join and participate in as a Mixed Reality developer. That said, I consider there to be two primary online communities. We've already talked about the first one – the HoloDevelopers Slack Team. The second is the "HoloLens Developers" Facebook group, located at the following URL: `www.facebook.com/groups/winholographicdevs/`.

From the description on this Facebook group, the HoloLens Developers group is an "open group to share thoughts, information, everything you want about the Microsoft HoloLens, Mixed Reality and how to develop with these technologies."

As of this writing, it boasts over 6,400+ members and is the largest Windows Mixed Reality developer group on Facebook. Figure 12-3 shows an example of what you'll see when visiting this group. Facebook will prompt you to become a member of this group before you are allowed to post or comment in this group. One of seven administrators will grant you access, typically within a few hours of requesting to join this group.

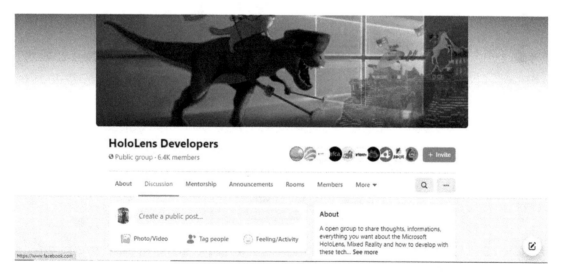

Figure 12-3. The HoloLens Developers group is the largest Windows Mixed Reality Developer group on Facebook

There's a certain degree of user overlap between this group and the other popular online communities we've covered so far. Most days, each group has different sets of active contributors, and different content is shared and covered across each of these groups. For this reason, I typically monitor these (and other) communities on a weekly basis.

The Facebook group is generally more useful for the sharing and consumption of Mixed Reality news and experiences. New users can see the group's photos, links, and history easier than on Slack or the Forums. It's also convenient for developers who are comfortable on Facebook and frequently use the platform. This group is not ideal, however, for real-time chat and discussion. Extended developer discussions may also be difficult to follow on Facebook.

There are dozens (if not hundreds) of HoloLens- and Mixed Reality–related groups on Facebook. Figure 12-4 shows a small sampling of groups that appear when I searched for "Windows Mixed Reality" Facebook groups. Some of these groups have several thousand members. I've not had the opportunity to explore each of these groups – but if you are looking for a certain niche Windows Mixed Reality community, you are bound to find something relevant on Facebook.

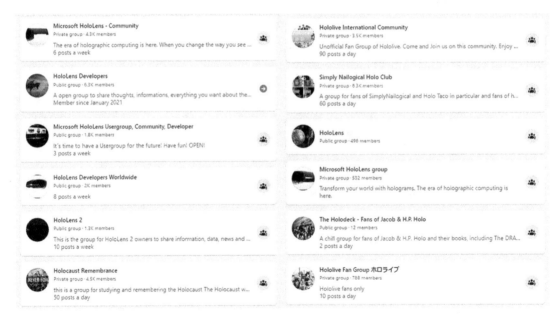

Figure 12-4. *There are many HoloLens and Windows Mixed Reality groups on Facebook to choose from*

Unity and Unity HoloLens Forum

One of the most powerful development resources for any Unity-based application (including Windows Mixed Reality applications) is the Unity Forums. You can find the Unity Forums at https://forum.unity3d.com.

When asking your favorite search engine any Unity-related question, you will most likely be taken to the Unity Forums for your answer. Outside of the Mixed Reality world, Unity is widely used for game development. This is excellent news, because it means that there are years of tutorials, resources, and forum discussions to help answer almost any question you may have as you are developing your Mixed Reality applications.

HoloLens Subreddit

If you're not familiar with Reddit (`www.reddit.com`), it is the 18th most popular website in the world (at the time of this writing). Reddit is popular because users "vote" relevant news and content to the top of users' feeds, instead of being presented curated content by unknown search engine algorithms or handpicked by media agencies.

There are countless topic groups on Reddit, called "subreddits." The HoloLens subreddit (`www.reddit.com/r/HoloLens/`) is the most popular subreddit for HoloLens and Windows Mixed Reality, boasting roughly 9238+ subscribers as of this writing. Figure 12-5 shows what you can expect to see when visiting the HoloLens subreddit.

The HoloLens subreddit is an excellent resource for filtering out relevant Windows Mixed Reality news from irrelevant or unimportant content. Naturally, any important or relevant posts will receive a higher number of upvotes and rise to the top of your feed.

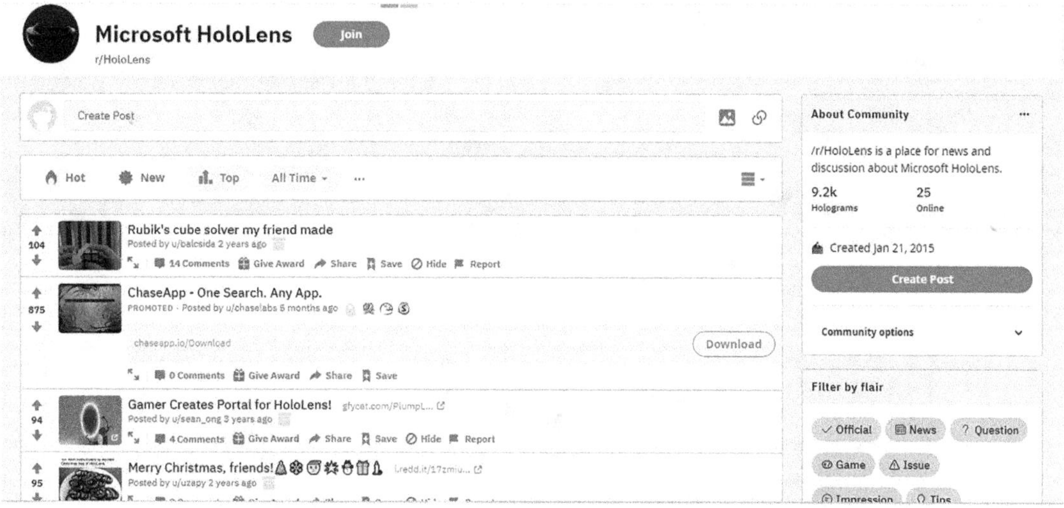

Figure 12-5. *Subscribe to the HoloLens subreddit to stay up to date on the most relevant and exciting HoloLens and Windows Mixed Reality news*

Reddit also has a useful feature to sort by most upvoted posts for various time periods. As you can see in Figure 12-5, I've listed the top posts all time by clicking "Top" in the upper menu and then "All Time" in the lower menu bar. This allows infrequent visitors to check in every few days/weeks/months and make sure that they did not miss any big Windows Mixed Reality news or content.

Don't forget to read the comments section of important posts! Reddit boasts an active community of "commenters" who share opinions and valuable insights, adding rich context and humor to most submitted posts.

Next Reality News

Of the vast number of technology-related news websites available, I've found that Next Reality News (`https://next.reality.news/`) consistently provides the best coverage of Windows Mixed Reality headsets and software. They also regularly publish tutorials that are helpful for HoloLens and Mixed Reality developers.

Next Reality News is a great place to read in-depth coverage and hear opinions on Windows Mixed Reality (and other Augmented/Virtual Reality) news with a special developer perspective that you'll be hard-pressed to find at any other news source. Figure 12-6 shows what you can expect to see when you visit Next Reality News.

Figure 12-6. *Next Reality News is an excellent community and source for Windows Mixed Reality and other VR/AR news*

YouTube

The best way to quickly visualize and learn about another Mixed Reality experience is to watch a video. This is why YouTube has been a valuable platform for developers to share their Windows Mixed Reality apps with the world. Here are a few YouTube channels worth subscribing to in the HoloLens and Windows Mixed Reality space:

- *Sean Ong's YouTube Channel*: A shameless plug for my YouTube channel, where you can find relevant content on my latest Windows Mixed Reality projects. With over 50500+ subscribers as of this writing, my channel is best known for technology-related tutorials, tips, tricks, and news with a special focus on Windows Mixed Reality and Microsoft products. Find me at `www.youtube.com/c/seanong`.

- *Official HoloLens YouTube Channel*: Follow Microsoft's official HoloLens YouTube channel for tutorials, app features, and inspiring examples for your next project (`www.youtube.com/channel/UCT2rZIAL-zNqeK1OmLLUa6g`).

- *Matrix Inception's YouTube Channel*: With 773 subscribers as of this writing, Matrix Inception's rising YouTube channel features some of the most innovative concepts in Windows Mixed Reality, including beaming lasers through portals, a keyboard you can use in your own application, room scanning tricks, reviews, and more! See this channel at `www.youtube.com/channel/UC5WLFKmv6BPFTBzOcZQzVag`.

Local Events and Meetups

In this section, I'll introduce some ways you can get involved with local Mixed Reality events near you. While online communities and group provide a quick and easy way to communicate with a large number of developers across the world, there's still immense value in meeting fellow Windows Mixed Reality enthusiasts, and developers face to face at a venue.

One popular resource for finding local meetups is the Meetup website, found at `www.meetup.com`. In the following, you'll find a non-comprehensive list of HoloLens and Windows Mixed Reality meetups for cities around the world. Some of these may be broader developer or VR/AR groups, but are known to have a one or more Windows Mixed Reality developers in the community.

Europe Meetups

- Valencia, Spain Valencia Virtual AVRE

- Stockholm, Sweden Coding After Work

- Amsterdam, Netherlands VR 020 Meetup (Virtual Reality Amsterdam Meetup)

- Milano, Italy 3D/VR/AR//Khronos Milano Meetup

- Paris, France Paris Glass User Group

- Ivanovo, Russia Ivanovo IT Garage

- Paris, France Paris XR

- Berlin, Germany Reality Hackers VR/AR

- Sofia, Bulgaria VR Lab BG

- Rijswijk, Netherlands Mixed Reality User Group

- München, Germany HoloLens Meetup Germany

- Rijswijk, Netherlands Global XR Talks

- Amsterdam, Netherlands B Talks

- Stockholm, Sweden Mixed reality Sweden

- Dundee, United Kingdom Dundee Tech Talks – All Things Technology

- Amsterdam, Netherlands HoloLens Augmented Reality Fanatics

- Basel, Switzerland Basel AR & VR Group

- Berlin, Germany Football Technology Berlin

- Mechelen, Belgium HOLUG

- Stockholm, Sweden Stockholm AR Meetup

- Dublin, Ireland Industrial and Commercial Applications of VR & AR

- Paris, France NUI Day Conférence et Meetup

- Göteborg, Sweden Gothenburg Hololens Meetup

- Barcelona, Spain ERNI Innovation Community

- Villingen-Schwenningen, Germany XR Trainingszentrum (XRTZ) | Digital Mountains Hub

North America Meetups

- San Francisco, California Microsoft HoloLens and Mixed Reality

- Santa Monica, California XReality: Future Technology and Beyond

- Québec, Canada Meetup CGI Québec

- Los Angeles, California XRLA (Legacy)

- Nashville, Tennessee Spatial Nashville

- San Francisco, California Microsoft HoloLens and Mixed Reality

- New York, New York Microsoft Makers & App Devs of New York City (#MMADNYC)

- Dallas, Texas Dallas Immersive Design and Development – AR/VR/MR

- Seattle, Washington VR and AR in Architecture, Construction and Real Estate

- Austin, Texas AR/VR Tools & Tech

- New York, New York NYC HoloLens Developers Meetup

- Redmond, Washington Windows Holographic User Group Redmond (WinHUGR)

- Austin, Texas Austin Microsoft Developers

- Iselin, New Jersey Microsoft Makers & App Devs of New Jersey (#MMADNJ)

- Portland, Oregon Portland HoloLens Meetup

- Culver City, California Exploring Mixed Reality

- Los Angeles, California Los Angeles AR & Mixed Reality

- Vancouver, British Columbia AWE Nite Vancouver

- Québec, Quebec Meetup CGI Québec

- New Brunswick, New Jersey NJ Unity User Group – Learn VR/AR/360 Development Here

- Knoxville, Tennessee VARDNet – The Virtual/Augmented Reality Developers Network

- Austin, Texas Austin XR Meetup

- Washington, District of Colombia DC Augmented Reality Meetup

- San Antonio, Texas San Antonio Virtual Reality

- San Antonio, Texas PH3AR: San Antonio – Geeks and Gamers

- Vancouver, British Columbia Vancouver HoloLens User Group

- New York, New York Immersive Arts and Tech || XR, VR, AR, MR

- Halifax, Nova Scotia Halifax Augmented/Hyper/Mixed/Virtual Reality

- Mountain View, California Silicon Valley HoloLens Developers Meetup

- Seattle, Washington Seattle XR

- Houston, Texas AWE Nite Houston

Asia Pacific Meetups

- Jakarta, Indonesia Mixed Reality Community Indonesia

- Sydney, Australia Mixed Reality Fundamentals

- Sydney, Australia Microsoft events in Australia

- Melbourne, Australia Augmented Reality Melbourne

- Hangzhou, China Reality Hangzhou(啥现实?来玩转"现实")

- Melbourne, Australia Melbourne Holographic

- Beijing, China HoloLens User Group China

- Adelaide, Australia Adelaide Augmented Reality Meetup

Again, if you don't see your city or region represented in the preceding list, be sure to check meetup.com or perform a search on your favorite search engine to find meetups near you. Microsoft also maintains an updated list of community resources and meetups here: `https://developer.microsoft.com/en-us/windows/mixed-reality/community`.

You may also consider joining or following the local chapter of the VR/AR Association. You may see a list of local chapters and chapter leaders here: `www.thevrara.com/team/`.

Hackathons

A hackathon is an event where people come together for one or more days to quickly develop an application. A hackathon forces you to solve problems, leverage team members' expertise, and ask for help from experts. A hackathon will typically give you access to volunteers and experts that can help you out of tricky situations and show you optimal solutions to challenging development problems. Getting out of a coding problem that might take you a few hours of searching and reading online typically only takes a few minutes when you're able to have an expert show you what to do in person.

Attending a hackathon requires some commitment (typically a weekend) and stamina, but it is an extremely valuable experience that you won't get anywhere else. I highly recommend that you find a relevant hackathon, even if you must travel to attend it. Relevant hackathons include HoloLens, Mixed Reality, Virtual Reality, and Augmented Reality hackathons. VR and AR hackathons will typically include a healthy number of HoloLens and Windows Mixed Reality devices and developers.

Hackathons are often planned a few months in advance. The best place to find a hackathon is on a community calendar of your local meetup group. You may also find them occasionally advertised on any of the online community groups I mention in this chapter. You can always ask members of your local or online community groups if they are aware of any upcoming hackathons, and you will be sure to get several responses for a range of hackathons.

Notable Industry Events

Industry events and conferences are an excellent way to keep a pulse on the Mixed Reality industry. Conventions and Expos give you a chance to educate yourself during informative sessions, experience countless demos in person, build your network, and have a chance to meet up with people you typically communicate with online in your community groups.

There's no shortage of conferences, conventions, expos, and other events locally, nationally, and globally. As I mentioned with hackathons in the previous section, you can find out about upcoming events through community calendars and through your local or online-based groups.

I've also compiled a list of notable industry events as follows, recognized for being especially important for HoloLens and Windows Mixed Reality developers:

- *Unity Unite*: Unite is a platform which brings together developers across the world to get inspired and learn. Get inspired by people and projects through Unity's Unite social networking events and spaces, discover new technology in the expo, and connect with partners all in one place. The events include live sessions which are on demand, keynotes which are loaded up with inspiration, strong tips, and amazing workflows. Link to the latest Unite 2020: `https://unity.com/events/unite`.

- *Augmented World Expo*: The Augmented World Expo (AWE) is the largest AR and VR event in the world. AWE includes a range of Mixed Reality technologies, with a focus on Augmented Reality. I attended the 2017 AWE and was surprised to see that a vast majority of booths in the expo featured HoloLens experiences. AWE is also known for being more enterprise and commercial focused. Many other VR/AR conferences tend to be social, and gaming focused. Learn more about AWE at `www.augmentedworldexpo.com/`.

- *Microsoft Build*: Microsoft Build is Microsoft's premier event for developers of Microsoft's various software and hardware products. Microsoft typically includes academy sessions on Windows Mixed Reality, makes major Mixed Reality announcements, and provides in-depth sessions on a wide range of topics. Microsoft Build tickets typically sell out within minutes, but keynote sessions are streamed online, and all sessions are made available on demand for free after the event. Find out more about Build here: `https://news.microsoft.com/build2020/`.

Summary

Congratulations! Not only have you made it to the end of this chapter, but you've also completed the book. In this chapter, I walked you through ways you can keep informed and stay connected as a developer. I've introduced the best online communities to participate in, the most informative sources of Windows Mixed Reality news, ways to get involved in person at your local meetup groups, and notable events and hackathons that you can attend. As mentioned at the beginning of this chapter, being plugged into a community of developers is imperative, especially since Mixed Reality is still an emerging field with a lot of best practices still being learned by the development community.

Our journey with this book may have come to an end, but your journey as a developer is just beginning! There are countless ways to sharpen your skills as a developer, from mastering physics in Unity to being a shader optimization pro. There's still so much to learn and so much that's yet to be discovered in the world of Mixed Reality.

I wish you the best on your new adventure and cannot wait to see all that you will create. Now, let's start building our holographic future together!

Index

A

Additive displays, 240
Allow far manipulation, 129
AudioInfluencerController.cs
    script, 165, 168
AudioOccluder.cs script, 162
Audio Source component, 163
Augmented World Expo (AWE), 270
Awe-inspiring experience, features, 219
Azure Spatial Anchors
    buttons configuration, 179, 180, 182,
        183, 185
    definition, 175
    download and import tutorial assets, 177
    inbuilt unity packages
        installation, 176, 177
    scene connection to Azure
        resource, 186, 187
    scene preparation, 178
    testing application, 187
    unity scene, creation, 176

B

Behavior settings, 124
Boundary system, 103
Bounds control, 122, 124, 125, 241
Button Config Helper (Script) component's
    OnClick() event, 182–185
Buttons, 104

C

Camera System, 105, 106
Cloned profile, 151
Community resources
    HoloLens Developers Facebook
        Group, 261, 262
    HoloLens Subreddit, 263
    Next Reality News, 264
    Unity and Unity HoloLens Forum, 262
    YouTube, 265
Constraint system, 124, 129
Content scenes, 102
Contract, 253
CreateAzureAnchor Button OnClick()
    event, 212
Culling, 230
Cutoff Frequency parameter, 162

D

Deads-up display (HUD) UI, 243
DefaultMixedRealityToolkit
    ConfigurationProfile, 149
Default plane distance, 235
DirectionalIndicator, 99

E

Events, 124
EyeGazeCursor prefab, 117

© Sean Ong and Varun Kumar Siddaraju 2021
S. Ong and V. K. Siddaraju, *Beginning Windows Mixed Reality Programming*,
https://doi.org/10.1007/978-1-4842-7104-9

F

Field-of-view (FOV) limitation, 9
FindAzureAnchor button, 184
Frame rate, 220, 223
Frames per second (FPS.), 220
Freelance opportunities, 252
Frustum culling, 230

G

GazeProvider, 117
Gaze tutorial
    add scenes to build menu, 114
    components, 120
    cursor functionality, 120
    scene understanding, 116, 117, 119
    set up unity scene, 113
    try the scene, 114, 116
Gestures tutorial
    bounds control, 122, 124, 125
    implementation in app, 131
    load test scene, 120
    object manipulator, 128–130
    press and touch interactions, 126, 127
    try it out, 121
GetAzureAnchor Button OnClick()
        event, 214
GitHub, 109
Graphics processing unit, 5

H

Hackathon, 269
HandConstraint, 99
Hand menu, 104
Hand tracking, 97, 98
HandTrackingProfile, 97
Hardware input, 142

High-poly 3D models, 225
HoloDevelopers Slack Team
    description, 258
    discussion channels, 258
    HoloLens and Windows Mixed
        Reality developers, 259
    join, 259
    participating, 260
Hologram
    cube
        creation, 69
        move, 70
        resize, 71
        zoom, 70
    installation in HoloLens, 73–83
    persistence, 7
    testing, 72, 73
HoloLens
    Hologram app installation, 73–83
    inside-out tracking, 6
    spatial mapping, 7
    spatial sound, 8
    transparent *vs.* immersive headsets, 8, 10
HoloLens 2 cameras, 6
HoloLens Developers Facebook
        Group, 261, 262
HoloLens Subreddit, 263
Host transform, 129

I, J, K

Immersive headsets, 8
InBetween class, 99
Input data providers, 94, 116
Input methods, Windows Mixed Reality
    benefits and limitations, 111
    gaze (*see* Gaze tutorial)
    voice (*see* Voice command tutorial)

Inside-out tracking, 6
Inspector panel, 165
Interactable.cs script, 131
Invisible audio sources, 170

L

Lerp power closer, 234
Lerp power farther, 234
Level of detail (LOD) rendering, 229
Lighting scene, 102
Local events and meetups
    Asia Pacific meetups, 268
    Europe Meetups, 266
    North America Meetups, 267, 268

M

Magic
    try it out, 246, 247
    Vuforia installation, 244–246
Manager scenes, 102
Manipulation events, 129
Manipulation type, 129
Microsoft Store, 250
Mixed Reality design, practices
    bounds controls, 241
    colors, 242
    design experiences to avoid, 243
    distance from user, 239
    resources, 243
    shadows, 239
    sharp text, 240
    spatial mapping, 237, 238
    toolbars and app bars, 242
    voice commands, 240
Mixed Reality development
    Mixed Reality Toolkit
        scene preparation, 61–68

Mixed Reality Toolkit Unity
    package, 58, 59, 61
    system specs, 4, 5
Mixed Reality Toolkit (MRTK), 24, 26,
    57, 86
    components
        boundary system, 103
        camera system, 105, 106
        hand tracking, 97, 98
        input system, 94–96
        multi-scene manager, 100, 102
        profiles, 106–108
        solvers, 98–100
        spatial awareness, 102
        standard shader, 109
        UX controls, 104, 105
    definition, 85
    online
        GitHub, 109
        help and documentation, 109
    repositories online, 86
    setup
        importing MRTK asset files, 86, 88
        unity package manager, 89, 90, 92
    Standard Shader, 109
Multiple users connection
    Avatar, creation, 203
    configuring PUN, 206
    Prefab, creation, 204, 205
    scene preparation, 199, 200
    user, create and configure, 201, 202
Multi-scene Manager, 100, 102

N

Negative shadowing, 240
Next Reality News, 264
Notable industry events, 270, 271

O

Object Manipulator component, 128, 129
Occlusion, 152–154
Occlusion culling, 230
One-handed manipulation properties, 129
Operating system, 5
Orbital class, 98

P, Q

Packages, 26
Performance
    best practices
        culling, 230, 231
        level of detail rendering, 229
        optimize polygons and
          textures, 225, 227, 229
        optimize shaders, 232
        single-pass instanced
          rendering, 231
        start monitoring and optimizing
          early, 225
    HoloLens, 224
    metrics, 223
    monitor, 222, 223
    optimizing, 221
    simplygon, 232
    stabilization plane, 233–235
Photon Unity Networking (PUN)
    application creation, 195, 196
    assets, importing, 193, 194
    enabling additional
      capabilities, 190, 191
    installing inbuilt unity packages, 191
    tutorial assets, importing, 192, 193
    unity project connection to PUN
      application, 196, 198
    Unity Scene, creation, 190

PlaneModifier, 234
Pressable.cs script, 131
Processor, 4
Profiles in MRTK, 106–108
Publishing App to Microsoft Store
    free apps, 250
    freemium apps, 251
    free with ads, 251
    paid apps, 251

R

RadialView, 98
Random access memory (RAM), 4

S

SetFocusPointForFrame()
    function, 234, 235
Shaders, 232
Shadows, 239
ShareAzureAnchor Button OnClick()
    event, 213
Shared experiences
    Azure Spatial Anchors Integration
      buttons configuring, 210–214
      scene connection to Azure
        resource, 214–216
      scene preparation, 210
    PUN (*see* Photon Unity Networking
      (PUN))
    spatial alignment, 217
Sharing object movements, 207–209
Simplygon, 232
Slack, 257
Slate prefab, 105
Sliders, 104
Smoothing behavior, 124

SoC power, 223
SolverHandler, 98
Solver system, 98–100
SoundEmitter game object, 163
SoundOccluder, 162
Spatial awareness
    definition, 145
    navigation, 146
    occlusion, 145, 152–154
    persistence, 146
    physics, 145
    placement, 145
    scene understanding, 154
    tutorial
        scene understanding, 148–150
        set up unity scene, 146
        spatial mapping in
            application, 150, 151
        try it out, 147
Spatial mapping, 7, 237, 238
SpatialObjectMeshObserver, 150
Spatial sound, 8
    design considerations and best
        practices, 169, 170
    guide users, 169
    tutorial
        enabling in your
            application, 165, 167, 168
        scene understanding,
            161–163, 165
        set up unity scene, 158
        test scene, 159, 161
Spatial understanding, 102
Stabilization plane, 233–235
StartAzureSession Button OnClick()
        event, 211
SurfaceMagnetism, 99

Target object, 123
Target override, 235
Track velocity, 235
Transparent *vs.* immersive headsets, 8, 10

Unity
    installation, 15–24
    Mixed Reality workflow, 29
    pricing tiers, 30
    Windows Mixed Reality
        experiences, 10
Unity and Unity HoloLens Forum, 262
Unity application
    ball
        add physics, 47
        creation, 40
        raise, 42
        zoom, 42
    color, ground blue, 42, 44, 45, 47
    enable keyboard control, 48–52
    ground plane
        creation, 35, 37
        scale, 39
        zoom, 38
    new project, creation, 31–34
    rename, ball, 41
    rename plane, 37
    reset ball's position, 41
    reset ground plane position, 38
    scene save, 34, 35
    testing, 53
Unity editor, 33
Unity Joystick, 94
Unity package manager, 89, 90, 92

T

U

Unity Touch, 94
Unity unite, 270
UX controls, 104, 105

V

VisualProfiler, 224
Visual Studio
    deploy, app, 11
    installation, 11–15
Voice command tutorial
    add your own voice, 137, 139, 140
    enable voice commands, 140
    load scene, 132

practices, 141, 142
scene understanding, 134, 136
try it out, 133
Volume Pass Through parameter, 162

W, X

Windows Device Portal, 222
Windows Mixed Reality (WMR), 94
Windows Speech, 94

Y, Z

YouTube, 265